THE INTIMATE MALE

Linda Levine, ACSW,
and
Lonnie Barbach, Ph.D.

THE
INTIMATE
MALE

*Candid Discussions
About Women, Sex,
and
Relationships*

ANCHOR PRESS/DOUBLEDAY
Garden City, New York

To Stuart—my very own super-man.
Linda

To the many loving men in my life—
especially my father and my brother.
Lonnie

FOREWORD

In the avalanche of books on sex that have appeared in the last twenty years, there have been a lot of bad ones and a few good ones. The bad ones pass off personal opinion as scientific fact, attempt to make everyone fit into a particular model of sexual functioning, and serve to confuse people and make them feel inadequate. The good ones provide useful information, leave room for differences between people and between relationships, and support us in accepting ourselves or making desired changes. *The Intimate Male* is one of the good ones.

The responses of the men ring true. Although Levine and Barbach's sample is not representative of American men in general —if for no other reasons than these men are well educated and middle-class and were chosen because their sex lives are good— what they say is similar in content and style to what I have heard from over a thousand men I have worked with in sex therapy and talked to about sex in other contexts. One thing that will surprise those people who think all men are the same when it comes to sex is the wide range of responses given to various questions. Men, like women, are different in many ways. What is pleasing, arousing, or satisfying to one may be just the opposite to another. *The Intimate Male* conveys well the diversity found in contemporary men.

While the differences among men are important and require attention, there are also significant similarities. Men are changing. Most of them have learned the value of intimacy, of sensitivity and consideration, and of relationships with women who are their equals. They are also aware, at least to some extent, of the obstacles

put in the way of attaining these goals by the models of masculinity
and sexuality they were raised with. And they know what it means
to struggle—to try to choose between what they now think is right
and what they were taught was right. These men know about the
pressures of the macho stereotype and are not fond of them. They
don't like having all the responsibility for sex on their shoulders
and penises. They ask why they alone should have to initiate, orchestrate, and be responsible for the results, and they appreciate
women who can share the burdens and joys of lovemaking.

The men in this book are real flesh-and-blood human beings, with
concerns and compassion, feelings and fears, and with decency and
thoughtfulness, in contrast to the insensitive abusers of women
written about in some sex books and the ignoramuses written about
in others—for example, men who don't know what a clitoris is,
where to find one, what to do in case they should discover one,
and who don't care about their partner's satisfaction in the first
place. Like most of the men I have worked with, they want to have
sex with women they care about and who care about them, they
are reasonably knowledgeable about sex, and they very much want
to satisfy their partners. Despite what they learned while growing
up, scoring and "Slam, Bam, Thank You Ma'am" sex do not mean
much to them. They have learned about the significant tie between
emotional closeness and good sex, and about the importance of
clitoral and other stimulation for their lovers.

Although there are macho elements in what these men say—
which is not surprising, considering how they were raised and what
the culture reinforces—by and large they are not the silent,
"problem-free" macho types we have heard too much about. They
worry about the size and performance of their penises and especially about the possibility of not getting it up and not satisfying
their mates. Most have experienced sexual difficulties at one time
or another, and the vast majority found ways of alleviating the
problems without professional help (which should be good news
to people who are beginning to lose confidence in their own ability
to solve problems). These men know that establishing and maintaining intimacy is not easy, and they also know how hard it is to
talk to their partners about feelings and about sex. It is particularly
difficult for men to say no to sex, and some of them would rather
fake enthusiasm and orgasm than tell their lovers they are not in

the mood or want to stop. Nonetheless, most of them try to talk to their lovers about sex and try to do what is necessary to maintain intimacy and a good sexual relationship.

Although most of these men are not politically radical, they do question cultural models and are receptive to exploring new ways of living and relating. This should be a hopeful sign to women who worry about finding men who are their equals. These are men who have given some thought to what they want from life, from relationships, and from sex. Since women often complain that men aren't very specific about what pleases them sexually and brush off questions with a vague "everything feels good," specific sections of *The Intimate Male* where the respondents do talk about what they like—everything from atmosphere and ways of being touched to the use of sexual accoutrements—should be of special interest to women readers. While the preferences of these men should not be taken as universally applicable, they may provide a basis for experimentation and discussion.

In its own unpretentious way, I believe *The Intimate Male* is a significant contribution to the literature on male sexuality. It provides a wealth of information about the sexual thoughts, feelings, and behavior of an important group of men—in the men's own words. There is much we can learn from this volume. If we are willing to listen, I think we will find that macho is mortally wounded and that men, or at least some of them, are joining the women who are challenging accepted notions of what it means to be feminine and masculine, and what it means to be with another human being, in bed or out. Good sex—learning about it, talking about it, integrating it in a meaningful way in our lives and relationships—is neither as easy nor as natural as many of us think. More and more people, I believe, are beginning to understand this, and Levine and Barbach's fine book makes it clear that men are having many of the same questions, fears, and difficulties that women have. Knowledge of this simple fact may help to generate understanding and sympathy for ourselves and our lovers, especially when sex, and perhaps the relationship, are not going well. I believe and hope that this book will encourage such understanding and sympathy.

Bernie Zilbergeld
Berkeley, California

ACKNOWLEDGMENTS

Writing is often described as a labor of love. For us, the love was in the conception of *The Intimate Male: Candid Discussions About Women, Sex, and Relationships* and the illuminating interviews that followed. The labor was in the actual writing, which could have been overwhelming without the loving assistance of friends and colleagues. We wish to acknowledge those who supported us in the creation of this book.

We are indebted to both Loretta Barrett, our editor, and Rhoda Weyr, our agent, for their support and guidance throughout this project.

We are also indebted to Bryan Arling, Larry Brain, Clark Clipson, Warren Farrell, Mark Glasser, Richard Haddad, William Maxted, Barry McCarthy, Judith Wallerstein, and Bernie Zilbergeld, who drew on their professional experience in the fields of psychiatry, sexuality, medicine, and male role scripting and shared their thoughts with us.

Special thanks to Suzan Richmond for her substantial contributions in the writing and editing of portions of this book and also to Cherie Franklin, who helped with the editing. Since all the interviews had to be typed and the manuscript retyped many times, we are also indebted to Sharon Bauman-Leach, Mickie Denig, Tom Gartner, and Rosalie Moore. We also appreciated the help of those who arranged interviews, provided technical expertise, and gave of their time and energy during various stages of the project: Rosalind Andrews, Martha Batchelder, Larry Beinhart, Sandy Bremer, David Bullard, Cheryl Chisholm, Marian Cuomo, Norma Davidoff, Pat

Delorme, Edith Dolan, E. Lee Doyle, Sue Eichler, Jerry Franz, Caroline Fromm, Donna Gerdin, Julian Graubart, Caroline Griffin, Martha Gross, Charles Hansen, Susan Haskins, Jerry Hieb, Phyllis Hirschkop, Paul Lange, Ray Larsen, Jeri Marlowe, Jeanne Mitchler-Fiks, Gail McEachern, Kevin Powers, Heddy Reed, Michelle Rosenberg, Peter Rosenthal, Richard Sablowsky, Fred and Kathy Scott, Danny Slomoff, Diane Weathers, Fred Weiner, and Doug Williams.

Finally, we are indebted to all the men who were willing to share with us the intimate details of their sexual relationships. Without their trust and willingness to make themselves vulnerable, this book could not have been written.

CONTENTS

THE INTIMATE MALE

INTRODUCTION

When we first started interviewing men for this book, our goal was simply to write the male version of *Shared Intimacies: Women's Sexual Experiences*. *Shared Intimacies* provides an exchange of intimate sexual attitudes and activities of one hundred and twenty women who feel good about their sexuality. It supplies information few women have access to: how other women keep their long-term relationships sexually vital and how women successfully handle problems that arise in the normal course of daily life that affect their sexuality, such as pregnancy, parenting, aging, and illness.

Women all over the country told us that reading about the range of female sexual preferences and practices and how other women had resolved obstacles to their sexual enjoyment had made them feel less isolated and more knowledgeable and confident. Surely, we reasoned, there was a need for a similar book about men who have satisfying sex lives and who have resolved similar conflicts.

But in the process of gathering information from one hundred and twenty men across the country, we discovered more than solutions to problems and an exchange of sexual techniques and ideas. We discovered that men, regardless of age, life-style, or economic circumstances, want more intimacy in their lives—especially in their sexual lives. As a consequence, the men we interviewed were rethinking the definition of what it means to be a man, particularly in the area of sexuality. They were taking a second look at how culturally accepted macho images influenced their behavior in and out of bed and limited their ability to be intimate. These men were aware, concerned, and articulate.

Given these qualities, you may wonder how representative of American men the men we interviewed really are. But for the most part, they represented the general population. They were ordinary in the sense that they faced everyday problems and confronted their share of sexual difficulties. Their ages, life-styles, and professions were diverse. The youngest man was nineteen, the oldest eighty-eight. Some were swinging bachelors, others family men. We interviewed men who were students, artists, ministers, lawyers, dentists, doctors, mechanics, government workers, retired, executives, and even media stars. Approximately 10 percent of the men were nonwhite; the rest were Caucasian. We recruited interviewees predominantly from the two coasts, the San Francisco Bay area and the New York–Washington, D.C., megalopolis, but we also interviewed men in Kansas, Ohio, Washington, Texas, Colorado, Georgia, and Florida. Only four of the one hundred and twenty men were so-called "liberated men" who attended consciousness-raising sessions aimed toward self-actualization.

The interviewees may *not* have been representative in that most were college-educated, career-oriented, and middle-class. In addition, they all felt good about their sexuality. We chose men who were satisfied with their sex lives for a number of reasons. Most books on male sexuality are written by professionals who tell people how to solve problems. In this book, we wanted the men themselves to share what they felt was important to their sexuality, as well as their unique solutions to familiar problems. We also wanted men who had successfully grappled with the changing male expectations imposed by society so they could be role models for other men. Finally, we felt that men who could live emotionally satisfying and successful lives while dealing with the conflicting issues typical of a transition period within society could point to trends that might later become mainstream.

How did we find these men? Initially we began by asking friends and colleagues around the country to suggest men who met our criteria. We also solicited volunteers from audiences across the country as we lectured on sexuality and publicized *Shared Intimacies*.

As we accumulated more information for our new book, we searched for men in situations of particular interest, for instance, handicapped men; men whose wives were pregnant; men over sixty or under thirty; and single fathers with custody of their children. And, as we found with the women in *Shared Intimacies,* the men we interviewed were often delighted to suggest the names of friends, willing to be interviewed, who also felt good about their sexuality.

In the beginning we interviewed homosexual as well as heterosexual men, thinking, as we had in our earlier book on women, that the basic concerns of the two would be similar. However, unlike lesbians, who generally shared the same aspirations of intimacy and monogamy as heterosexual women, we found the lifestyle of gay men to be substantially different from that of gay women. A high degree of variability characterized the gay male population, ranging from monogamy to stand-up sex, and from leather to limp wrists. Since we thought that we could not do justice to this varied range of gay male sexuality, we concentrated on heterosexual men.

Our intention, similar to that of *Shared Intimacies,* was not to conduct a statistical study or make any grand pronouncements about the differences in attitudes and experiences of men of various ages, marital statuses or locales, but rather to present a range of sexual thoughts, attitudes, experiences, and problem-solving techniques used by the men we interviewed.

Each interview we conducted took at least two hours. The questions we asked were pointed and specific, which necessitated establishing a rapport with each interviewee as rapidly as possible. As a result, the interviews were warm, intimate, and in-depth. We encouraged men to be open and candid as we elicited personal and practical information from them.

While working on this book, we were constantly taken aback by one concern that was expressed repeatedly, sometimes even by the interviewees themselves: "How do you know that the men you interview will be honest?" One man even facetiously suggested we use lie detector tests.

The underlying assumption was that men exaggerate, embellish, and brag, but rarely, if ever, tell the truth about their sexual experiences. Since this was never a concern while interviewing women about their sexuality, we began to wonder why men's sexual images were so important that they would lie to protect them. But as we completed the interviews, we began to realize how strongly our culture defines a man's masculinity in terms of his sexual prowess. Any chink in this armor—any apparent insecurities or failures, for instance—could make a man doubt his entire masculine self-image.

Consequently, any dialogue among men concerning sex is often reduced to exercises in he-man breast-beating. Spike and his best friend, Paul, for instance, have traded inflated stories about their sex lives for fourteen years. In the privacy of the interview, Spike shed some light on one of the games men play:

> Whenever either of us would go out with a woman, we'd call each other first thing in the morning with the "deets"—details. No "hello," just the deets. We would graphically describe what had happened the night before. Knowing Paul would call in the morning meant I had better make it a good, long, hard one. Paul and I had a real need to perform for each other. So sometimes I would tell him we spent forty-five minutes to an hour fucking rather than say what really happened. Finally I realized I'd gotten so wrapped up in the bullshit with him that it was affecting my relationships with women.

In our quest for honest responses, we did not feel we had to resort to using lie detector tests. Between the two of us, we've had over twenty years of clinical experience, and we trusted our professional judgment to discern the validity of the men's responses. In all but a few cases, we truly believed these men gave us the "deets." There were some, however, who bragged of Herculean sexual exploits, marathons, and the like. And when we felt a man was not being honest, we discounted his interview accordingly. For instance, one man claimed his insistent sexual appetite could not be satisfied by the three times a week he and his wife had sex. He supposedly compensated by keeping four mistresses.

Many of the men we spoke with confessed that they had rarely, if ever, talked as candidly and openly about sex before. Said one man: "I don't talk about sex with anyone—not my wife or my friends." And another: "I've never talked to anyone the way I've talked to you, not even to my analyst."

Some men were obviously embarrassed by some of the questions and had difficulty answering them. In response to being asked

about his sexual turn-offs, forty-year-old Verner replied: "I'm trying to think if I really know the answer to that, and then if I have
the courage to tell you. I think we'd better pass on that question for
now." Other men were willing to share areas of sexual difficulty and
to reveal themselves in far less than a perfect masculine light.
Thirty-four-year-old Drew admitted:

> Sex is such a loaded topic that it's hard to talk about it without
> either exaggerating or covering up. I think there's a natural
> tendency to want to highlight the good experiences and not to
> talk about the bad ones. I found it a little bit difficult to be re-
> ally honest, because some things aren't very flattering and it's
> difficult to talk about things that aren't flattering.

But basically the men decided to be honest more often for themselves than for us or our research. "I decided when I came in here,"
said thirty-four-year-old Joseph,

> that I was going to be as open as I could be, and talk to you as
> much as I could. It might be a little difficult for me to get into
> it, since I don't know you, so if you hear me stumbling or see
> me looking up at the ceiling, please understand.

Even though we guaranteed the men we interviewed confidentiality, we were sometimes astounded by, yet always grateful
for, the trust some men placed in us. The men's names have been
changed in the manuscript and all identifying material has been
carefully deleted. With this promise of anonymity many men took
this opportunity to divulge things they had never shared with anyone else. Some welcomed the interview as a chance to unburden
themselves without having to worry about being judged. In the
process, some men could have jeopardized their relationships.
There were those, for instance, who confessed to having extramarital affairs of which their wives were unaware. Others shared
secrets which could have proved embarrassing if made public. For
example, one man confided: "Everyone thinks I'm really sexy, but
my wife and I haven't had intercourse for a couple of years."
At first, we felt the men had been more honest and candid than
the women we had interviewed for *Shared Intimacies*. But upon
later reflection, we realized that unconsciously we had accepted the
stereotype that says men don't talk about fears and are afraid of

being vulnerable. Therefore, when the men responded openly to our questions, their candidness seemed more dramatic, more revealing, and more trusting than that of the women.

Interviewing men about sex was undeniably different from interviewing women. The fact that we were women asking men the most personal questions about their private sex lives created a sexual tension that had not been present when we talked with the women, and we were unprepared for it. We found it difficult to acknowledge, even to ourselves, that any feelings of sexual attraction existed. We distanced ourselves from these feelings initially by maintaining a professional stance. Later on, as the interviews progressed and we became more at ease with the sexual feelings elicited by the subject matter, we were able to relax and talk more explicitly than we had dared in the earlier interviews. Our comfort, in turn, seemed to allow the men to be more relaxed and open about their own feelings.

Sometimes, as the men relaxed, we found ourselves taken aback—particularly in response to their language. The sexually explicit language used by some of the men caused us some discomfort at first. At the outset of the interview, the majority of men restrained themselves and used clinical words such as "penis" and "vagina." But as they became more comfortable, they slipped back into their familiar vernacular, and used words like "cunt," "pussy," and "dick" more frequently. And while sometimes we inwardly winced at language our ears were unaccustomed to hearing, outwardly we maintained a "we've heard it all—nothing can shock us" demeanor.

It was reassuring for each of us, conducting these interviews separately, to compare notes and discover we had similar reactions. We both were uncomfortable with the sexual tension in the interviews. We also found it difficult to listen without reacting to some of the slang terms the men used that sounded chauvinistic to us. But by squelching our initial responses, we were able to focus on what the men said about their sex lives rather than how they said it. In the end, we felt that by listening carefully we had significantly increased our awareness of how men experienced sex. We had also come to understand that some of their slang expressions, which could be construed as being offensive toward women, were used simply out of habit.

Even with this awareness, we wondered as we analyzed the data at the extent to which our unconscious biases remained and whether they would influence the way we presented this very sensitive material.

Basically, we wondered if two women could really write a book about male sexuality. Would our analysis accurately represent the male point of view? Our first response was that for years men have declared themselves authorities on female sexuality. Why not the reverse? We were well-trained therapists, skilled in perceiving the world through the eyes of our clients. But this justification was not really satisfactory. After all, men who have held themselves up as experts on female sexuality have frequently missed the mark. So we wondered whether we could truly present this material without experiencing firsthand what it is like to be a man in this culture. And while we were concerned, we felt we could sidestep some of the potential pitfalls by allowing the men we interviewed to speak about the male experience in their own words. Certainly, we chose which material to include, and any unconscious stereotypes we held had to influence to some degree the information we highlighted or left out, but that would be true of anyone who put together a book such as this one. So to check ourselves more closely, we asked the men how they felt being interviewed by a woman and how different it might have been had a man been asking the questions.

The overwhelming majority of the men we interviewed stated that our being women was a positive factor that made it easier for them to open up. They saw women as being more accepting and less judgmental than men. If a man interviewed them, some said, they might be preoccupied with their image. "You know, competing like dogs pissing on their territory," was how one man put it. Some even said they had consented to the interview *because* we were women. They would not have consented to being interviewed by a man. Many said it might have been easier initially to talk to a man but believed that their responses would have been more superficial. They felt that talking honestly and openly was easier to do with a woman. Most of their relationships with men were of the good buddy variety—sharing activities as opposed to feelings. If deeper feelings and sexual intimacy were discussed at all, it was with women: first with mothers and then later with lovers and wives with whom it was safe to share and feel vulnerable. Spike summed it up this way:

> It's an intimate thing talking about your sexual experiences and although I have an easier time being friends with men, I have a much easier time being intimate with women.

Still, the reaction was not unanimous. Some men found that our being women had an inhibiting effect. They felt they had to censor their language because we were women. For example, Greg, a fifty-three-year-old teacher, explained, "I have a whole other set of words I use with men that's much more graphic." And some men felt they had to explain things that another man would immediately comprehend. Because we were women, some men were concerned with pleasing us and appearing sexually attractive in our eyes. According to Barry:

> No straight man is going to look at me sexually and think that I'm either repulsive or desirable, whereas a woman might. Because you're a woman, I'd like to be sexually attractive to you. I have no intention whatsoever of doing anything about it but, still, it would be nice if you found me sexually attractive. If you were a man sitting there, it would be irrelevant.

Some men even openly shared their feelings of attraction toward us. One man admitted, "I had fantasies of going to bed with you, and I wouldn't have if you were a man." Responses such as these had to affect the material we elicited in the interview. For example, to some extent we may have elicited more liberal, liberated, or feminist attitudes because some men may have exaggerated these aspects of their beliefs and behaviors in an attempt to please us or to be found sexually desirable.

But the large majority of men responded to aspects of our femaleness that were not specifically sexual: our warmth, acceptance, understanding, and concern. In fact, the number of men who found the interview sexually titillating were few. The majority of men experienced the interview as a learning experience. Many told us that having to formulate answers to our questions provided them with some genuine insights into their feelings and behavior patterns. For example, one man during the course of the interview realized why he had stopped feeling sexual toward his wife during her pregnancy. His favorite sexual fantasy had always been one of deflowering innocent virgins, and when his wife began to really "show," that fantasy didn't work anymore.

Some men wrote letters telling us that they had shared impressions from the interview with spouses, friends, or lovers. Some felt the experience had enhanced their communication with their partners. One sixty-seven-year-old man admitted that he had never discussed these issues with anyone before. At the end of the interview he was pleased. "It felt good to say these things," he said. "I'm sorry the interview is over."

The men we talked with were not the only ones who felt they had learned something. We felt we had had the opportunity to be exposed to a vast storehouse of information that most people classify as "top secret." These men had shared their most intimate hopes, fears, anxieties, and triumphs. They told us how they had worked through problems they encountered in their sexual relationships and revealed details about male sexuality that rarely, if ever have been documented before: for instance, what strategies they used to seduce a partner, how men fake orgasm and why, how their wives' pregnancies affected their libidinal drive, what advice they would give others about resuming sex after their wives gave birth, and how the aging process affected their sexuality.

Much of what we learned forced us to confront some of our unconscious biases about men. Initially we felt we were beyond stereotypic thinking. But in hindsight we realized we had begun the interviewing process believing that men were more interested in the physical excitement and variety than in caring and intimacy. We believed that, while women often had sex in order to be in a relationship, men entered a relationship in order to have sex.

The men we interviewed said otherwise. The overwhelming majority of men treasured their intimate relationships and their ability to communicate with their partners. For them, a sense of mutual sexual satisfaction was a key concern. "After all," said one man, "good sex is a kind of glue that holds a relationship together." Another described a good sexual relationship as "the most intimate form of communication between two people."

Stepping out of our own prejudices and coming to understand the anxieties, pressures, and expectations an American male faces in today's society was itself a powerful learning experience. It enriched our personal lives and added to our professional skills. But more importantly, it provided the necessary information to help us dismantle the he-man myth that figures so strongly in relationships between the sexes.

DEMOGRAPHIC DATA

Number of men interviewed: 120

AGES		GEOGRAPHIC AREA	
Under 20	1	East Coast	39
20–29	19	South	17
30–39	50	Midwest	22
40–49	18	West	42
50–59	13		
60–69	13		
70 and up	6		

RACE

Caucasian	108
Third World	12

MEN CURRENTLY MARRIED OR
LIVING WITH PARTNER: 62

NUMBER OF YEARS TOGETHER	
Under a year	6
1–10 years	32
11–20 years	10
21–30 years	6
31 years and over	8

CHILDREN*	MARRIED OR LIVING TOGETHER	SINGLE
Expecting or child under 2	18	0
Children ages 2–11	17	11
Children 12 and older living at home	11	13
Children grown	19	16

	LIVING WITH A PARTNER	LIVING ALONE
No children	11	29

* Twenty-three men have children in two age groups and are counted twice. One man has children in three age groups and is counted three times.

OCCUPATION

Administrators/supervisors	8
Artists/photographers	3
Businessmen	7
Clergymen	6
Consultants	7
Educators/teachers	15
Hairdressers	1
Lawyers	7
Mental health professionals	15
Military personnel	1
Office personnel	1
Physical health professionals	5
Planners/environmentalists	2
Politicians/lobbyists	3
Retired	10
Salesmen	4
Scientists/economists/engineers	3
Students	14
Waiters	1
Writers/editors/producers	7

CHAPTER ONE

THE NEW SUPER-MEN

America was looking for a hero in 1938, the ninth year of the Great Depression. And find one they did:

> Look! Up in the sky!
> It's a bird!
> It's a plane!
> It's Superman![1]

The legendary comic strip hero Superman is hardly a real-life role model, yet the image he evokes is etched upon the consciousness of the majority of Americans. A cartoon character, the man of steel, as we all know, has "powers and abilities far beyond those of mortal men." Omnipotent, with X-ray vision, Superman assumed control in situations gone haywire and, in doing so, won the admiration of men and the love of Lois Lane. He epitomized the stereotype of a truly masculine man. Put into sexual terms, Superman is the quintessential macho symbol. Larger than life, he stands for power and dominance. His strength is legendary and he is always in control. Were this comic strip to have been X-rated, Superman would have been a sexual star, with unmatched prowess and enduring skill.

Clark Kent, in contrast, was Lois's buddy—considerate, vulnerable, kind, polite, a bit of a bungler. Certainly he was no one to rave about. Always seen as a Milquetoast kind of guy, Clark Kent is antithetical to the macho man and would be considered anything but a sex symbol.

The Superman/Clark Kent dichotomy represents, for our purposes, the perfect metaphor for the contrasting poles of male sexuality. Although each is a stereotype, particularly Superman, together they stand at opposite extremes of the wide-ranging spectrum of male experience.

Superman has been the unconscious and sometimes conscious role model, molding men's sexual self-concepts. Clark Kent has been the ultimate weakling men have steeled themselves against becoming. But today things are changing. We interviewed men who are finding the Superman/he-man image suffocating, with its emphasis on power, control, perfection, and incredible strength. They say their relationships have suffered, and that the man-of-steel image was not necessarily the most conducive to establishing and maintaining sexual intimacy. Clark Kent, on the other hand, had qualities necessary for building intimacy with a mate. The sensitive, considerate, trustworthy, and vulnerable aspects of his personality are those that women have complained most vociferously about men lacking. Consequently, because of the problems inherent in this conflict, many of the men we interviewed were in the process of rejecting or redefining aspects of the traditional view of the masculine male. Part of this process included taking a new look at the previously unappreciated qualities of the mild-mannered reporter. As men reevaluated their masculine images—by making a more realistic appraisal of the Superman expectations and by tapping into the feelings and emotions of their Clark Kent side—they were giving themselves many more options in expressing themselves as sexual beings.

Many of the interviewees consciously wanted to integrate both the Superman and Clark Kent aspects of themselves. Others, during the course of the interview, realized their attitudes and behaviors had been shifting of their own accord. From our perspective, we could see that men were picking and choosing from the full range of options available between the two symbolic extremes. They did not want to have to sacrifice one set of attributes and emotions for the other. They wanted to be able to pick and choose from the entire spectrum, when appropriate, in order to feel like a more complete human being.

For most, the redefinition of their masculinity was a painful process that came in response to the breakup of a relationship or a marriage. For others, it was a gradual change that took place over years, often in response to the women they were relating to or changes in the culture. But like our super-hero, who darts unobtrusively into a phone booth to switch into his disguise, most of the men we interviewed have been making these changes quietly, and often in isolation, without the advantage many women have had of being able to reach out to their peers for support. Part of the macho ethic, after all, calls for silent, stoic self-sufficiency.

The ways in which the one hundred and twenty men we interviewed perceived these changes, although individually unique, when taken together pointed to an unmistakable change in men's beliefs about their sexuality. To better understand the history of this trend and the need for making these changes, we must first understand the source of men's sexual identity—machismo—and examine its effect on men's lives.

TODAY I AM A MAN

Every culture has some form of a rite of passage that indicates arrival into manhood. It may be loosely defined, such as when young men leave their families and enter the military or move into their own apartments. Or it may be strictly ceremonial, as with the Jewish Bar Mitzvah, when the rabbi proclaims. "Today you are a man." But regardless of the ritual and the culture's stamp of approval, the truth is that men often continue to wonder whether they measure up. It's almost impossible to measure overall achievement —feats of strength, power, success, or satisfaction—in areas of a man's life other than the sexual. Standards for Real Manhood are, except for monetary success, ambiguous, and high achievers occasionally have nagging doubts that they've indeed "made it." But in the sexual arena the criteria are clear-cut. They have to do with fulfilling the sexual requirements of "machismo." And few men measure up at all times to every criterion.

Machismo is a Spanish term meaning maleness, dominance, courage, virility, and aggressiveness—the opposite of tenderness, passivity, vulnerability, and sensitivity. Above all, it is sexual prowess and control. Macho men, according to this script:

always are ready to have sex

always have rock-hard erections

always have unending staying power

always satisfy their women

One man we interviewed, Verner, age forty, describes a macho man as a "cocksman who brings quarts of Gatorade to bed and who is able to just get down . . . just ball for forty-eight hours. Then he looks over and says, 'I can tell you're not getting enough.' And goes at it some more."

The essence of machismo lies with always having to prove oneself. And the key word here is "always." In every instance a man is trying to live up to a set of idealized standards. They are impossible dreams, those set up by the machismo ethic, in which performance counts for everything. In the sexual encounter, it means a man is the lead actor, scriptwriter, director, and producer, all rolled into one. He runs the entire show, from beginning to end, and is expected to perform with the strength and endurance of a machine. And although men intellectually scoff at these myths and are quick to say they recognize how impossible they are, inwardly they wonder whether the guy next door is more of a man in bed than they are. After all, the myths and messages continue to be perpetuated in our culture today. They are alive in our minds and are reflected in our books. This titillating passage from Harold Robbins's *The Betsy* is an example of the ultimate in macho performance:

> Gently her fingers opened his union suit and he sprang out at her like an angry lion from its cage. Carefully she peeled back his foreskin, exposing his red and angry glans, and took him in both hands, one behind the other as if she were grasping a baseball bat. She stared at it in wonder. *"C'est formidable. Un vrai canon"* . . .
>
> Naked, he looked even more an animal than before. Shoulders, chest, and belly covered with hair out of which sprang the massive erection . . . She almost fainted looking down at him. Slowly he began to lower her on him. Her legs came up . . . as he began to enter her . . . It was as if a giant of white-hot steel were penetrating her vitals. She began to moan as it opened her and climbed higher into her body, past her womb, past her stomach, under her heart, up into her throat. She was panting now, like a bitch in heat . . . His hands reached and

grasped each of her heavy breasts as if he wanted to tear them from her body. She moaned in pain and writhed, her pelvis suddenly arching and thrusting toward him. Then he entered her again.

"*Mon Dieu!*" she cried, the tears springing into her eyes. "*Mon Dieu!*" She began to climax almost before he was fully inside her. Then she couldn't stop them, one coming rapidly after the other as he slammed into her with the force of the giant body press she had seen working in his factory . . . Somehow she became confused, the man and the machine they were one and the same and the strength was something else she had never known before. And finally, when orgasm after orgasm had racked her body into a searing sheet of flame and she could bear no more, she cried out to him in French. "Take your pleasure with me! . . . Quick before I die!" A roar came from deep inside his throat and his hands tightened on her breasts. She half screamed and her hands grabbed into the hair of his chest. Then all his weight seemed to fall in on her, crushing the breath from her body, and she felt the hot onrushing gusher of his semen turning her insides into viscous, flowing lava. She discovered herself climaxing again.[2]

Sensible men scoff when they read about "a giant of white-hot steel . . . penetrating her vitals." Still, this exaggerated version of a star-studded sexual performance is but one of thousands that might make even the most secure man wonder whether such bedtime scenes are common and why he is missing out. Men put an enormous amount of pressure on themselves. They are anxious about their performance and particularly about the performance of the main actor, their penis. As with athletes and musicians who rely on top-notch equipment, many men feel they need the perfect "instrument" to make love. One sex expert says the perfect mythical macho penis is "two feet long, hard as steel, and can go all night."[3] Popular literature has them thick, long, throbbing, and perpetually erect. They are also described as rods, shafts, machines, and swords that are ready at a moment's notice to plow, plunder, or penetrate their partner.

With men having internal anxiety over whether their penis is large enough, firm enough, and sufficiently powerful, it is no won-

der that the myth of the gargantuan penis keeps getting perpetuated in art, advertising, and even in humor. For instance, the following is just one of the endless variations of the familiar
man/horse/penis joke:

A man goes into a rough-looking bar in a small town in the Old
West. As he sits down he notices a horse seated at the end of
the bar holding a hatful of money in front of him. The man
pulls the bartender aside and asks: "What's that horse doing
with all that money?" "Well," explains the bartender, "we have
this contest going. If you can make the horse laugh, you win all
the money in the hat. If you can't, you put in ten dollars."
"Hey, that's easy," the man says as he gets up, walks over to
the horse and whispers something into his ear. Suddenly the
horse bursts out laughing. The bartender is amazed but hands
over the money.

Two weeks later the same man goes into the same bar and
sees the same horse sitting at the end of the bar, this time with
a larger hatful of money. The bartender tells the man, "This
time it's much harder. This time you have to make the horse
cry." "Nothing to it," says the man and proceeds to take the
horse aside. A few minutes later he returns with the horse
whose eyes are streaming with tears. The bartender is incredu-
lous. "How the hell did you do it?" he asks. "Easy," the man
replies. "First, to make him laugh, I whispered, 'My penis is
bigger than yours.' Then, to make him cry, I showed him!"

While no man would expect his penis to be as large as that of a
horse, this joke does reflect the message many of the men we interviewed had learned during childhood. Because the male genitals
are external, readily visible, easily touched and experienced, boys
have grown up equating their masculinity with their penises.
Unlike little girls whose genitals are hidden, most boys fondled and
experimented with their penises from infancy on. As youngsters,
some even had nicknames for their penises and proudly showed
them off to friends. Boys got together and held competitions to see
who could pee the farthest. Later on, the emphasis was on who
could ejaculate the fastest. One man facetiously defined a macho
man as one who comes in first *and* third in a circle jerk. Another

man we interviewed told us his father reinforced this macho mentality when talking his sons into eating tomatoes. He encouraged them by saying, "They'll make your dick hard." Imagine a girl hearing something comparable about her genitals from her mother.

George, a thirty-four-year-old builder, remembers when his father made the same penis-equals-man connection for him:

I was in the car with my father and I had an erection, as often happens to a little boy. I remember sticking my hand in my pocket and kind of pushing my penis down, which felt pretty good, when he noticed it and said something like, "Well, I can see you're becoming a man." There it was! A stiff dick means becoming a man.

George goes on to say that despite everything he has learned intellectually about what it means to be a man, he often still measures himself in terms of the performance of his penis:

If anyone had said to me that you measure your manliness by how you think, how you conduct yourself, how you communicate, how responsible you are, I would have thought they were terrific concepts. But I would have still said, "No, you measure yourself by how big your penis is and how much sexual satisfaction you can get." I think this is a real sickness. It means you don't go looking for a relationship, you go looking for a chance to demonstrate that you're sexually capable.

These childhood impressions left at least some imprint on all the men we interviewed. Regardless of age or education, men viewed their virility, in part, according to the form and functioning of their penis. For them each and every sexual encounter was yet another test of manhood. It mattered not how well they did the night before or that they had received a standing ovation a month earlier; they had to surpass that performance or at least equal it each and every time they had sex. Says Verner, age forty:

The stakes are so high when it comes to sex. It's becoming one of the most difficult things when it should be the easiest. My God, our whole dignity and sense of self-worth, adequacy, everything, is measured by it.

Men who became wrapped up in this philosophy came to see performance as their primary consideration. Before Nathan, age forty, and father of a three-year-old daughter, had married, he recalls feeling:

> I continually had to strut. You know, I had to show the woman I was involved with that I could screw her more times per night than she could screw back. I had to literally screw her into the wall.

In this macho scenario, with sex as the ultimate proof of manhood, women fit in primarily as objects. And this objectified state is directly reflected by the harsh words used to describe women, such as "piece," "pussy," and "cunt." Ned, age thirty-four, recalls going out with his father during his adolescence. Whenever they spotted a woman in a tight dress, his father would inevitably say, "How'd you like to get a piece of that?" Ned says that although it took him some time to figure out what he meant by a piece, his response was always, "Yeah, I'd love it."

This mentality encourages men to think of sex with women as conquests that not only prove their manhood, but also give them status among their peers. Emmitt, now fifty-eight, admits that this used to be his attitude toward sex. He says: "It was the familiar slam, bam, thank you, ma'am. I used to think, 'Get it over with, get out and get the next one.' The process was similar to the concept of acquiring notches on your belt."

Sex, for a man with this mindset, can become so impersonal that one man described it as using "a cunt to masturbate in. You so depersonalize that human being that sex literally becomes a masturbatory act."

Some of the men we interviewed had been raised to believe that women actually preferred this one-way sexual experience. They learned that a woman didn't get much pleasure from the sex act itself. They believed her source of pleasure came from satisfying her man's insistent sexual urges. Gary, a thirty-one-year-old psychologist and writer, says:

> I was taught at an early age that a woman gets off by getting a man off. I thought what a woman most enjoys about sex is witnessing your earth-shattering orgasm. Now I know that's

not true at all, but that's how I was raised. And so, of course, I was never taught to give a woman pleasure.

Men with this sexual consciousness faced the obvious contradiction: they were supposed to "score," but with whom? The women they expected to marry, according to the traditional ethos, were supposed to be chaste. So who were going to be the objects of their sexual desires? The way these men resolved the obvious contradiction was to split women into two groups: "good" (respectable, decent, moral, and sexually innocent) and "bad" (loose, indecent, immoral, and sexually promiscuous). Respectable women "saved" sex for marriage and then they did it only to fulfill their obligations as a good wife—to satisfy their husbands and bear children. Prior to marriage, these chaste women were potential conquests, and a man who managed to seduce one might feel as if he had hit the jackpot. It was different with "loose women," who had no qualms about "doing it" before marriage, and, contrary to their "respectable" sisters, often enjoyed sex. These women did not represent a challenge.

While these stereotypical categories may sound absurd and antiquated to many contemporary men, they often prevail on an unconscious level. And for some men such as Dan, a thirty-one-year-old doctor, they can cause ongoing emotional conflicts:

My mother and father raised me to believe that you should never have sex with anyone other than your wife. And that you should always marry a virgin, which I did. The thing I keep hearing in my head is, "If she did it once, she'll do it again." My parents didn't know any better. But I've grown up with these very chauvinistic and conservative attitudes. Once I became a young adult, my parents had changed to more moderate and liberal attitudes. But I was still stuck with this basic sexual philosophy formed twenty years ago.

Those whose sexual philosophies have been molded since the women's liberation movement (with its now accepted premise that even respectable women enjoy sex) are less attached to the old stereotypes. However, in some ways, these changes in female sexuality have put even more pressure on men. Not only do they still feel they have to be the sexual teachers, initiators, and orchestrators, but also, with contemporary women who expect to be satisfied and who have had other partners to whom they can be compared, the stakes have doubled. In the past, a man only had to get an erection and last long enough for the performance to be considered a success. Now, no matter how well he performs, if he doesn't "give her an orgasm," he thinks he has failed and fears she will look elsewhere. And so, during sex, men often remain emotionally outside the experience, observing their partners for signs of pleasure. Did she moan, groan, contract, or flush? "Did I make her come?" they wonder.

The sexual performance has moved to a larger, more awesome arena and men such as Jason, a thirty-six-year-old consultant, say they have gone through a difficult period. "I felt very inadequate as a result of the women's movement and the increased emphasis on female sexuality," he says. "All of a sudden, women were telling me, 'Hey, you're not giving me enough, I need more stimulation.' Or 'You're rolling over in bed and leaving me hanging.' So I felt I had to produce more, deliver more."

By substituting the old set of macho expectations for a newer but equally debilitating burden, many men continue to feel emotionally distanced from their partners. Because these men aren't fully involved in the sexual experience, they don't feel emotionally close to their partners. Their need to prove their virility during sex often reduces them to sexual machines and their women to objects. By concentrating so intently on having and maintaining erections and pleasing their partners, these men often lead sexual lives lacking in intimacy. This situation is particularly sad, since sex is one of the few socially acceptable avenues men have to be physically held, stroked, and nurtured.

Our society practically forbids men the opportunity to be physically expressive in any way other than in a sexual setting. Men are expected to be always logical, always in control, never needing a hug or a shoulder to cry on. Their training from the very beginning dictates the suppression of their softer, more emotional, side. Research shows that male babies are touched, talked to, and handled less than female babies.[4] When a young boy falls, it is not uncommon to hear, "Don't cry; be a man." Brad, now fifty-two, learned early on from his father to withhold his feelings and always be in total control even when it came to sex:

My father didn't raise any emotional questions about anything having to do with feelings, particularly about sex. Even more than that, he led me to believe that you shouldn't let yourself be a feeling person. His message was, "Just control yourself, son."

Men who adhere strictly to the macho ethic—with its emphasis on control and performance—find they are paying a stiff price for their abstractions.

NEW SCRIPTS/NEW OPTIONS

The good news is that men are changing. The men we interviewed are recognizing that the macho role scripts aren't sacred (even if they've been around for a while) and that any deviation from them won't challenge the very foundation of their masculinity. It's not as if men are discarding their Superman costumes to show the Lois Lanes of the world their mild-mannered sides. Macho men don't suddenly become soft and sensitive. Instead, men are cautiously exploring options: the option at various times to be passive, to receive, to be nurtured, as well as to be the aggressor and to concentrate exclusively on their own or their partner's sexual satisfaction. They want to feel free to explore and express a variety of feelings and in the process to choose among the various dimensions of their personalities and to have more intimate relationships with women.

"Who are these incredible men?" you might ask. Even those we interviewed might pause here and question the way they are being represented. The fact is, very few of the men we interviewed have transcended the old attitudes completely. But almost every man, in bits and pieces, has made changes in this direction in his personal life.

These more enlightened attitudes were most prevalent among the younger men, men in their twenties who weren't raised with the "notch on the belt" mentality, where women were conquests to be tallied. The women's movement and the sexual revolution have left their mark most noticeably on them. With more women feeling good about their sexuality, coupled with the advent of the pill which has lifted the threat of pregnancy, more women are sexually available. With more women available, "scoring" has lost its allure and men have been able to be more selective about the partners they choose to have sex with.

Observes Bernie Zilbergeld, a sex therapist, who authored *Male Sexuality:*

> The talk among younger men is different nowadays. It's not like it was in my high school when a group would get together and say things like: "Boy, we got to get some." Or, "I got some last night." Now they talk about the relationship and the fact that you have to care for each other first. A lot of that is just talk, but I think there's also something else there. I think mutuality is coming sooner and the slam-bam thing may be on its way out altogether.

Men in their thirties and older, however, are also rethinking their ideas about what it means to be a sexual male. Some of these changes were prompted by divorces or failed relationships. For these men, the macho sexual philosophy—emphasizing control and performance, while bereft of intimacy—was often an instigating factor in the breakup. Other older men said their change in attitude toward machismo came about because of personal discontentment. The straitjacket of the Superman costume left them feeling emotionally empty, unfulfilled, isolated, and sexually dissatisfied. Because of this, men today are moving from the macho model of proving oneself to one of self-acceptance.

Nowhere is this shift toward self-acceptance more welcomed than in the arena of sexual performance. The pressure to perform sexually has been one of the most crippling demands of machismo. Almost every man we interviewed spoke of the anxiety and pressure of the male role. In the words of forty-year-old Verner:

> I suppose there are some men who can short-circuit their anxieties when it comes to sex; they can get great big cocks. But all the men I know are subject to a kind of silent terror that runs through their minds—like the terror of a person who has a $16,000 bassoon and finds out the night of the concert that the reed doesn't work!
>
> Every man in the world is shitting in his pants, up to, during, and after having sex. We need to remove sex from some

sort of combat or performance arena where dignity and worth are at stake and make it into what it is supposed to be—one of the most refined and pleasurable experiences there is.

Men once preoccupied with scoring reviewed their sexual history for us and concluded that such an obsession ultimately led to dissatisfaction and dehumanization. Gary, age thirty-one, recalls:

When I was nineteen I had sex a few times a year. At twenty it became a few times a week; at twenty-one a few times a day. But I really didn't enjoy it. Up until then I just felt I had to perform. I had to get laid. I felt judged as a man by how often I got laid, or by how many women I could seduce. Inside I felt like a whore, like a prostitute, for doing it so I didn't get any fulfillment from it. I even thought I was gay for a while.

Gary, along with others like him, eventually discovered that the antidote to his dissatisfaction was genuine intimacy. He says, "Everything changed when I met a woman who I really fell in love with. That made all the difference."

Others said their sexual satisfaction grew when they stopped worrying about giving a stellar performance and, instead, concentrated more on getting pleasure from the experience. When they changed their goal from earthshaking orgasms to just enjoying sex, sexual satisfaction was more likely to occur.

Wayne, age twenty-three, compares his new attitude toward sexual play with his favorite game, basketball. Trying to be the best, he says, makes for a competitive and not necessarily enjoyable game:

I find out when I play basketball, if I play for competition, if I'm worried about beating someone really bad, it's not fun. I'll be only concentrating on dribbling and getting it through the hoop. But when I'm playing for fun, I just relax and I'm much more open. It's the same with sex.

Wayne says that when he's not trying so hard to be "the best," he veers away from his programmed pattern of heading straight for intercourse. Now he says:

I have a wider view of sex. Once I even went so far as sucking between someone's toes. Or while I'm having oral sex, I'll put my finger in her at the same time. When I'm thinking of it as enjoyment instead of competition, I'm more able to think of new ways to satisfy her . . . or myself.

Men who shifted their focus in this way also realized their masculine identity hinged on more than their penis and its ability to perform. They recognized that a penis does not a man make, and began to understand that their sexuality encompassed their total being. Many, like thirty-four-year-old Dean, were concluding, often for the first time, that each part of themselves—body, mind, and soul—worked together to make their sexual relationships good or bad.

The thing I always have to remember is that the sexy thing about myself, as a man, is my mind, my personality, who I am. The most important sexual organ is between my ears. It's my personality and my conversation that turns her on and makes me a good lover—not just my cock.

Men who cut themselves off from their true sexual potential by believing that the penis is the only important sexual organ, place undue emphasis on its performance. As a consequence, if anything goes wrong with their penis, it is viewed as a fate worse than death. But Blake, thirty-eight years old and physically disabled as the result of an accident, has no sensation in his body from the waist down. He has no erections and no ejaculations. Yet this has hardly ended his sex life. He has personal proof that men's entire bodies are erogenous and sexually responsive. He has retrained himself to obtain sensual and sexual pleasure through the physical stimulation of other parts of his body and is orgasmic again.

Before my injury, getting off was like twenty or thirty seconds of sexual current. But now, an orgasm can last for almost as long as I want it to, for as long as I am able to put up with the intensity, and it is far better than anything I've ever known before. My injury helped me realize that the obsession with this one organ, the penis, is absurd. I finally got out of my shell and realized that the fact that I have a hole in my side and my penis doesn't get hard is not that important. Eventually I began to realize that people are not with me because I've got a ten-inch dick or because I'm good-looking—it's because of who I am.

The genital focus of most men usually hampers their ability to experience overall sensual pleasure and to recognize other erogenous zones. And this genital orientation, coupled with the macho role script that says men should take charge and please their partners often means they aren't able to relax and allow their lovers to explore their bodies and pleasure them fully.

Having to take the lead and assume responsibility for satisfying a partner created a kind of performance pressure that detracted from their own sexual enjoyment. Leif, thirty-seven, explained how he has tried to overcome this newest version of machismo.

Women now say they have the right to pleasure and now demand sexual satisfaction. And even when they say, "Hey, you're great," it still caters to my performance scenario. Because then I have to continue to do it well or even better than before. And I end up feeling like I did a great job, but I didn't get anything out of it myself. I don't think the desire to be touched, to be close, to enjoy sex, is a very important part of what's considered masculine in this society. The pressures are to perform, to be strong, to satisfy someone else—not to know what I want or how I feel. So now, I try to sit back and not get into my performance thing, but to become aware of what I'm feeling, which I think is equally important.

Those men we interviewed who had persevered through the initial discomfort of experimenting with the passive role found they enjoyed being on the receiving end. One man said that when he and his girl friend switched roles and she took the lead in giving him pleasure, he experienced "a sensual awakening." He had never realized how many erogenous zones he had other than his penis.

Yet, according to the macho ethic, there should be no need for a sensual awakening. Any experience that includes a partner and orgasm should be fulfillment enough. A true he-man needs no prerequisites for enjoying sex. However, many of the men we interviewed were able to admit that there were certain conditions that made sex better for them. These men wanted a more complete sexual experience, mentally, emotionally, and physically. And to achieve this, they said, they needed more sensual and erotic stimulation during lovemaking. But since most women aren't aware of their partners' need to be more fully aroused, men who want more must be willing to overcome the script that prevents them from asking. Roger, married three years, feels that it has been hard for him to learn to open up without embarrassment or shame and to ask for the things that give him pleasure.

Because men get raised to be pretty selfish in a mechanical way about sex—just get it on, score, come, and go to sleep—I had to feel close enough with my sex partner to really feel free to do and ask for what I wanted.

Another change men are making in the male script includes sharing the full responsibility for orchestrating the sexual act. As a result, most men appreciated female partners who were making corresponding changes in their scripts. Seventy-year-old Riley feels that having a partner who participates equally in the lovemaking results in greater intimacy as well as in a greater range of sensual and sexual experiences:

I wish a lot more men knew some of the things I've been learning over the last eight or nine years. When I was younger I was doing a proper man's trip and I was good at it. But it wasn't so goddamn fine. I was always in charge. I made sure I orchestrated the whole thing, that my wife had an orgasm every time. If I was tired or bored, I might have to fantasize about other people and other places to keep from ejaculating for whatever the hell time it took—and in her case it took forever. I didn't realize the benefits of experiencing both sides of sexuality, the giving and the getting. I didn't realize that until I stopped having to be macho and run the whole trip. So I've encouraged my partner to feel free to assert herself sexually, and I've discovered I dig it. It has broadened our sexual life enormously. Before that, there was a whole half of the process I never got, and the same was true for her. Now, we both get to experience the whole spectrum of sexuality. We both get to initiate and we both get to receive. And I find this equality has enhanced our level of intimacy.

Accepting an active sexual partner often meant unlearning certain attitudes about the way women ought to be sexually. According to Leo, age fifty-four:

Somewhere I learned it was okay to have sex with some girls, but not with others. For instance, there were some girls you could play around with or even sleep with. But others were nice girls, so you couldn't do that with them. And you certainly didn't sleep with someone you were going to marry. Then all of that changed and I had to learn that it was okay and, in fact, more fun to sleep with people you loved, and it was even okay to marry them.

Vince, age thirty-seven, says he was not even aware of how he had objectified women until an awful one-night stand made him reexamine his attitudes. When Vince was twenty-one, he met two women who were roommates. One was beautiful, the other quite unattractive. While talking the entire evening with both of them, he secretly plotted how to go home with the pretty one. Later in the evening, her boy friend came by to pick her up and Vince was left with the "loser." Even though he had his mind set on the pretty one, after a couple of drinks the one who was left over suddenly started looking good to him. He didn't know her name but figured she'd have all the requisite parts, and so, why not go to bed? But when he rolled over in bed the next morning and found the nameless female next to him, Vince felt less than proud of himself. "No more of these vacuous sex episodes," he resolved. From then on he wanted a deeper sort of intimacy with women.

This desire for deeper intimacy was typical of the men we interviewed. They cared about nurturing, affection, and a sense of closeness with a woman. Sometimes experiencing these feelings was totally satisfying and even made the physical sexual experience unnecessary. When Alan, thirty-eight and separated, slept with a woman for the first time without having sex with her, none of his friends believed him:

When I was younger, sex was everything. It didn't matter where I was, what I was doing—I wanted to get laid. Whenever I was out with a woman, I was busy plotting. But that changed in the last nine months or so because I have since had experiences of being totally affectionate with women without having to have sex. Boy, is that different. And they have been some of the nicest experiences I have ever had. The first time it happened, this woman and I were sleeping together, naked, but not having sex, by agreement. And I really got aroused. I just enjoyed getting hard. Then you know what happened? I got soft and that was okay. It didn't matter. And then a little later on I got hard again. And it was great not having to do anything about it. There was no pressure. It was one of the most enjoyable evenings I ever spent and I didn't even get laid.

As a consequence of breaking down sexual barriers with women, some men have discovered that they are also able to be more intimate with their male friends. They can share with other men topics which were previously too intimidating. As a result, they feel more nourished and less emotionally isolated. Art, thirty-four, says the advantage of having close male friends is that:

> It's good to just have somebody to talk to, somebody to share with, somebody to either piss and moan with, or to learn from by hearing what helped them. Being able to verbalize seems to help me put things into perspective.

Spike, age thirty-one, says that, in talking over sexual problems, he and his best friend have been able to help each other through some rough times:

> Dillon had his first sexual dysfunction this year. He couldn't get it up. He was terrified. Really terrified. And it meant a lot to him that I was there to say, "Welcome to the club. Where the hell have you been for the last ten years?" I could tell him to relax, that it comes and goes, and not to worry about it, it'll be back. And that helped.

Even though men told us they were reexamining their traditional Superman-like role scripts, it was evident that they were not adopting an entirely new set of Clark Kent behaviors. Instead, they were going through a growth process of incorporating qualities that were somewhere in between the two extremes. They wanted the option to choose from being sensual, playful, vulnerable, passive, or uncertain without feeling these were inadequate or feminine attributes that had to be repressed. Yet they also wanted to retain the powerful, active, even forceful qualities of machismo whenever they wanted. Both had their assets and some men were more naturally disposed to some qualities than others. What was desired then was the freedom to express the emotions that fit for the particular man and under those circumstances that were appropriate.

Making these ongoing changes isn't easy. According to Clark Clipson, who did his doctoral research on men's evolving roles, men use one of three ways to give themselves psychological permission to express these various sides of themselves. First, they might redefine the term "masculine" to include all parts of themselves, even those parts they once automatically labeled inadequate or feminine. The second way some men might be able to accept these nonmacho aspects of themselves is to accept the fact that men have *feminine* as well as *masculine* parts to their personality and that it is acceptable to have both. Finally, others might totally dismiss any notion of labeling behaviors. They would just consider their various attitudes and actions as different aspects of a human being.[5]

The result of this growth process is anything but a new cartoon character. Instead, we are seeing a composite picture of men who are becoming increasingly multidimensional. Because the he-man messages run deep and constantly reassert themselves on levels below awareness, making these changes is often not easy. Still, these men clearly felt good about the strides they had made and the direction in which they were going. As people they felt more complete because the level of emotional and sexual intimacy in their lives was more fulfilling.

CHAPTER TWO

LEARNING
TO BE A GOOD LOVER

Like Superman, who was born with superhuman powers, men in our culture are expected to magically land on this planet knowing how to be consummate lovers. No wonder, then, the worst thing one man can do to another is to impugn his lovemaking skills. This is the ultimate below-the-belt assault on a man's masculinity. When Vince, a thirty-seven-year-old therapist, was an adolescent working on a construction crew, he recalls the men ridiculing each other by undermining their sexual prowess. He remembers the foreman yelling out, "If you screw as badly as you sweep, no woman will ever want you around."

The foreman's words implied what the men we interviewed continually expressed: the test of manhood—whether as measured in the past by how much you scored or currently by how well you satisfied your woman—was proved in terms of sexual competence. And the macho myth that underlies this assumption is that men are expected to be accomplished lovers right from the start. But the reality, according to the one hundred and twenty men we interviewed, was that it took years of experience with women and input from them to become good at lovemaking.

In "The Regular Way," comedian Bill Cosby reminisces about his first opportunity to "get some" with the popular and savvy Rosemary when he was thirteen years old. Some of *what*, Cosby didn't quite know. But even at his tender age he believed he was a man, which obviously meant he couldn't possibly ask someone to explain the mechanics of sex. He was already supposed to know it all, yet all he knew about sex was the word "pussy," which he had seen boldly scrawled on walls and sidewalks. As he walks toward Rosemary's house for their first date, he tries to figure out how one goes about getting "it":

I've been thinkin' all week about this p-u-s-s-y, and I'm tryin' to ask people questions about how they get some p-u-s-s-y. And I don't want guys to know that I don't know nothin' about gettin' no p-u-s-s-y. But how do you find out how to do it without blowin' the fact that you don't know how to do it?

So I come up to a guy, and I say, "Say, man, have you ever had any p-u-s-s-y?" And the guy says, "Yeah." And I say, "Well, man, what's your favorite way of gettin' it?" He says, "Well, you know, just the regular way." And I say, "Yeah, good ol' regular way . . . good ol' regular way of gettin' that p-u-s-s-y."

So now, I'm walkin', and I'm trying to figure out how to do it. And when I get there, the most embarrassing thing is gonna be when I have to take my pants down. See, right away, then, I'm buck naked . . . buck naked in front of this girl. Now, what happens then? Do you . . . do you just . . . I don't even know what to do . . . I'm gonna just stand there and she's gonna say, "You don't know how to do it." And I'm gonna say, "Yes I do, but I forgot." I never thought of her showing me, because I'm a man and I don't want her to show me—I don't want nobody to show me, but I wish somebody would kinda slip me a note.[1]

Even at that age Cosby was strutting about in his Superman suit, thinking that a guy like him should already know how to "do it." Many of the men we interviewed felt the same way. In most cases their First Time was as awkward and uncomfortable a rite of passage as Cosby's. Not only were they anxious and scared but they were also sexual novices. And they faced the same dilemma: because of the tremendous pressure of machismo myths, these men believed they should be sexual experts the very first time they went to bed with a woman.

As twenty-nine-year-old Bernard recalls:

I certainly wasn't breaking any records to make it known to the girl that I was a virgin. You see, in my neighborhood, the macho ethic was law and men just didn't admit they were vir-

gins. It was like admitting you were soft or less than a man.
You had to always come off as a very experienced man of the
world.

Yet, how does a sexually inexperienced adolescent know enough
about sex to come off as an experienced lover in bed? Most women
assume that men had privileged access to sexual information and so
did we. After all, there are such traditional avenues of learning as
the fabled father-son talks, peer group discussions, courses in
school, and books on sex. But we wondered, how genuinely useful
were these sources? How much helpful information did they provide? Not much, according to most of the men we interviewed,
whose First Times paralleled Cosby's in that they were entered into
in virtual ignorance. As for those supposedly privileged sources of
sexual information, here is what the men we interviewed say actually happened and what they actually learned.

FATHER KNOWS BEST—OR DOES HE?

According to the myth of manhood, fathers pass on special information about sex to their sons. Robert Young of "Father Knows
Best" perhaps best exemplifies this well-intentioned and expressive
fatherly type who is expected to take his son aside and talk to him
intimately about sexuality. Not only does he explain the birds and
the bees, the mechanical aspects of intercourse, but he also shares
all the subtle nuances of sexual know-how he has accumulated over
his many years as a lover. This scenario, however, seems to be nothing more than a cultural myth.

Actually, most men grow up in families where sex rarely, if ever,
is mentioned, and no one takes them aside and helps them prepare
for their roles as sexual experts. Almost all of the men we interviewed, when asked if they had ever had that famous "father-son"
talk, answered no. As Billy, a thirty-one-year-old graduate student,
said:

> My parents said nothing aside from "don't get in trouble." I do
> remember my mother once saying to my father, "Marvin, you
> gotta have a talk with this boy sometime." But my father was
> much too embarrassed.

If the subject of sex was broached between father and son, more often than not, nothing more than a book passed between the two. Twenty-seven-year-old Raymond remembered:

My father walked in my room one day when I was about ten and dropped a copy of *For Boys Only* on my bed. And that was it. And then another time I asked him, "How would I know when I could produce sperm?" And he said, "When you get a girl pregnant."

It's an ironic situation. Men are traditionally given the role of sexual authority and are expected to initiate women sexually. Yet parents rarely give their sons any more instruction than they give their daughters—who are expected to be sexually naïve. Even when men do discuss sex with their parents, they are given only the most basic information—namely that the man ejaculates in the woman's vagina. Usually the information is technical and devoid of any sense of emotion. There is rarely any discussion of orgasm, of the importance of foreplay, and, perhaps most importantly, no discussion of the emotional or psychological aspects of intimacy. All in all, these talks provide almost no really useful information about sex and certainly no preparation for being a good lover.

According to Adam, who, at age ten, had such a talk with his father:

I remember when my father gave me The Sex Talk. I already knew that the man inserted his penis into the woman somehow, but I thought that sex consisted of his peeing inside her. I didn't know that the penis could do anything else *but* pee. I didn't even know that you had to have an erection. So I got the basic sex talk: the man inserts his penis into the woman's vagina, ejaculates sperm, and fertilizes the egg. Then the woman becomes pregnant, the egg grows into a baby, and the baby's born. It certainly let me know that the penis did more than just pee, but there wasn't any discussion about feelings.

In fairness to the fathers, some might have been willing to delve into the subject more deeply, but their adolescent sons were often even more embarrassed than they were. Scott, a twenty-seven-year-old teacher, whose parents came from Russia, explained why he couldn't talk about sex with his father, even though he was hungry for information:

> When I was about twelve or thirteen, the boy across the street told me something about jacking off, and so I went home and tried it and I thought I was having a heart attack. My body was out of control. It was terrifying. I immediately went out on the sunporch, where my father was resting, and I said, "Papa, I masturbated." And he looked up and said, "Did you enjoy it?" And I said, "No. I didn't like it at all." He said, "Okay," and nothing more. Well, the next day he brought home a plain brown bag with four books in it from the library about puberty and sexuality. He said, "I want you to read these. If you have any questions, let's talk about it." The books were pretty obvious. They explained the physical side of sex but didn't cover the questions I had such as, "How do you get a girl in the sack?" "How do you make masturbating enjoyable?" These were issues I didn't want to discuss with my father. I was too embarrassed. I wanted more information about the emotional side of sex, but my father was not my friend, he was my father, and I just couldn't talk to him about it!

In theory, men said that if they would have considered talking to one of their parents about sex, it would have been their mothers. In general, mothers tended to create a warmer atmosphere that allowed for the discussion of feelings and more emotional subjects. But in practice, very few men had talked with their mothers about sex. Especially during adolescence, there is often an acute awareness of the sexual feelings which are lurking just beneath the surface in most mother/son relationships. Oedipal feelings naturally rise to the fore as the hormones begin surging through a young man's body. And while acting on these normal feelings is generally quite out of the question, both parent and child remain somewhat concerned that these feelings are abnormal and could get out of control. Rather than risk opening them up further by directly talking about sex, they prefer to avoid the subject altogether.

Despite all these complications, some parents still managed to convey attitudes about sex that helped men become better lovers as adults. Barry, a sixty-seven-year-old professor, said he learned to be a good lover, not through any direct communication from his parents, but through their ongoing display of affection over the years:

> I was lucky. Even though my parents had some Victorian ideas about sex, when you come right down to the core of their beings, they were good, tender, loving people. I saw that and copied it. How else can you learn to be sexually loving?

Parents like Barry's acted as role models for their sons, showing by example that sex is intimately tied with affection, tenderness, and love. While this was an important message, it still did not prepare men technically for their first sexual experience or for being a good sexual partner.

SEX EDUCATION COURSES

If men did not get accurate and pertinent information about sex from their parents, what did they learn in formal sex education courses? Was preparation for the role of lover transmitted through classroom lectures? Most men clearly felt it was not, and they related humorous anecdotes about the inadequacies of sex education classes to back their point. Edgar, age twenty-seven, remembered:

> I was in the sixth grade of a Catholic school when the teacher announced that they were going to tell us about the "birds and the bees." They ushered all the boys into one room and all the girls into another room. They took turns showing us this movie that was supposed to tell us all about the facts of life. There was a question-and-answer period after, with the experts being a priest and a male teacher. What a big joke! Of course, the movie never said how the sperm in the man got to the egg in the woman! So one of the guys asked about it. Well, you never saw a bigger shuffle in all your life. They never answered the question. And that was that!

The quality of sex education was not necessarily better if acquired later in life. Chris, a military officer with two grown children, laughed as he recalled the sex education film he viewed in the military:

> I got my wings and my commission in June of fifty-four, and I

got married in December of fifty-five. The only formal sex education I had was in the military. They had this "classic" film
where this cadet goes out and gets VD. This, of course, causes
him to crash and almost get killed. And that's all they taught
us about sex!

A number of the men observed that they didn't really have a
complete understanding of human sexuality until they took classes
in college, long after they had become sexually active. As one man
put it, "Everyone heard stuff on the street, but as far as the truth, I
never heard that until I took college anatomy and physiology. And
by that time it was too late."

STREET TALK

Another supposedly important source of sexual knowledge is the
"information" picked up in the streets. Kenneth, a thirty-year-old
sales manager, says neither of his parents talked to him about sex,
nor, as far as he knew, did they discuss it between themselves. He
says, "I learned about sex through riding the school bus, talking at
the playground with other kids, in the streets, in the gutter."

However, the more we explored this source of sex education, the
more apparent it became that street talk was little more than
inflated accounts of sexual conquests or totally unfounded boasting.
"The bald truth of these peer talks," says twenty-seven-year-old
Raymond, "was that everybody was trying to prove how many people they'd slept with and of course none of us had ever slept with
anyone!"

Spike, a thirty-one-year-old investment banker, remembered that
"it was more like putting on a big show. 'Then I did this to her and,
yeah, it was great, and then I went back into her.' And stuff like
that. So it wasn't instructional." And, while enthusiasm was high,
little usable information was actually gleaned through such experiences. If anything was learned, it was how to cover up their ignorance. For example, even though Spike didn't have any real sense
of what his friends were talking about, he said, "I sure kept shaking my head like I knew what was going on."

Boys pretended they knew, even when they didn't. For example,
Cosby never did do it with Rosemary. He managed to avoid sex by

saying his mother wanted him home by twelve o'clock and they wouldn't have enough time because when he does it, he does it for three or four hours! As he returned home, Cosby ran into his friend Rufus and bragged about the "gooood" sex he got. When Rufus asked how he did it, Cosby first said, "If you don't know, I ain't going to tell you!" And then he added, "You know, the regular way."

So Rufus was led to believe that Cosby had in fact scored and really knew what he was doing. Like Rufus and Cosby the men we interviewed agreed that it was the appearance of having sexual expertise that automatically put a boy ahead of his peers in status, even if the stories were filled with gross misinformation, if not outright lies.

Even if most of these sex talks with peers lacked the vivid details boys could one day apply to their real-life experiences, something was gained from them. For instance, thirty-seven-year-old John, while quite aware of the limitations of these adolescent conversations, still found them to be important:

The conversations in my youth were not explicit, detailed descriptions of techniques, like "I stroked her very softly" or "we kissed for an hour and a half." They were more general conversations about what had happened. There was talk of oral sex, talk of what you had done and where you had been. So I still picked up new ideas of things to do, things that might not have occurred to me, had I not had those conversations.

In addition, these talks tended to cultivate special friendships, often of the mentor sort, in which a more experienced, often older boy became teacher to a younger boy. It seemed as though most men had at least one sexual mentor while growing up who stood out in their memories. Often an interviewee would get a glazed, far-away look in his eyes as he fondly recalled "good ol'" . . .

Burt Harris, God he was a crazy man! He loved oral sex. And I can remember guys talking about it, older guys, when I was younger, talking about eating women. I thought it was kind of a strange thing, and might even be a little disgusting, but Burt said no. He compared it to eating fried chicken—greasy, but delicious! I figured I'd give it a go, so I could say I had done everything! Of course, I didn't know that there were still other things you could do.

The stories they traded were often a source of fond memories. Harry, age thirty-four, laughed as he recalled childhood conversations with his sexual confidant, Frankie:

My parents never talked to me about sex. My first lesson about sex came from my friend Frankie, who was in the fifth grade when I was in the third. We would walk through the woods and he would tell me all about fucking and sticking your cock in a cunt and it was really a wonderful introduction. He also taught me how to light matches!

In retrospect, Harry conceded that what was "wonderful" was not the specific information shared, but the camaraderie of those experiences. Perhaps even more important was the implied message that sexual intercourse was a grand adventure awaiting them as adult males. This message was significantly different from the one most females received that said sex was "wonderful" only within the context of marriage and for the specific purpose of making babies.

Also in direct opposition to the experiences of most girls, most boys talked about masturbation, instructed one another, and even masturbated with friends as a part of their sexual exploration. In this way, peers were helpful in teaching each other how their genitals functioned physically, long before they were capable of sustaining the kind of emotional relationship that might develop with a female—that is, if they could find one who would be willing to explore with them.

Many men recalled group masturbation scenes as a natural extension of their male friendships. Several of the men remembered masturbating together between football practice sessions:

In high school, masturbating with the other guys was real common and fun to do. I remember in the fall, when we started double football practice. There would be one practice session between three and five in the afternoon, and then there would be an hour break or so, and then we'd come back and continue from seven till nine. In between those football practices, about half of us would go out to a local gravel pit and swim nude and jerk off together. Somebody would be telling a fantasy story while two or three others would be jerking off, seeing who could come the farthest. So jerking off was something that was fun to do in high school. But somewhere along the way I learned that it was a "bad" thing to do, that you shouldn't get caught or you'd get teased.

David was thirteen when he learned about masturbation from his roommate, who had him ejaculate in his mouth. Says David:

The first time I didn't know what was going on at all. I didn't know why he wouldn't let me pull out of his mouth, because I thought I was peeing or something but it felt great. And then he insisted on doing it once or twice a day for the next six months. I didn't learn to masturbate for about two years after the first experience with my roommate because there were so many accommodating boys at my school. Later on I had girl friends and we played with each other and rubbed against each other. I may have even come once or twice on top of one of the girls but I still didn't know that you could do it yourself.

While most men recalled these early sexual experiences with other boys without guilt or concern, some heterosexual men harbored fears that such experiences indicated they had latent homosexual tendencies. Don, age sixty-eight, confided that, because he couldn't share his feelings about the following incident, he carried scars of self-doubt about his masculinity well into adulthood:

I got very drunk when I was seventeen years old, and I got involved with some gay guys at a party and had a homosexual experience. I carried that trauma around with me for about ten years. Nobody had ever really talked to me about any of that stuff and I certainly couldn't talk to my parents about it. To my older brother I was just a kid, and we had very little communication. At least that's one way the world has changed. You can talk about these kinds of things now and not carry around those feelings like I did.

BOOKS

While sexually explicit information now abounds in the media—in books, magazines, television, and films—the men we interviewed who are now thirty or older remember a scarcity of such materials while they were growing up. Reflecting over the father-son talk that didn't quite do the job or bravado-filled peer group sessions, many men said that the most useful sources of accurate sexual information were contained in the few books they did manage to get their hands on.

Often, young men aggressively sought out written material on sex. Some mentioned ferreting out these coveted books from under their parents' beds or in their father's dresser drawers. For instance, Dean, a thirty-four-year-old psychologist, says that discovering his father's collection of sex books hidden under his socks was very healthy for him:

> I think he knew I was doing it, but he didn't say anything. He had stuff like *Lolita,* and books by Henry Miller, and even some more old-fashioned-type books. Reading these books had a very positive influence on me because it showed me that there were many different sexual possibilities. When I first started having sex as an adolescent, I had a sense that there were lots of different ways to pleasure and satisfy each other—like oral sex, for example. Not only did those books give me material for a lot of masturbation fantasies, but they also gave me incentive to get a real-life partner so I could try things out.

Not having the information at home didn't stop some boys from hunting down books about sex elsewhere. Jonathan, age thirty-seven, relentlessly pursued his quest for sexual information even in the public library. "When I was eleven or twelve years old," he recalls:

> I tried to check out *How to Teach Your Daughter About Sex* from the library, but the librarian wouldn't let me. It didn't matter though, because children could go into any section they wanted, so I just sat there and read it. That's basically how I learned about sex.

Reading books for sexual information doesn't stop at the adolescent stage. Men who are reluctant to admit they aren't sexual experts can get information from books without having to reveal they don't already have all the answers. As one man put it, "My sexual knowledge or lack of it is nobody else's business." He says:

There's always the fear that someone will find out that you're ignorant, that you're in the dark sexually. So one thing that worked for me was to read books by people who were knowledgeable. I started with Masters and Johnson and then went on to *The Joy of Sex.*

Even men with prolific sex lives picked up pointers from books that enhanced their lovemaking. Seth, a thirty-six-year-old lawyer, says that it wasn't until he was twenty-five and very active sexually that he learned through reading books that clitoral stimulation was important to the female orgasm.

When these new books on sexuality began appearing on the market, older men such as Chris, who was divorced at age fifty, became introduced to "a lot of things you'd classify as technique." Chris admits:

This is funny to say, but I was really naïve as hell about sex when I got divorced. I think I learned more about sex after I was divorced than I had known my entire life before that. One of the first gals I went out with after my marriage ended had a book called *The Sensuous Man*, which I read one day while I was at her place. That book was an eye-opener for me. I really learned a lot from it. It was always important to me that sex contain caring and tenderness, but the book taught me a lot about technique. Before then I had not tried oral sex.

Clarence, a sixty-seven-year-old college teacher, unlike his peers, wasn't afraid to drop his he-man mask and admit he was a sexual novice. He and his fiancée read marriage manuals together in preparation for their wedding night:

I was married at age twenty-four, and being a person who hates to fail at anything, I didn't want my marriage to be one that would go sour. So Carlene and I did a lot of reading together. We read such books as *Married Love* by Helena

Wright, and one by Mrs. Exner. During our courtship days, we would read these books together in preparation for marriage. We discussed sex in theory rather than just doing it, as young people do nowadays. Most of my friends were amazed; they said, "We wouldn't dare discuss that with our fiancée." "But," I said, "what are you going to do? Just approach your fiancée on your marriage night and say, 'Well, here we are!'?"

FIRST TIME

Because most men acquired the information they needed to become skilled lovers *after* they became sexually active, the first time they had sex was often fraught with conflicting emotions. But the first awkward experience was worth it if for no other reason than just to get it over with. For a male, being a virgin is tantamount to having some terrible disease. So men wanted to rid themselves of it as rapidly as absolutely possible and without letting anyone know. Virginity was a sign of inadequacy. Real Men, the myth goes, are experienced lovers; certainly, they aren't virgins.

Because of this stigma, many men, such as twenty-seven-year-old Scott, went through their first sexual experience pretending that having intercourse was old hat. Says Scott:

I had sex for the first time when I was a seventeen-year-old college freshman. The girl I was dating was a strikingly attractive person, with high cheekbones. She was elegant, almost like a model. I remember I went over to her apartment and we started drinking. Eventually we went to bed. But I didn't want to get into an emotionally involved relationship with her. I just wanted to get the sex over with—so I could *tell* someone about it. I wanted to run out and tell the world that little Scott Stevens from Atlanta, Georgia, had lost his virginity. In other words, then all the lies I'd been telling up till then would have had validity.

Almost every young man felt tremendous pressure to get that First Experience over with. It became a milestone of sorts for Spike the day before his twentieth birthday, when a friend insisted "you need to get laid at least once while you're a teenager; after all, you can't be an American if you don't do that." To help him overcome his strict Roman Catholic upbringing, his friend fixed him up with his girl friend's roommate. Looking back on it, Spike says, "She wasn't the most beautiful woman in the world, or the sexiest, or the most attractive. But I'll never forget her. I was relieved that I was no longer a virgin and was thankful to her for putting up with me and my inexperience."

Sometimes it was nice to have other male friends present for the event so they could corroborate the experience. Dean's first time was unusual. He lost his virginity in a hotel room filled with friends who were waiting their turn to make it with twenty-year-old Monica. "The whole thing was crazy," Dean recalls:

She had this pathological need to screw as many guys as she could. She met some friends of mine and said she would take on as many guys as we could bring. She really wanted virgins. For me, the whole thing lasted about one minute. I got into bed with her and there were about three other guys in the room, waiting their turn or recovering from the last one. It was not very intimate. On the other hand, it was incredibly exciting. It was my first sexual experience—the real thing. I was going to lose my virginity. There was this incredible sense of breakthrough. And having the fellows around, in a sense, enhanced it. I mean, it proved that it happened, because if anybody doubted me, he could ask Allen, because he was there.

Having sex for the first time with a prostitute often had this flavor of male camaraderie and male validation. Richard, now fifty-three, recalls his first sexual experience, which took place in a whorehouse, as being somewhat distasteful; but he was eighteen, in the Navy, and he and his two buddies had big plans "to go drinking and get laid." As Richard recalls it:

The place was real seedy. A hut with a dirt floor. I remember the gal, too. She had auburn hair and would have been a very pretty woman, except that she was worn out and hard-looking. What stands out in my mind was her saying, "Come on, hurry up, I got the next customer." It was business, strictly business. She went through certain motions as if to say, "I have to do this, what a drag." I mean, she made it hard for me to even *pretend* that she was really feeling it.

"Still," Richard says, "it was a good experience because at least I could say I had been laid! And I had a great time with my buddies."

There were other reasons why men we interviewed felt good about being initiated into manhood by a prostitute. One reason was that female partners weren't readily available to men growing up before the 1960s. The "good girls" they dated were off-limits sexually, and so a prostitute provided a socially sanctioned way to lose their virginity. Besides, the sex was anonymous and the men weren't going to be judged—at least not by someone whose opinion mattered. Perhaps most importantly, they didn't have to worry about their performance. The role of sex expert belonged to the professional. If things didn't work out smoothly, it was her fault for not doing her job well. Explains Verner, age forty:

> When you have sex with a woman in that profession, it's up to her to prove herself by making *you* excited. If she doesn't, then *she* has failed, not you. So you can go in and say, "Okay, get me off." If she doesn't, she's not a good whore—that way the whole performance business is removed from your shoulders.

And some men found that while the experience lacked intimacy, sensuality, and often ended only too quickly, at least they learned how to do it. "My first and only time with a prostitute," recalls sixty-seven-year-old Barry, was "a loathsome kind of thing—window-shopping in a whorehouse! The madam would trot out all the available young women for you to look at." Yet, he wouldn't say his first sexual experience was entirely negative. "The woman I picked was quite thoughtful," Barry said. "You see, I didn't know how to go about having sex and she showed me."

Aside from the excitement of finally ridding themselves of their virginity, the men recalled that the actual sex involved in the first sexual experience, whether with a professional or a friend, was often a real letdown. They worried they would come off as novices—not as the accomplished lovers the macho myth prescribed. One man describes the loaded emotional baggage he brought to his deflowering:

> On the one hand, no one told you anything of substance about sex. On the other hand, sex was touted as the most wonderful

experience of your life. On top of all that, there was enormous pressure just to do it—to get it over with and prove that you were a real, red-blooded American man! You were obsessed, terrified, and in a state of heightened anticipation all at the same time!

The spontaneity and confidence that come with experience were obviously missing from their First Time and, consequently, most men remember the experience as a genuine comedy of errors. The sex was generally awkward and self-conscious, and their attempt to use a condom was often looked back upon with humor.

Tom, now nineteen, made love for the first time a couple of years ago but says he had a condom rolled up in his wallet in preparation for eight years before that. When a girl he had been dating a couple of months indicated to the frustrated virgin she was willing to have sex, Tom reached for the condom, but to his chagrin, he recalls, "I couldn't get the damn thing unrolled because I'd been sitting on it for so long!"

Bernard, age twenty-nine, also remembers being awkward at age fourteen when he—not so smoothly—invited a precocious peer downstairs to his family's rec room. "My very first experience was really a humorous one," he recalls. "And was I ever awkward!" . . .

I remember all kinds of funny things about the first time, like leaving my socks on and having one of my legs still in my pants. I didn't even know that people completely disrobed! Besides, I was worried that my father would wake up and come downstairs and I did not want to be totally undressed. This girl was very nice so she kind of pretended not to see my awkwardness. I remember kind of ripping and tearing at her clothes trying to find the right areas. In my awkwardness I was just kind of falling all over the place. I somehow managed to get it in and come, as I recall, fairly soon. But it felt wonderful and she, thank God, acted like she liked it too!

With little accurate information and a lot of religious and parentally instilled guilt, some men who were incredibly excited about the prospect of having sex were also tremendously anxious about it —particularly if they didn't know their partner well. Hank, at seventeen, was especially worried about contracting some disease after

his first sexual encounter. While initially he was feeling grateful
that the young woman he had just met was letting him play with
her breasts "right in the middle of a restaurant," he had concerns
later on when they had sex. At the time, however, he remembers
thinking:

> "Heeey, my prayers have come true. I've been praying for this
> since the third grade! Thank you, Lord." She was an attractive
> girl with short, curly blond hair and seemed reasonably clean
> as far as you could tell. What I mostly remember is hearing my
> knees and teeth shake! I guess it was just the newness of the
> experience and not really knowing what was expected of me. I
> remember thinking, "Shit, am I going to be able to perform?
> Will I be able to enjoy it? Are my bowels going to get so loose
> from anxiety that I'm going to shit all over us both?" But I put
> it in and I got about three strokes when I had an orgasm—
> which surprised the hell out of me.
>
> I remember I went home and I took my clothes off and
> threw them all in the hamper. I took a bath and scrubbed my-
> self and really scrubbed my penis to make sure I was not going
> to get any type of disease. Now that I think of it, I'm glad I
> didn't come up with any blindness a couple of years later, or
> some terrible welts on my body.

Yet some men have only the fondest memories of their first sexual
experience. Peter's was with a woman he had loved from afar. "It
was uniquely romantic, because it was with the woman I'm now
married to." Says Peter:

> I remember she had a cold, a real bad cold, and she called me
> up. It was December twenty-seventh and it was raining. I got
> a bottle of wine and drove to her house. She gave me direc-
> tions on the phone but I got lost. I was driving all around and
> it was raining. It was a funny scene. I finally found the house
> and went down the stairs into the bedroom. There was a big
> brass bed with satin sheets on it and she was sitting in bed
> watching television in a long nightgown. She was real sick. She
> had a bottle of Chloraseptic on the table next to her. So I came
> into the room and put the bottle of wine down and got some
> glasses. Why would anybody want to drink wine when they're

sick with a cold? Anyway, we drank some wine. Then I mustered up my courage and leaned over and kissed her. And she said, "Why don't you take your clothes off." And so I did, and we made love for the first time—twice in fact. It was the first time I'd ever made love. It was classic. I was so innocent, so incredibly innocent. I didn't know what I was doing. I'm sure it was incredibly crude. And she was so sick. But it was really wonderful, because it was so kind of offbeat romantic, and, of course, because it was my first sexual experience. Now, every time I see a bottle of Chloraseptic, I remember that night.

LEARNING FROM WOMEN

Before their first sexual encounter, men could only rely on secondary sources for information about sex. But once they lost their virginity, women became their primary source of information. It was their continued sexual experience with women that ultimately expanded and enriched men's sexual repertoire. Their skill at the game of love evolved over time, through trial and error. Each experience left them with a clearer sense of themselves as sexual men. But until they acquired this sexual confidence, many men were reluctant to drop their he-man façades and reveal to their partners that they were less than skilled lovers. Some men found creative ways to conceal their ignorance and yet still get the woman to assume the instructional role. Edward, for instance, who lost his virginity at the ripe age of twenty, says:

In the early stages of having sex I didn't know much about what I was supposed to be doing. Still, I pretended to know but I would claim some sort of infirmity so that I wouldn't be expected to do much. I claimed to have a sprained muscle or bad back so that the woman would take over and I could learn something in the process. It wasn't until I was in graduate school that I started having good sexual experiences.

The one relationship that made it easier for men to relinquish the conventional sex-expert role and allowed them to relax and assume a more receptive one was when they had sex with an older woman. For the most part, those who were initiated into sexuality by an older and more experienced woman remember the relationship with a great deal of gratitude. Usually these women were sensitive teachers who gently led their young lovers through what otherwise could have been some very awkward moments. Because this initiation was carried out in a tender, caring way, not only were the men's emerging sense of masculinity protected, but they were provided with some valuable guidance.

Raymond, age twenty-seven, remembers how grateful he was for the invaluable learning that he received as an inexperienced fifteen-year-old boy from an older, more sexually sophisticated woman of twenty-eight:

I used to play in a rock 'n' roll band at a nightclub in Santa Fe, New Mexico. A woman who danced there left a note on my piano that said, "I want you to come home and spend the night with me." I didn't know what was going on, but everybody else in the band, who were much older, thought it was just wonderful. It was going to be the kid's initiation!

We were sitting around in her apartment, after our band had finished playing that night. She had a girl friend over, who had invited one of the other band members home with her. The four of us were sitting around talking. Somehow it came up that I was only fifteen, which blew her out. She was teasing me about how much hair I had on my chest for a fifteen-year-old and how many ladies I must have gotten because of it. I realized that there was no way I could lie at that point, because I would only get caught later. So I told her the truth. She was just marvelous. I didn't know what to do at all, and she just took over. She took it upon herself to teach me all about sex, and what women like. She explained a woman's anatomy and how it works and that this was her clit, and that you sort of stroke it slowly and gently at first. She just went through the whole thing with me. It was really neat. And I've always been told by women I've been with, especially when I was younger, that I was much more sensitive about what to do than most men. Because of her I think I have been.

Released from the responsibility of taking full control of the sexual interaction, men who had sex with an older woman felt more open to learning, and also appreciated one aspect of sexuality that is generally considered off limits for men—the pleasure of being passive. Dean, age thirty-four, felt that his relationship with an older woman fifteen years earlier had set forth a positive precedent which enabled him to loosen up some of his rigid sex-role expectations and learn to allow the sexual control to flow back and forth between his partner and himself. He recalls:

I had a very positive relationship when I was eighteen. Carol was twenty-one. We went together for about a year, and that was my first real sexual relationship. She was much more experienced than I was. I was essentially still a virgin. Having an early sexual experience with a woman who was a little older and a little more experienced helped with a lot of my anxieties. It also got me out of the more conventional male role of having to be in charge and having to perform. There was much more of a give-and-take in our relationship. I learned to let the woman run the show if she feels like it.

Gene, sixty-six, said the experience he once had with an older woman expanded his sexual repertoire and helped him develop an open-minded and guilt-free attitude toward sex:

I lived with a woman prior to meeting my first wife. I was twenty-seven and she was fifty-three. She was experienced, brilliant, and well known in her world. She had lived for many years in Europe, had had two husbands and many affairs, and was very sophisticated. You might say that she taught me a hell of a lot. Frankly, I had never engaged in the vagaries of sexual pleasure—the eccentricities of sex beyond the missionary position. From her I discovered that there were other ways to make love that were exciting. I learned about foreplay, byplay, different positions, oral sex—everything. She took away any feeling I might have had that what we were doing was bizarre or wrong by being so totally open about using her body.

It is not necessary to be older to be appreciated as a sexual mentor. Being open sexually, regardless of age, was what most men considered the most important quality in a partner they could learn from. As opposed to the stereotypical expectation of the passive, demure, naïve, and innocent sexual novice, men appreciated a knowledgeable and assertive lover. They particularly were grateful for women who were confident enough to openly convey sexual information yet sufficiently sensitive so the man never felt inadequate or put down. Spike, thirty-one, said that a relationship he had had a few years earlier with a self-assured and communicative woman provided him with valuable sexual information that was of tremendous help with subsequent lovers. He remembers:

> She was a woman who was a good-enough partner to slow me down, tell me what she liked, ask me what I liked. She was really vocal. She led me through lovemaking by saying things like, "Place your hand here, place your tongue here, kiss me here, suck this. Does this feel good? Does this hurt?" And it wasn't like an instruction manual, either. It wasn't, "Do this. Do that." She didn't emasculate me by telling me, "You're doing it wrong. Do it this way." She said things gently. Sexually it was not only very exciting but fun. And then, later on, even after the feelings had kind of faded a bit, and the strong emotions weren't there, I still appreciated the relationship because I had learned so much from her.

Through many different routes, the men we interviewed had all arrived at the point where they considered themselves confident, comfortable lovers. Each had acquired enough experience and information to get beyond the mere mechanics of lovemaking. Most men attributed this growth process to relationships with women they could learn from and with. But to reach this point, the men agreed they had to be willing to discard the strict macho ethic that says they should already know everything about sex and always perform perfectly in bed. In order to develop their skills as good lovers, they had to feel free to grow and evolve as sexual partners without experiencing it as a threat to their male identity. Raymond, age twenty-seven, had this attitude: "I always allowed women to teach me about sex. And I always thought that was a good thing." Still, he represents men in the forefront of this revisionist thinking about traditional male roles. "It's an advantage I have over most of my friends who are so into proving something that they aren't even sure what they are trying to prove," he says. "I just ask my partner what she wants. Even when I was younger, I gave up the notion of acting like a real pro when clearly I wasn't. And I found it worked better that way."

Declining the role of sexual expert was a relief to almost all the men we talked with. And even those who often found themselves reacting automatically by taking charge sexually were aware that the lovemaking was more enjoyable and they were more sensitive and better lovers when they could relax and enjoy rather than perform. Since this aspect of many of the men's sexual identities had changed, we wondered whether their preferences in bed had also changed. To help men focus on this issue we asked them to recall their best sexual experiences and to highlight the factors they considered most important to good lovemaking. We were interested in learning what particular qualities were salient in producing especially good sexual experiences.

CHAPTER THREE

WHAT MAKES FOR GOOD SEX

Emotions are everything when it comes to sex. There's no greater feeling than having an emotional attachment with the person you're making love to. If those emotions are there, it's going to be fabulous—no matter whether you do it in the missionary position or in position four hundred of the Kama Sutra. You know it will be great. They don't call it "making love" for nothing.

That was thirty-one-year-old Spike's response when we asked him about what factors make an ordinary sexual experience into a truly superior one. As the men we interviewed recounted their best sexual experiences and analyzed why they chose those to be among their all-time greats, their responses sounded strikingly similar to Spike's. The overwhelming majority of men felt that their emotional attachment to the woman they were making love to made the critical difference. Men described the importance of having relationships in which there were love, gentleness, caring, and warmth. Although the physical aspect of lovemaking was important, it was mainly seen as a vehicle for expressing love and caring.

Scott, age twenty-seven, described this special quality of lovemaking as a shared intimacy:

The giving and getting of pleasure is a greater gift and more truthful and longer lasting than mere physical pleasure.

And fifty-three-year-old Richard said:

You can have the formula—know all the spots to touch—but if there's no feeling behind it, it's not really exciting.

We were surprised. Above all, we had expected men to emphasize the physical aspects of lovemaking. We reasoned that men raised with the traditional he-men expectations would recount endless stories of protracted lovemaking sessions, earth-shattering orgasms, and a continuous parade of new and exciting partners. But they didn't. Only a few men put their strictly physical sexual sessions in the exceptional category. These included some descriptions of fantasy-come-true sexual adventures. Franklin, for instance, recalled "tightly packed, well-stacked Carolynn," the answer to a lonely soldier's dream:

I was in South Carolina on my second tour of duty for the Army. I hadn't had a "piece" for a while and I was going crazy. So I went to the NCO Club and Carolynn picked me up. She was beautiful. Nineteen years old and built like a brick shithouse. Oh, Carolynn! I was broke. Here I was on my second tour of duty, just got off leave and I didn't have a dime! I was drinking water at the bar! Carolynn came over to the bar and said, "Soldier, do you want a drink?" "Yes, you're doggone tootin', I responded. And we sat and talked and she said, "You're awfully good-looking," and I said, "You don't look too bad yourself, baby." And we went on from there. She had a car and took me out to a motel. I spent all night with Carolynn. Man, did she have staying power! As long as I could make love, she could make love back. Her hunger was just like mine. It was mutual—we were both electrified. We had sex time after time after time. I would come and Carolynn would play with me until I got hard again. Then Carolynn would come. We just went on like that all night long. It was the hottest time I ever had.

Yet when we went back to men such as Franklin, asking whether they would choose these experiences above the others, they said no, the best times were with partners they really cared about. More important than numerous partners and marathon sexual experiences, Franklin said, is "being with a woman who really loves me, so it's not one-sided. It's best when I'm totally infatuated, because then sex is warm, tender, slow, and ultimately more gratifying. The explosion at the end is awesome."

Similar thoughts were shared by other men we interviewed. Although they treasured memories of voluptuous experiences, these weren't considered the very best ones. When asked to examine which qualities made a sexual experience fantastic, they didn't describe all-night sessions or bodies built like "brick shithouses." And they did not want innocent, chaste, submissive partners who would resist until overwhelmed by their magnetism.

Instead, they focused on emotions. They talked about their feelings, a sense of being cared for and loved, the bond of intimacy with their partners. Ultimately, the emotional aspects of the sexual experience were what propelled a "good time" into the ranks of "the best." And while men talked about other factors, first and foremost they rated the emotional relationship as the most important quality leading to supersex.

THE RELATIONSHIP

Men of all ages, life-styles, and sexual philosophies thought that making love with a partner with whom there was intimacy on other levels, where there was trust, comfort, and a strong emotional bond, produced a sexual experience of a significantly higher quality.

Sixty-one-year-old Mark expressed it this way:

Sexuality as an end in itself is becoming less and less important to me. Techniques and things of that kind seem to be trivial. The quality of the relationship, how we relate to each other, is much more important. As the quality of the relationship improves, the sexual experience improves.

Even at nineteen, Tom thought that his peak sexual experiences were more the result of the emotional warmth and closeness in the relationship than mere physical attraction:

I just don't get that much real emotional satisfaction out of a purely sexual experience. The important thing in a peak sexual experience is the closeness. I have to feel open on all levels. As a matter of fact, my best sex was with a woman for whom I did not have a strong sexual attraction. It just felt really good to be with her, to hold her and to touch her, rather than what you would normally think of as strictly sexual feelings. I felt very close to her and I really cared about her. There was a lot of mutual warmth and love in this relationship.

And as the relationship deepened, the sex seemed to get better. According to thirty-one-year-old Billy:

I guess like any relationship, the more you care for the person, the more attractive they become to you. The physical sensations are enhanced over time and with caring. The sex gets better and better, assuming the relationship gets better and better. Boundaries become more diffuse and there is an inter-mingling—like the Vulcan mind meld, if you're a "Star Trek" fan. You're wrapped up in someone else's arms, and they're wrapped in your arms, and it's a really nice feeling.

Part of the reason the sex was better in an emotionally involved relationship was that the caring and comfort facilitated a level of communication that enhanced the physical experience. With time came a sense of safety and security that enabled the partners to risk communicating specific sexual information that was often necessary in order for the sex to be especially fulfilling. This is what college professor Charles, age forty-five, found:

The best sexual experiences I've had have been with women I've been quite deeply involved with emotionally. That's been important to me. The longer I get to know someone, the greater the intimacy and the better the sex. In my experience, women's sexual preferences vary, and most women are loath to simply announce their preferences right off. Given enough time, these discoveries are made, and consequently sex gets better.

While most men felt that a close emotional relationship took time to develop, some men said that, with the right person, the emotional level of intimacy could be established rather quickly, sometimes as soon as the first date. Nicholas, a fifty-year-old social worker, who has been separated for two years, had an interesting theory to support his belief that "it's either there or it isn't":

I almost always get a very quick feeling of intimacy. I immediately feel like I really know this person—I feel comfortable and I don't have to strain or anything. It just flows. And I think it's almost biological. I think people have different biosocial templates and two people fit together like pieces in a puzzle, depending on their background, how they were brought up, their energy, and other things. I can feel the fit in my bones. It has to do with very deep feelings and a very deep kind of energetic flow. When both people feel this, there's a kind of intimacy, a kind of understanding which is immediate and somewhat beyond words.

For others, it was not biological, it was the result of a friendship that had its roots in shared interests, activities, and values. According to forty-four-year-old Claude:

I've changed over the years. I guess I think of women differently now than I did when I was younger. The days of the airline stewardess are over for me because it's not worth the hours at motel bars talking about how senior you are and where your base is and all that shit. In order to have good sex, I need someone I can talk to and someone I feel close to. Then sex is just the frosting on the cake or the culmination of the rest of the relationship. I think the first good sexual relationship I had was with a woman I still know. It started out as a purely intellectual relationship. She was a reporter, and we were covering an in-depth story together, so we were in each other's company every day for three months. It was a relationship where we were really able to talk to each other. There was a meeting of the minds long before we ever went to bed.

Thirty-five-year-old Howard found that his relationships followed this pattern:

The sexual relationship fits into a greater whole. We had a friendship that was fun. It wasn't pursued just for sex. The friendship developed slowly, and eventually turned into a sexual relationship.

This feeling of friendship and fun that characterized the nonsexual relationship clearly enhanced the lovemaking. Fifty-three-year-old Greg added:

For me, a big part of sex is what I call "pillow talk." When you go to bed with a person, it isn't just slam, bam, thank you, ma'am. There's a lot of talking, fooling around, teasing, and tickling. That kind of companionability is a very important part of creating enjoyable sex.

All of the men who had been lucky enough to experience a genuinely loving relationship agreed that when friendship and emotional caring deepen into full-blown love, the lovemaking is unsurpassed. According to fifty-year-old Nicholas, "Love is really the best aphrodisiac."

Spike, a thirty-one-year-old bachelor, described sex with love as bombs bursting and bells ringing:

Sex is always fun, especially the first time you have sex with someone, but the excitement and fun is heightened logorythmically as the emotional state deepens. The sexual experiences I've had with women I've been really in love with were incredible in every sense. Where there are emotions and there's loving, it's not just fucking or some kind of masturbation. It's actually "making love." The orgasms are better for some reason. They come more frequently. It's easier to become aroused, even just after you've climaxed. That feeling, that emotional attachment, and physical attachment, is so marvelous, that everything else kind of pales in comparison. I've caught a touchdown pass in a football stadium with twenty thousand people watching. That was great. So is a great meal, great pot, Christmas dinner at home. They are all good feelings, but there's just nothing quite like sex with someone you love. It's the bells, the whistles, the emotion, the feeling that you never want to stop. You just want to save that moment, and it's a moment that you don't forget.

For some men, love equaled commitment. And it was this commitment to weather the storms of everyday life together that created the intimacy which often turned routine lovemaking into truly memorable experiences. Justin, a forty-three-year-old minister who has been married twenty-three years, declared:

I'm a very monogamous person and have been all my life. I'm married to the woman I really love and, when we are making love, I think back to the experiences my wife and I have shared—the crises, the illnesses, being with the children, problems at home, anger, frustrations—which just made us more intimate and more sensitive to each other. Each experience brought us closer and broke down more barriers so that now we're much more inclined to share everything. There is no holding back now. And that is true with our sex also. All the experiences we've been through over the years come together and mushroom and make it a tremendous experience!

After twenty-three years of marriage, Justin and his wife are able to draw from their years of shared intimacies to recreate honeymoon-like sex:

I try to make one auto trip a year to the West Coast so that my wife and I can be together, and on this particular occasion we stopped off at Little America, Arizona, to spend the night. We walked into the lobby, and the lady sitting behind the desk said, "You're a honeymoon couple," and I said, "You're right." So she asked if we wanted the honeymoon suite and I answered, "If the price is right." My wife said, "We're not on any honeymoon. We've been married twenty-three years." But the lady said we looked just like a honeymoon couple. And I agreed. "As far as I'm concerned, this is my bride," I said. "Well, for that you get the honeymoon suite for twenty dollars," she answered.

We went up to the honeymoon suite, had supper, took our showers, and jumped in the sack. We were just lying there reminiscing about the day's trip, thinking about home, and suddenly we found ourselves in each other's arms. I said to her, "Girl, I just appreciate you so much." And I went on like that telling her how much I loved her, how happy I was to have her. The beautiful thing about my wife is that I really believe God hand-made her for me. Anyway, even though we had traveled six hundred miles that day, it was one big, fantastic night.

SPIRITUALITY

While not a typical response, some men mentioned the word spiritual to describe the sexual quality that, for them, was most important. These men felt that the physical sexual experience was often just a vehicle for experiencing something much more profound. It seemed to be a dimension of sex beyond the physical sexual act and even the emotional aspect of caring. To describe this process men used words like energy, oneness, and unity in their attempt to explain what spirituality meant for them.

Some described it as a conscious decision to make all of themselves available to the other person—body, mind, and spirit. This decision often resulted in a special sense of oneness. Peter, age twenty, who has been married six months, experienced this altered state of merging or unity on his wedding night:

> In the contact of two bodies, there is a sense of oneness that happens. You stop being two separate beings and become one. It's a bit cliché, but I think that that does happen. It actually happened on my wedding night and it was probably the most intense sexual experience I've ever had. There is definitely a sense of merging. And at times, it's like being enveloped in something, and at other times it's just kind of like melding together. Sometimes, in sex, there is such a remarkable exchange of pleasure and sensations that it's like the two organisms become one, because there's all this energy going between the two people.

A number of men saw it as a greater opening of the heart. Mark, a sixty-one-year-old practicing psychotherapist, described it this way:

> For me, the most important thing has to do with bringing the heart into the experience. That's where I experience the greatest amount of tenderness and sense of oneness with my partner. I may feel that my being is embracing her, even though she may be some distance from me. I feel connected heart to heart. It's profound. It involves some altered sense of consciousness. It involves qualities that are beyond my words at this moment.

For some men, like seventy-two-year-old Alvin, the spiritual element was so important that, "without it, it isn't sex. To me, sex is not just a physical experience. A good sexual experience is when my partner and I fully enjoy this deeply spiritual aspect of love-making."

PARTNER QUALITIES

Next to the emotional relationship which included caring, love, and in some cases even spirituality, the second most important factor men mentioned that contributed to really good sexual experiences were certain qualities possessed by their partners. Attributes such as physical attractiveness, sexual responsiveness, sexual knowledge, and assertiveness could make all the difference in creating a sexual experience that was particularly good.

Physical Qualities

None of the men we interviewed denied that physical attributes were an important aspect of partner appeal, but very few could separate out a specific feature that was salient. And as long as he found her attractive, the size of her breasts, her height or hair color were really quite secondary if not totally unimportant. Said Barry, age sixty-seven:

There is something in the woman that turns me on and there's no way I can describe it. It's like describing a flavor—either it's there or it isn't.

As another pointed out:

I can't describe why I'm strongly attracted to some people but not others. It probably depends on the chemistry or temperature of the body or the way the body sweats or doesn't sweat. Some bodies are attractive and others just aren't.

Mutual Interest and Responsiveness

A man could be satisfied physically as long as a woman was sexually appealing. Beyond physical appearance, however, it was the woman's personality and her attitudes toward sex that determined whether or not the lovemaking experience would be outstanding. In opposition to the cultural myth, men repeated again and again that they preferred a partner who was as interested in sex as they were. They wanted a woman who was comfortable with sex, who was uninhibited and sexually knowledgeable. Rather than demure and passive women who required the men to assume totally the role of active and interested aggressor, men clearly preferred partners who were assertive and responsive in bed. They wanted a woman who was an equal participant and, as such, equally reaped the pleasure.

Men who desired a mutually active and responsive partner said they had grown tired of carrying the whole sexual load. They were turning away from the traditional macho role of initiator and orchestrator and were learning to enjoy a more receptive role in their lovemaking. Eric, age forty-four and divorced, explained why he found mutuality so important:

The phrase "mutual participation" comes to mind. By that I mean that I'm not doing all the work, and she's not doing all the work. It's half and half. I did all of it in my marriage. I felt I had to prove myself. I was always trying to get my wife to the right emotional stage. That didn't work. So I don't do that anymore. If my partner is not willing to do some work, then I'm not either. I'd just as soon go home and read a good book.

Having an affair with a sexually responsive woman marked a turning point in Alex's sexual confidence. "My wife and I did not have a good sexual relationship," said Alex. "As a result, I had extremely low self-confidence, few lovemaking skills, and a very poor sexual self-image." Then he met Peggy:

This was the first woman who seemed to want to make love with me as much as I wanted to make love with her. And I felt that throughout the experience she was enjoying what was happening as much as I was. I didn't have to do anything in order for her to get this pleasure; I was just there being myself and she was loving it. That was an exhilarating experience. She was tremendously assertive sexually. She knew what she wanted and she didn't need my permission to take it. I never had the impression that she was waiting for me to do something. If my clothes were in the way she took my clothes off. We seemed to take turns at fondling each other's body. I just felt that I was in bed with a real partner. She was not passive and receiving while I was supposed to be the machine that turned her on. This woman was having fun with me. And it blew my mind.

Furthermore, a partner who was as interested in sex as they were freed men from a sense that they were forcing her to do something against her will. As one man put it: "I don't want anyone in bed with me if she doesn't freely choose to be there."

Many of the men were very sensitive to the feminists' message that for centuries women have been sexually taken advantage of by men. To assure themselves that they were in no way exploiting their partner, men preferred women who were clearly responsive. Tom, age nineteen, confided:

> I feel really good about pleasing my partner. It is very important to me to feel like she is getting satisfaction out of our lovemaking. Otherwise, I feel like I'm exploiting her. Then it's not a complete experience for me, because, to be really complete, it has to be shared.

Some men had more selfish motives. They wanted a sexually responsive partner because they found that their partner's turn-on significantly increased their own sexual arousal. Paxton, age thirty-three and married eleven years, described this element nicely:

> I just like to see Candy move. I find that very exciting. Also, I really like the way she enjoys her breasts. I love to see her get excited when I stroke or kiss or suck on her breasts. That's very stimulating for me.

While vaginal lubrication, hardening of the nipples, noises of pleasure, and erotic movements during lovemaking were almost always appreciated, some men preferred making love to partners who were also orgasmic. These men often saw a responsive and particularly an orgasmic partner as a barometer of their own sexual expertise. As thirty-one-year-old Billy put it:

> When a woman has an orgasm, it's almost like I've performed a mitzvah. I've done something good. I have given something to someone else. And doing that makes me feel good about myself.

Some men candidly admitted that knowing their partner had

climaxed bolstered their own ego. Paul, age forty-two, told the following story:

I was about thirty-three and living in England at the time when this woman I knew from the States came over. She was black, exotic-looking, and very sexy. I picked her up at the airport, we went to my flat, and spent the weekend in bed. It was a weekend of uninterrupted sex with no demands. It was very sensual. There wasn't a great deal of intellectual conversation, simply because we were so taken up with each other's sexual needs. She was as sexually aggressive as I was. She had no inhibitions and we did everything. I think the reason why this weekend stays with me is because she was so satisfied. I knew I had completely fulfilled her, so the question "Was it as good for you as it was for me?" was never asked. It was just obvious by what she said. It was a bacchanalian feast and, after it was over, my ego was enormous.

In addition to being responsive, they wanted a woman who was assertive, uninhibited, and sexually knowledgeable, basically all those things a nice girl is trained not to be. The less inhibited she was, the greater the pleasure the man derived from the experience. According to fifty-two-year-old Bruce:

I like freedom, the lack of inhibition, the flexibility to interact sexually in a variety of ways. So I really enjoy a partner who is equally uninhibited, who has freed herself from the hangups she learned while growing up.

If she was uninhibited enough to be assertive, that was a real plus. As Billy stated:

It's a relief to have somebody who will initiate things. It's nice to have somebody who likes to explore, who's inventive, and who will say, "Come on, let's do it," when I'm feeling ambivalent.

Not only was it a welcome change, but for many men it made sex more exciting. As Jim, a twenty-seven-year-old bachelor, said:

I'd say I'm usually the instigator of sex. But when my partner takes the aggressor role, it really turns me on. I find that particularly arousing.

A woman who felt secure about her own sexuality and had enough confidence to display her skills at lovemaking was a very desirable partner as described by Bernard, who is twenty-nine and single:

I like being with women who really are quite good at the lovemaking process. They really know how to help you relax by taking a bath together, washing together, using a gentle technique at lotioning, drying down, massaging, maybe some soft kisses everyplace from in between the toes to around the ears and licking my eyelids. I enjoy oral sex, and a woman who knows how to do that well is really special.

Wanting knowledgeable, active, uninhibited, and responsive partners resulted in many men preferring older women as lovers. The reason, explained Joshua, a twenty-eight-year-old graduate student, is that "older women play fewer games. They are less inhibited, and they tend to have more confidence in themselves. Therefore, they make better lovers."

Most men had lost interest in the role of sexual teacher and experienced that role as a burden. According to Basil, a twenty-one-year-old student:

The best sexual experiences I've had have been with women who were older. I've never wanted to be in the position to instruct anybody. I've never had any interest in that. I do not want to instruct someone who's eighteen and wet behind the ears! That's just not my bag.

In fact, many men preferred the reverse role. Wayne, a twenty-three-year-old student, enjoyed learning from a more experienced, older woman. The role reversal, he found, was not only highly erotic but quite useful in expanding his sexual repertoire. Wayne says:

Older women are a little more experienced, and they tend to do crazier things. They teach me, and then I go back and try it out on other women. Like with oral sex, they tell me how fast or slow they want me to move with my tongue. Sometimes they say, "Where's the fire at? Slow it down." Or they show me how they like the clitoris touched or how to touch their breasts real lightly with my tongue.

Preferring older women was true not only for men in their twenties but also for some older men. When we asked the men to elaborate on why they felt women became better lovers over time, fifty-year-old Chris hypothesized that older women were more comfortable with themselves sexually because they had had time to overcome the various sexual inhibitions they grew up with:

When a woman becomes less conflicted about her sexuality, she is freed up emotionally and is more likely to be in touch with her libidinal drives. It seems to me that when a woman gets to her middle thirties, she is more at ease. She's more comfortable with herself, and she's more comfortable with sex.

"Before then," says Ron, age twenty-four,

sex is one of the things that they do in order to be close to a male. It's just something that is expected of them in a relationship. I'm not saying women don't enjoy it. They enjoy it to some extent, but they certainly don't seem to have the same appetite that develops as they get older.

There were a few men, however, who preferred younger women as sexual partners. They found the role of sexual teacher ego-gratifying. They liked it when a woman looked up to them as the powerful, more experienced one. In addition, younger women helped some men feel youthful and more sexually desirable. This was true for fifty-two-year-old Bruce, whose best sexual experiences have been with younger women.

With few exceptions, women closer to my age seem to grow old faster than I do. And the things that appeal to me and stimulate me just aren't there as much with an older woman as they are with a younger one. Of course, I need a younger person with maturity who can learn fast and adapt well. But I meet a lot of women like that. Also, I like being a combination of lover, big brother, and father rolled into one. I like meeting the needs of women who enjoy the company of a more mature man.

Dean, age thirty-four, said he also preferred liaisons with younger women, even though the idea of it left him a bit uneasy:

> I am susceptible to young chicks. I've had one recent girl friend who's ten years younger than I am, and I'm aware that a big part of the attraction is her youth. She very much looks up to me, and I'm the dominant older male. That whole trip turns me on but also troubles me, because it doesn't really fit with my values.

PHYSICAL EXPERIENCE

For a few men, far fewer than we had anticipated, neither the emotional relationship nor specific qualities in a partner were primary in achieving a good sexual experience. For these men, pure physical gratification was the major factor. Such was the case for forty-five-year-old Charles:

> Obviously, there are more important things between people than an orgasm, but I think when two human beings are fucking, they ought to be thinking about that. I would call that physical gratification. And I think that human beings should be able to lose themselves in that enterprise.

Ben, a thirty-five-year-old rehabilitation program consultant, who is himself disabled, gave us a wonderful example of the sexual abandonment that makes his sexual experiences good ones:

> Knocking off a quickie to stay in touch and show you still care is not as much fun as abandoning yourself sexually. I love it when I roll around and when I'm finished my head's down at the foot of the bed and the blankets are all on the floor and one leg is hanging off the bed and I wonder how I got there. That's when it's the most fun.

Sometimes certain prerequisites are necessary before a man can achieve this level of physical abandonment. For example, forty-five-year-old Clint, a management consultant, said he needed to feel relaxed and free of stress:

> What makes sex good for me now is my ability to relax, to let go. When I'm able to do that, everything about the sexual act

is magnified. My orgasm is longer and more powerful. Sometimes I even feel like I'm being physically lifted up when I'm coming.

But in order for me to feel relaxed and be able to let go, we have to have no hassles between us. If there's something left unfinished or something I need to talk to my wife about, and I don't get it off my chest before we have sex, I feel distracted.

Sometimes it was necessary for the couple to spend some time together before making love in order to overcome the stresses of the day and reestablish the intimate connection. Clint continues:

There has to be enough time to establish good contact. I need time to relax and get in touch with Esther. That might entail talking a little bit, just holding each other, touching and making eye contact. I need time to realize where I am and what I'm doing, so I'm not just rushing in mechanically to make love. There have been times where just rushing in and screwing has made a lot of sense and has been right for me, but more and more, in this relationship, what seems to be appropriate is being in good contact with each other.

Paxton, age thirty-three and married eleven years, described it as "getting back in sync" with his wife:

My best sex is when I'm feeling really attended to by my partner. Often, this requires time. Those good times usually evolve after a period where things haven't been going too well, where our communication has been off and undercurrents have developed. So our best close sexual times evolve out of one of us noticing that things have gone awry and making a decision to spend some time getting back in sync.

Sometimes the time of day or night a man chose to make love was crucial because he could count on being more energetic or more relaxed during those hours. Albert, age forty-two, thought that his best time to have sex was in the afternoon:

I'm not very good sexually at night, but I love to have sex in the afternoon. I can almost predict that I'll have a good sexual experience if it happens in the afternoon. That's a real turn-on.

As opposed to the time of day, the amount of time available made a difference to some men. These men wanted to have enough time to thoroughly enjoy their partners through prolonged foreplay. One man said:

I think you have to build up to good sex. It's got to be tender. I love to be touched and I love to touch and hold, and snuggle and cuddle and all that. That doesn't just happen quickly. It takes time and preparation.

Men gave us numerous examples of physically outstanding sexual experiences that were still vibrantly alive in their memories. Emmitt, age fifty-eight, said:

I'm going to brag a little bit. When I was twenty-eight, I had this experience that I have never forgotten. I was stationed in an isolated area in Japan. And I went out with this woman one night. It was incredible. I went five times that night from about six in the evening to about six in the morning. I never achieved that before and I've never achieved it since. I've tried to duplicate it but it never works. It was the most fantastic evening I ever had.

For forty-four-year-old Eric, "there is a level of joy and intensity that stands out" in his best sexual experiences. The physical intensity he describes here took place while he was attending a conference with an old acquaintance:

After dancing, my partner and I went back to the room and lit some candles and put on some music. That kind of romantic atmosphere is important to me. Sex began slowly with kissing, caressing, touching, and talking. We sort of lost track of the time as we mutually stimulated each other. We spent considerable time at that. She had an orgasm and we went on to some oral sex, where she had another orgasm. The whole process kept getting higher and higher and more and more intense. I finally entered her. Again, there was more playing, different rhythms, different strokings, different kinds of caressing. I withdrew for a while and we stroked each other some more. I guess she had another orgasm, and finally, after a time, I did too. Then, after caressing, kissing, and lying back and enjoying one another for a while longer, we repeated the process.

My best sexual experiences are like that. There is a level of joy and intensity about them that stands out. It's like there are a lot of beautiful days in California, but some of them are really special. The sky is *really* blue on those days. It's a matter of intensity, of degree.

PLAYFULNESS

While "having fun" during sex does not exactly fit the he-man image, a number of the men we interviewed listed playfulness and spontaneity as important qualities of lovemaking. These men were opening up to the idea that, as sixty-seven-year-old Dennis put it:

Sex can be and should be just a hell of a lot of fun. It doesn't have to be more complicated than that.

When men described this quality in more detail, it seemed that they were usually referring to playfulness as the ability to be spontaneous and uninhibited in the way that is natural to children. Larry, age thirty-eight and married fifteen years, said:

A number of times recently our sexual experiences have been fun and playful beyond belief, like five-year-olds running around in a sandbox without any adults around.

Eric said:

A sense of humor is really essential because sex is really mutual playing. Sometimes I find myself laughing and just enjoying the playful aspects of sex. Afterwards there's the same kind of joy and satisfaction you get when you've played a sport well. As a matter of fact, I get the same high from running that I get from making love. It's a feeling of total exhilaration! One experience that brought particular joy to me was the time that my partner stood up in bed after sex and applauded. It was such a high; I laughed and laughed.

Fifty-two-year-old Jim agreed:

I think that the best sexual experiences I've had are those that were humorous. I remember one situation in particular where just as we were about to reach a climax she came up with some wonderful comment like, "Tell me, did you ever screw a girl who had a doctorate in journalism before?" My response was to laugh and say, "No, and if you don't stop talking I don't think I'm going to finish it either." It was the capacity to laugh at ourselves and what we were doing that added to our enjoyment. I know some people say you ought to be serious about sex, but I think it's most enjoyable when it's lighthearted.

For some men, the emotional security of an intimate relationship was the key to being able to enjoy a childlike spirit of playfulness during sex. Gary, age thirty-one, married one year, said:

A deep connection with the person that I'm involved with enables me to laugh more comfortably and not feel like I'm onstage. The fact that there's familiarity, comfort, and caring means that I don't have to be in a script that's really rigid. I could stop and go get some ice cream in the middle of it if I want to and feel good about it, rather than feeling like I have to perform.

Billy, age thirty-one and single, concurred:

With somebody I care about there is a quality of fun. There is playing and teasing, tickling, the kind of stuff that doesn't happen if I don't know the person as well. I guess it's the safety that allows me to be kind of silly, like being able to put my thumb in my mouth, or whatever.

Scott, a twenty-seven-year-old teacher, offered some examples of how he and his wife incorporate playfulness into their lovemaking:

Sometimes, we lead up to sex by sort of play-acting. For instance, my wife might wear a nightgown or some thin underwear, or we might put on some funny music and dance. We do this as an icebreaker rather than for any sexual or sensual reasons. Otherwise, sex is too serious and it's not fun. The fun element should be integral to good sex, especially for an old married couple of two years. If sex stops being fun, and becomes heavy all the time, it can get to be deadly.

VARIETY

We expected variety and new partners to be among the major qualities men would think important for exciting sex. We misinterpreted the popularity of the stereotypical playboy image to mean that men would consider newness to be the penultimate in good sex. After all, if variety is the spice of life, surely a variety of sexual partners would spice up sex. But far fewer men than we expected gave this response.

Those who placed a high value on sexual variety were concerned that monogamy would turn into monotony and that they would soon grow bored waking up to the same face day after day and year after year. Bruce, for instance, fifty-two and divorced, believed his taste for diversity made it difficult for him to stay within the bounds of a long-term monogamous relationship:

I would welcome a more permanent sort of relationship, but only if it were tempered by the stimulation that comes from a variety of partners. I feel this so strongly that perhaps I need to reexamine monogamy for me. I wonder how going to bed and waking up with the same person three hundred and sixty-five days a year, unless it's a tremendously unique situation, can really hold its appeal once the novelty wears off.

Interestingly, the men who spoke most convincingly against exclusivity in relationships were generally unattached. These men found one-night stands where they could have peak physical experiences without emotional constraints very exciting. One forty-year-old single man explained: "As long as both partners understand each other's intentions, they can have a good time and no one gets hurt."

And a number of men related unique episodes where they were able to sow their wild oats and enjoy casual sex. For example, one man described the excitement of a quick encounter with a particularly uninhibited woman he met at a party:

Obviously she was attracted to me. We danced, and I guess we were both feeling pretty loose and pretty crazy. Anyway, we ended up in the bathroom where she sucked my cock. That was pretty exciting to say the least!

However, since most men were interested in an ongoing intimate relationship, they handled any need they had for novelty in a different way. To maintain the marriage, some men willingly suppressed certain needs. As thirty-three-year-old Gus explained:

I believe that no one person can ever fulfill all your sexual needs, just as one person can't fulfill all your physical or emotional needs. You can have your emotional needs supplemented by the outside—you can get a job, you can have a female or male friend to fulfill emotional needs that your spouse cannot meet—but we haven't progressed to the stage where we will allow another person to supplement our sexual needs. So I just have to accept it and deal with it. I'm a believer that I'll always have fantasies, but I have to establish my priorities in my own mind and not feel depressed or hold a grudge when I can't have something. It requires accepting what I can't have.

However, some of the men we interviewed were unwilling to just accept the limitations of marriage as Gus had. Their solution to the problem was to have what they called "safe" affairs. These were clandestine one-night stands or short-term sexual relationships that did not threaten the security of their marriages. Some men confined these experiences to times they were away from home on business. Others "worked" late at the office. For these men, affairs provided the sexual variety and excitement they needed. A new partner was not only a conquest and interesting because she was new, but these partners were often willing to try sexual activities that were taboo in their own marriages. As one man explained:

I love my wife but she's appalled by the idea of oral sex or anal sex or almost anything besides the missionary position. I don't want a divorce because I like our life together but I'd go crazy if I thought sex would have to be like this for the next twenty years. So having an occasional affair is one way to keep everyone happy!

Of course, some men found that these situations were not always gay and carefree. Sometimes they boomeranged and caused problems in their primary relationships. Charles found his own infidelity a very painful experience.

I got involved with another woman and it was a friend, which made it very painful. It was one of those foursomes where we were all friends, and I was tortured by the fact that the man remained fond of me. We were all so close that it was really awful. And so now, down in the depths of myself, I think that I would never allow such a thing to take place again.

Forty-two-year-old Albert also had a painful experience:

I consider myself a monogamous person, but I was screwing around while I was married to my wife. It took all my time and energy and I would never choose to do that again. I would sooner go to my partner and say, "I'm really feeling turned on to somebody else and I want to have sex with that person," and say it out loud and get it out, get it dealt with rather than carry it around until the point where I couldn't control it any longer. The juggling of schedules, the juggling of lives is exhausting. I think I paid too high a price.

Two of the men we interviewed were able to do exactly what Albert contemplated. They institutionalized variety into their marriage by maintaining open relationships. This seemed to be a good solution when both partners were in agreement. Dennis and his wife, who have been married forty-three years and have three children and several grandchildren, found that outside sex even increased sexual activity at home:

One of the reasons our sex life hasn't become routinized is that we have had a very open marriage for the last thirty-five years. So we have outside sexual encounters and that always reflects positively on our sex with each other—which always increases when one of us or both of us are having outside sex. I find it a pleasure to know that my wife is getting pleasure outside and this increases my pleasure. I also feel less guilty if I'm having outside partners and she is too.

Nevertheless, an open relationship took work and sensitivity. The two who were able to make it function agreed that the marriage always had to come first. Dennis continues:

Neither of us are jealous people and there just hasn't been any jealousy at all. But we do have certain ground rules. First, Ellen does not want me to bring anybody home while she's there. And, second, we're very clear that we have a primary relationship. So if I want to go out, I would double-check to see if I would be disappointing her, not because I was having sex but because I was going out with somebody. And if I had any feeling that it would upset her, then I wouldn't do it. In fact, there was a period about seven years ago where I was really worried that my outside sex was bothering my wife. Although she was insisting it wasn't, I got a sense it was, so for about four months I didn't have any outside sex at all. Finally, she said, "You're absolutely crazy not to." So I went back to it, but the very fact that I did that reassured her that we really had the primary relationship.

Dean, age thirty-four, married nine years with one child, found that it wasn't always so easy to maintain an open relationship:

Having an open relationship has caused a lot of ups and downs in the eight or nine years since we opened it up. What makes it work, I think, is a lot of sensitivity and consideration—a sense of fair-mindedness, of fair play. For example, let's say I was thinking of spending a weekend with someone else, or a night with someone else. I wouldn't even bring it up during a time that Beth was sick or our son was sick or when her parents were visiting because it's a sensitive issue. If she's sick and I walk in and say, "Mary just called me and I'd like to see her," she's likely to say, "Fuck you, all you can think about is getting laid, and here I am sick." And I would have the same response. So you just have to be sensitive about when to bring these things up and how to handle them.

However, the overwhelmingly large majority of attached men had monogamous relationships and preferred it that way. Riley, age seventy, who has been monogamous for thirty years, said:

Turning on with a new partner is exciting because of all the things you can discover about each other. But I've found that being monogamous is what is most comfortable for me. I'm not a good liar. I don't have a lot of energy for that kind of stuff. Besides, when I really care for or, better yet, love the woman I'm with, the sex is better. So it doesn't make any sense for me to have any casual sexual encounters.

Scott expressed his feelings about his marriage of two years:

When I got married, I was excited about devoting my life, my sexual life, my emotional life, to my partner. I knew there were going to be limits, and that being monogamous was going to close off some options. But at the same time I had an incredible sense of adventure and exploration about making this commitment. If I chose to play around, I would be sacrificing the most important part of my life, the part that makes me happy: the emotional support, the desire for a family. And I don't mean that being unfaithful would immediately and actually sacrifice what I have. But in my own mind it would, because I would be giving her less, and I want to give her as much as I possibly can. That's what you do through marriage—you find more and more ways to give a hundred percent, not just fifty percent.

These men who enjoyed variety but preferred to be monogamous found ways to build novelty into their lovemaking with their lovers or spouses. The men we interviewed had various suggestions as to how to do this. Jim suggested trying something novel:

Having sex in a different location, like a different room in the house or a motel or even camping, adds something to it. And then with the sex itself, it's important to experiment with different techniques.

Experimenting with different techniques, for Joseph, meant not focusing primarily on intercourse:

It's really nice to have variation. Sometimes I'll just masturbate Paula, which I really like doing. Or I might suck on her, or maybe I'll rub myself against her buttocks and her breasts. But it doesn't always have to be genital sex.

Others felt a break in the routine could be achieved just by the way they were feeling at that moment:

Sometimes we purposely build a sense of novelty or surprise into our lovemaking and that can be fun. And other times we don't do anything new and sex is still exciting. It can just be the way my partner and I are feeling about ourselves and about each other that makes it electric.

Many men felt that spontaneity was important in lovemaking because it added variety to their sex life. Gary, age thirty-one, married one year, said:

This morning, for example, I had a spontaneous sexual experience. It was really nice because it caught me by surprise. Suddenly I found myself making love to the woman I'm married to and it was lovely. Most evenings we go to bed exhausted. We've been so busy with work and with a lot of other things, we haven't had the time to have leisurely sex in the evening. What made it good this time was that I was relaxed and turned on all over. I felt cuddly, warm, and fresh. I didn't feel like I just had to get it over with so I could go to sleep, which is the way I sometimes feel.

Joseph, age thirty-four, found that the lovemaking could be different each time because of a kind of spontaneity that was a rewarding part of his relationship with his live-in lover:

There has always been a sense of spontaneity about our lovemaking. Sometimes it's a combination of mood and feeling, but our lovemaking is different every time. Sometimes sex will be extremely loving and gentle and tender; other times, passionate and lustful; other times, passive and sort of meditative. It won't just be flat. There's this special energy there every time.

RISKY SEX

Another quality that made for particularly exciting sex was lovemaking under circumstances in which there was a possibility of being caught. The frequency of this response made us curious about the appeal of this type of sex, so we asked our interviewees why they found this so exciting. Most of these men said that the lure of the forbidden, combined with a sense of shared adventure, were the major attractions of "risky" sex. Edmond, age forty-seven, confided:

I think there's a sense of intimacy that comes from taking a risk together. There's a kind of forbiddenness to it that's fun. It is something that only the two of us can do together, and nobody else knows about it. Doing this really requires trust. You need to trust someone to make yourself that vulnerable.

Forty-year-old Verner recalled a unique experience which transformed a boring dinner party into an illicit event:

I think routine tends to mitigate against exciting sex, so the danger of being caught or the possibility of being discovered can make for a special kind of excitement. I'm really very timid, so I have passed up myriads of such experiences and have actually acted on very few of them. The most exciting one happened at the height of my spontaneous philandering when I went out to an expensive restaurant with a group of fancy people. On the way into the restaurant, my date turned to me and said, "Come with me," and she took me into the ladies' room while everyone else was being seated. I had just met her, and there we were fucking in the ladies' room. It was fantastic. Then we returned to the table for this very straight, business dinner. That made it even more exciting.

Dusty, age twenty-one, had particularly erotic memories of his senior prom night:

We were pretty much shit-faced, totally drunk, and we went off to the Washington Monument. The elevator doesn't work after a certain hour, but I told the guard that this was our senior prom and we were supposed to be getting married or something like that. Anyway, he took us up and we made love standing up going all the way up and coming all the way down. My girl friend stood between me and the guard and I just lifted up her dress and came in from behind. He didn't seem to mind; in fact, he never turned around.

Another man remembered a time in high school when sex was heightened by the fear of getting caught:

We were upstairs in her room, sitting around studying. My girl friend's parents were downstairs. We got to petting and playing, and got sort of excited. We did not want to have her mother or father walk into the room and catch us so we got into the closet and closed the door. I picked her up and wrapped her legs around my waist and sort of held her by the buttocks and went to town. It was wonderful. The fear of getting caught made it more exciting—I guess because we were playing with forbidden fruits.

Chuck, a forty-three-year-old corporate president, separated now for three years, said he frankly enjoys lovemaking when "there's a real possibility of being caught." He said, "I remember getting under a table in a cocktail lounge full of people and I went down on this lady right there. I took off her underpants and ate her."

Chuck also remembered meeting a woman at a crowded dance bar:

One part of a woman that really intrigues me is the small of her back, and when I'm dancing it's easy to get in tune with it. I just played with her back, then slipped my hand between her blouse and skirt right down her shorts, and then started playing with her ass. Then I just kept going. We got so excited that her skirt was hiked up, and my zipper was open. We never did get to fucking, but I got her off, and it was real exciting!

Fifty-nine-year-old Mel, who has been married for thirty-four years, recalled an incident that stood out as one of the most exciting sexual experiences of his married life:

I think probably the most exciting sexual experience that comes to mind was when my wife and I rented a place with our kids for the summer. It was our custom in those days to have very sumptuous lunches. So after we all had a huge lunch in this beautiful setting out over the Pacific, with lots of wine and stuff like that, my wife and I started feeling aroused. We took a little walk and lay down on the ground, and then my wife said something like, "Come on, put it in," and I said, "We can't, somebody might see us." And she said, "Come on, what's the matter with you? Don't you have any guts?" So I did, and it was one of the most exciting experiences I ever had in my life. I don't think that we were observed, although we might have been. But that's what made it so exciting.

Jack, a thirty-eight-year-old engineer who has been married for fifteen years, also told us about the time he and his wife wandered away to grab some moments alone. They started making love on a fairly deserted beach but ended up as the star attraction for two Army helicopters circling overhead:

We had been married only about three or four years and had gone to the Gulf for a week. One afternoon we took a drive down the beach to a reasonably deserted part. I remember that we took our clothes off, and we started walking along the beach. At first another couple came toward us, so we ran out to the water and stayed there until they walked past. Then we came out of the water and started making love just along the edge of the water where the waves come in. And I can vividly recall that just as I was going to climax a couple of Army helicopters came flying right overhead. I can't remember if I waved or my wife waved, but I remember that they circled. The spontaneity of something like that adds a lot of spice to your sex life—and if somebody else happens to see it, well, I guess that's just part of it. That just adds to the spontaneity.

For some men, the sense of the illicit could be more subtle and still enhance their lovemaking. One forty-year-old man reported:

It seems to me that I experience increased interest if I suspect that someone else may be able to hear or perhaps catch me in the act of intercourse. If I go on a vacation with another couple, and there is the chance that maybe they can hear us outside in the living room, that turns me on. I've noticed that when my in-laws or other members of my family come to visit, my sexual interest in my wife increases dramatically. I wouldn't be interested in a squeaking bed or anything that obvious, but knowing that some other person is in the house and might hear us certainly increases my interest.

INTERNAL FEELINGS

While men talked about the emotional relationship, various partner qualities, a sense of fun, and variety or intrigue as being important to good sex, underlying all of these factors was a man's feeling about himself. None of these other qualities was sufficient to produce an outstanding sexual experience if a man didn't feel desirable or his self-esteem was low. Men who were not self-confident, who did not feel good about their bodies, or even those who had a bad day at work said they found that these feelings put a damper on their sex lives. These men reluctantly admitted that, contrary to the he-man myth, they were not ready to engage in exceptional sex at a moment's notice. They needed to feel good about themselves for really good sex to take place. They told us that feeling relaxed, physically fit, clean, and confident were some of the requirements necessary for experiencing intense moments of physical intimacy with a partner. Kenneth, age thirty and married five years, recommended:

Sometimes just going and getting my hair cut, whether it needs it or not, or doing something else that makes me feel really good about myself, helps me feel really good about somebody else. It could be exercise, a little personal hygiene, maybe a shower and shave before going out rather than going out directly from the office. Doing these small things helps me to feel a little extra good about myself and leads to better sex.

Forty-year-old Verner candidly admitted that his own feelings of self-worth colored his sexual experiences. When he felt confident about his work, he felt confident in bed:

Sex really is connected with how I am feeling about myself. Very exciting sex only happens to me when I am feeling very good about myself—when I'm doing some exciting work or when I feel like "hot shit." When I feel insecure or uneasy in my work, sex can be more of an ordeal than a pleasure. I can't imagine being free enough to be seduced by anyone at a time when I'm not happy about myself. When I'm not working well, I desexualize myself. I have no interest in sex at all, and the idea of taking my pants off fills me with a sort of deep despair.

Then I become rather anxious about sex. These cycles are very clear in my mind.

When men did not feel good about themselves and therefore were not interested in making love or when they were not involved in the kind of relationship that would make sex truly fulfilling, they still had an option. Solo sex or masturbation was one way they could attain release—and, according to a number of men we interviewed, it did not have to be just a quick physical release. When they wanted, they could turn their solo lovemaking into a fully satisfying sexual experience.

CHAPTER FOUR

SOLO SEX

What does practically every man engage in but few readily acknowledge? What is it that enables individuals to be sexually self-sufficient and allows them to derive immediate gratification and satisfy insistent urges alone? What enables men to privately explore and experience the range of their physical responses? Masturbation. Masturbation, that defamed singular sexual activity, has not until recently been accepted as a useful and important sexual outlet. Boys who grew up furtively stimulating themselves behind closed bathroom and bedroom doors to prevent being discovered participating in that "loathsome act" have naturally grown up with negative attitudes toward masturbation.

There are, however, signs of a change. For instance, Alex, a thirty-nine-year-old administrator, says,

When I was horny and needed a release I would use masturbation as a quick fix. Now, since my separation, I've learned to think of it differently—more as a way to pleasure myself.

Alex once held the common, deeply entrenched traditional view of masturbation as merely a "quick fix" to release sexual or other kinds of tension. Masturbation in our society is generally considered a second-rate activity. "It's a bore compared to the real thing," says Brad, a fifty-two-year-old psychotherapist. And many relegate it to a practice participated in only by "losers." "It's something you do when you can't get a woman," says Paul, a sixty-two-year-old stockbroker. "Masturbation is something a true he-man never has to do."

In carrying out our interviews, we noted a gradual shift in attitude on the parts of many men. They are coming out of the bathroom—out of the closet, so to speak—and acknowledging that masturbation can be more than a quick fix or a poor substitute for partner sex.

Masturbation is increasingly becoming a means by which men enjoy their own sexuality. However, this appreciation of autoeroticism was new to most of the men we interviewed. Men who viewed it in a new light had to overcome the societal messages that cast masturbation as somewhat of a necessary curse.

The conflict between men's qualms about solo sex and the real pleasure it gives them is the central theme of Daniel Rudman's play, *Hold Me Until Morning*. In the following excerpts, the main characters, a man and his penis, conduct a dialogue which describes some of the roots of men's ambivalence toward masturbation and how this ambivalence often leads them to feel estranged from their own bodies.

PENIS: When you were nine or ten and first realized that I could do more than help you piss . . . remember? . . . remember?

SELF: Nine or ten . . . (*Straining to recall*)

PENIS: You loved me then.

SELF: God, that was long ago [. . .]

PENIS: But it doesn't change the fact that I turned you on.

SELF: Long long ago . . . before I'd ever seen a vagina . . . long long ago . . . God, you were like some fantastic toy . . . all my own. A secret magic toy. The more I touched you the bigger and harder and hotter you got . . .

PENIS: [Then] suddenly everything changed. You didn't look at me the same way.

SELF: (*Threatened, getting glib*) Well, I guess that's what happens when you start getting interested in girls.

PENIS: No, it happened long before that, long before you got interested in girls. You started feeling guilty . . . You started feeling that it was wrong to play with me . . . Remember?

SELF: Well . . .

PENIS: Remember those horrible fantasies you used to have? If you played with me five more nights then you'd get cancer . . . a hundred more times and you'd wake up in the morning and discover that I'd split into two penises like the forks of a slingshot and you'd be a freak for the rest of your life . . . Remember that?

SELF: Yeah . . . yeah (*Getting upset*). Yeah.

PENIS: You never acted the same towards me after that.

SELF: Yeah . . . sure I remember. But it doesn't matter now . . . that's all over and done with.

PENIS: It matters to me!

SELF: No, what matters now is that I'm turned on by women . . . Women, not you, Prick. Not you.

PENIS: But if you were once turned on by me you could be turned on again.[1]

To be turned on again, however, men found it helpful to recall the negative messages that influenced their early views of masturbation. There were, for instance, all those horror stories about the evils of masturbation and how it would deform you for life. Those interviewed for our study reminisced and laughed at the absurdity of those childhood fears. At the time, though, they were no laughing matter. Farnsworth, a forty-six-year-old postal worker, says he remembers thinking:

> Oh my God, if my father knew what I was doing . . . He would have told me that it's bad, it's going to stunt my growth or that little red hairs will grow in the palm of my hand. I remember having all those fears. I think that was part of not being able to accept myself and what I was doing. But over a period of time, I began to accept myself and what I do a hell of a lot more. And masturbation was one of those things that I accepted.

Remember all those jokes about other people's mothers who warned their sons that masturbation would drive them crazy? Some of those jokes were real. Nicholas, age fifty, recalls:

> Masturbation was never talked about. My mother once found soiled sheets and she said I'd go crazy if I played with myself. But I didn't believe her. I had a tinge of guilt, but I never paid too much attention to my mother anyway, so it didn't matter.

Some mothers' admonitions, however, had an incredible impact on their sons. Lanny's mother instilled such fear in him that he didn't touch himself for years:

> My mother always said that it was bad to play with yourself. She once told me she knew a man who played with himself all the time and his penis grew so big, he couldn't fit through the doorway. So I was always afraid to touch myself. For about five years I wouldn't dare lay a hand on myself. But then I discovered you could get real erotic feelings by manipulating yourself, so I really started to get into it. And I think she worried because I spent so much time doing it.

Some of the obviously ridiculous fears—becoming blind, growing hair on the palms of one's hands, or having a penis so large that it has to be carried around in a wheelbarrow—were fairly easily discarded as bugaboos of childhood. However, prohibitions based on religious doctrine were, for some men, more difficult to shrug off. Many religions forbid masturbation, but men we interviewed who were raised Roman Catholic had an extra burden. Catholicism equates masturbation with mortal sin, and many Catholic boys were threatened with being tainted forever if they indulged. Thirty-one-year-old Hank remembers going to extraordinary lengths to prevent his hands from roaming:

> I didn't masturbate until I was eighteen, because I was convinced I would go to hell. So I had to play all sorts of tricks on myself. I even tied rosaries on my hands at night so I wouldn't play with myself.

Gary, a thirty-one-year-old writer, as with other men we interviewed, eventually resolved the dilemma by realizing that the forbidden fruit—masturbation—was actually a "God-given gift":

> The first time I masturbated I was about thirteen or fourteen. I couldn't get to sleep that night, so I took a shower. While I was in the shower, I played with myself, and I had my first ejaculation. It felt terrible. It felt like I had come in God's face. Literally. I felt like I had committed this horrible sin. And I felt so guilty, I cried. I was a Catholic in those days, so I went to confession the next day. The priest told me I had done a horrible thing and I should say three rosaries and never do it again. But

of course I did it again, a couple of days later. Each time I kept confessing it, and each time I religiously said three rosaries. Then, a number of years later, I figured out that God was probably getting off on it too, 'cause he knew it was good stuff. Suddenly I started feeling all right about the good feelings and I stopped feeling guilty.

Larry, a thirty-eight-year-old minister, says he came to realize that:

Our bodies were made for sexual enjoyment. God didn't give us these things not to use them. He didn't say, "You can have it but you can't touch it." And when I realized my arms were long enough to reach there, I thought that must mean *something*.

Shame and embarrassment almost always accompanied the fear of being caught masturbating during childhood. Gilbert, now a forty-two-year-old public school teacher, recalled his humiliation when his collection of "crunchy old Kleenexes," was discovered:

When I was little, I was terrified that I was going to get caught masturbating. I would jack off real fast and shove the Kleenexes in the hole under the mattress of the upper bunk bed. That hole became absolutely filled with crunchy old Kleenexes. Over a period of years there must have been hundreds and hundreds of them. Then one day I came home and found that my mother and my sister had cleaned my room and had cleaned the whole thing out. They never said a word to me about it, but I knew they knew.

As boys got older, adult fears took the place of those ingrained in childhood. Some of these fears were founded upon superstition, while others contained a measure of truth. Wayne, a twenty-three-year-old basketball player, believed that masturbating or having intercourse the night before a big game sapped his strength:

I'm never up to anything the day before or the day of a game. It'll cut down on my speed, my endurance, and it works that way with all fellows. Women I've talked to say it gives them energy. Fellows say it takes it away. Like when we play today, I can tell who's had some and who hasn't, because the ones who haven't will be flying up and down the court; they'll be up over the rim. But the ones who have, they'll be under the rim, slowing it down. The energy's not there. The same thing if I'm having sex with women regularly. Sometimes they get to draining my juices.

"Draining my juices," much like the Samson and Delilah myth, implies that a man's strength is cut off when he uses up his semen. What Wayne most likely observed among his teammates was exhaustion that was the result of staying up all night rather than masturbating or having intercourse.

Another fear, along the line of the drain-your-juice theory, was that masturbating while in a relationship would sap a man's sexual energy and kill his interest in partner sex. However, most men we interviewed did not find that masturbating took away from their interest in lovemaking as much as it took the edge off their sexual appetite. In fact, some men considered this to be a fringe benefit of masturbation, because it made their level of interest more commensurate with their partner's. However, some men, like thirty-four-year-old Joseph, did feel that it dampened their enthusiasm for sex:

If I masturbate the night before I'm with Paula, I don't feel like I want to make love as much. I mean, I may get into it anyway, but I won't be thinking as much about wanting to make love as I would if I hadn't masturbated.

Another fear on the part of many men is that autoeroticism will be so satisfying that they will become completely self-absorbed and will choose solo sex over a relationship. Masturbation has been depicted by many authorities as a narcissistic, immature act which is not compatible with adult sexuality. "I think one of the most damaging things I ever read," says fifty-four-year-old Leo,

was a sentence from what was supposed to be a scholarly work on human sexuality that said that while masturbation was okay, it was still an immature act. That was a very powerful negative sanction because I didn't want to be immature. But it didn't make sense to me. Somehow I was supposed to be more mature if my sexuality was always expressed with someone else. Many times when I have had a need for a release and have gone out and found someone to meet my need, the expe-

rience was not very personal. In my own judgment, it is sometimes far more mature to meet your needs yourself than to use
another person sexually.

But the most damning charge leveled against masturbation, according to the he-man script, is that it raises questions about a
man's ability to attract a woman. A true he-man doesn't have to
masturbate. A real man, after all, can find a partner for sexual
gratification whenever he wants.

Don's comments seem to reflect this traditional assumption. "Oh,
I suppose if I went for a month or so without sex with a partner I
might have at least some thoughts about masturbating," says Don,
age sixty-eight, a retired airline pilot. "But I'm lucky, I guess. I
have no problem finding partners. And I can't remember any period
when I did, other than during the gawky years."

The word one fifty-two-year-old psychotherapist used to describe
the importance masturbation plays in his life was "zilch." "I have
enough sexual outlets," he said. "I've only masturbated when I
didn't have a woman and was literally climbing the walls. I've
never used it as a way of making love to myself. Never. I can't conceive of sexuality without a woman."

To some extent every man has had to confront these negative associations with masturbation. In fact, only in the last decade has
the cultural attitude toward masturbation shifted from considering
it harmful and perverse to recognizing it as being widely practiced and at least benign if not positive. In fact, the current view
held by most sex experts is that masturbation is a healthy part of a
person's sexuality. Sex therapists and counselors often recommend
masturbation as a way to enhance a client's sexuality or to help
solve a sexual dysfunction. This dramatic shift in attitude understandably has left many people feeling confused, particularly men
raised with macho attitudes toward masturbation. How are men
who learned to consider masturbation as a sign of inadequacy and
a substitute for the Real Thing supposed to change their perception
and see it as a loving act? It's not easy to shift attitudes. Yet this
is precisely the transition men have been making.

A RELEASE

Some men, while feeling good about masturbation, did not yet see it as an expression of self love. However, they did see it as a positive "release"—release from the accumulated stress of daily living or from sexual frustration itself.

"When I have a day where nothing really works," said a hassled young businessman, "like when my car was in the shop and I missed the bus, the quarterly report was overdue and the taxes on our house had just doubled, I just wanted to come home and jerk off."

Riley, a seventy-year-old journalist, shares that viewpoint: "Sometimes when I'm troubled, I masturbate. It's a good way to go to sleep. Then masturbating serves more of a sedating and comforting function for me than a sexual one."

Howard, a thirty-five-year-old land use planner, says masturbation is "a sort of pressure valve for not wanting to spend all my time being horny."

AN ALTERNATIVE

Nowadays, some men are beginning to appreciate that a variety of personal and even interpersonal needs can be fulfilled through autoeroticism. In contrast to the old view most men have of masturbation—do it if you can't "get a woman"—many of the men we interviewed don't consider masturbation as a reflection of their inadequacy as men. In fact, some even preferred masturbation over unfulfilling partner sex. Dusty, for instance, a twenty-one-year-old student, says:

Until I find somebody I'm really comfortable with, whom I respect and who is knowledgeable about her own sexuality, I'll just keep masturbating and enjoying my own little world.

Other men, such as Edward, a thirty-five-year-old divorced college professor, thought similarly:

Sometimes I masturbate because there isn't any woman I'd really care about seeing, and I don't want to spend time with a woman just for the sake of having an orgasm.

Some men who were already in meaningful relationships found that when their partner was either not available or not interested in sex, masturbation was a natural way to accommodate their sexual drive. Edward adds that even while he is in a relationship, "I might just suddenly feel like I want to come and my lover either isn't around or isn't interested in sex. It's nice to feel free enough to masturbate right then and there."

There were also men who were in close relationships and had easy access to partners but who chose masturbation over partner sex when they wanted the physical release but felt the need to be alone or selfish. For some men this was difficult to do because of a belief that it is abnormal to masturbate once married.

The idea that a man in a steady relationship should not have to masturbate is yet another variation of the macho theme that masturbation is merely a second-rate substitute for the Real Thing. However, some men in our study were beginning to realize that autoeroticism was not antithetical to intimacy but often permitted a greater intimacy to develop later on. They understood that certain psychological states were not conducive to making love with a partner and, in those situations, used masturbation as their outlet.

Jerry, a thirty-two-year-old scientist who has been living with his girl friend for three years, notes:

Sometimes I'm in such a foul mood that I don't want to be around other people, and then I'm certainly not up to having sex. But by masturbating I can just let myself go and forget about everything. Psychologically it can be quite a boost and make me feel like I'm fit to be around people again.

These men acknowledged that, at times, romance, tender words, and soft caresses took more effort than they genuinely felt like putting forth. One man points out that sometimes "I don't feel like getting into a lot of heavy sex with my partner. I might be horny but won't feel emotionally ready to go through with the whole thing."

Most long-term relationships have periods of emotional discord. During those times, neither partner may feel like going through the charade of pretending to share in sexual intimacy. Many men said that solo sex was one way to avoid further burdening a troubled relationship. When not used as a weapon, masturbation could provide a way to release tension, thereby giving a couple time to work through their points of contention.

Masturbation was considered valuable by some men in close relationships for yet another reason. "Even though I love my wife," thirty-five-year-old John says, "I still get turned on to other women. But I'm not willing to act on that because it might seriously jeopardize my marriage. In those situations, my solution is to fantasize and masturbate instead."

Edmund, a forty-seven-year-old minister, has come to the same conclusion. He says he's comfortable with his masturbatory fantasies but is clear about their limits:

> My favorite fantasy is that an unexpectedly lovely woman, usually someone I know, wants to have sex with me. If that woman actually called me up and said, "Hey, come on over," it'd probably scare me to death because I don't want to mess up my marriage. I'm happy with my wife. But that doesn't stop me from fantasizing. That's what's neat about fantasy and masturbating, you can have all that and not jeopardize anything.

AN INSTRUCTOR

Even though many men can have an erection and ejaculate without difficulty, they are often unaware of the kind of stimulation that would change a fair orgasm into a great orgasm. They have accepted the macho belief that men should need no special requirements to experience satisfying sex. Sex for these men is often completely genitally focused, as is their masturbation.

But some of the men we interviewed reported that they sometimes use solo sex in a completely different way—not merely as a quick release but as a way to discover the subtleties of their sexual response and to learn greater ejaculatory control. They said that masturbation has helped them learn about their own bodies and their sexual responses without having to contend with the distraction of a partner. Afterward, they were able to take this information and share it with a lover.

Drew, age thirty-four, put it this way:

> The reason I've practiced masturbating myself is to understand my physical reactions. When you masturbate you don't have

the psychological dimension that sex with a woman adds. And when you don't have to deal with that, you can come to fully understand how you like to be stimulated physically and what will evoke the greatest purely physical response. Practicing on yourself and learning how you like to be touched makes it easier to teach someone else how to do it.

Masturbation was also a way for men to learn to control their ejaculation. During childhood, masturbation was an act shrouded in guilt, and the fear of getting caught made most boys masturbate quickly. Because their childhood masturbatory experiences tended to be furtive, fast, and fearful, adult men often found that they transferred this learning into partner sex and ejaculated too quickly during intercourse. However, through the use of masturbation, men can retrain themselves to control ejaculation.

The first step to learning greater ejaculatory control is to view masturbation as self-pleasuring rather than as a method of providing quick release. This means shifting the focus from a genital orientation to one that encompasses the entire body. This sexual self-exploration can be a guide in discovering areas of sensitivity not previously considered erogenous.

One man shared the way he explored the erotic potential of his body through masturbation:

I like to make my whole environment feel really sexy. I put a few candles strategically around my bedroom. And I have really sensuous music playing in the background. Also, I make sure none of my roommates are around. If they are, I lock my door so no one interrupts me. Then I lie down on my bed, take off my clothes, and spread massage oil on different parts of my body. Sometimes I fantasize that a beautiful woman is stimulating each part of my body until I reach a fever pitch of excitation. At other times, I just concentrate on the feelings I can produce in my body by either softly touching it all over or stroking certain areas with more pressure. Doing this, I've discovered parts of my body that are highly sensitive. For instance, if I stroke lightly under my arms, it sends a tingling sensation down my whole body. The same is true if I touch lightly across the inside of my thighs and the whole general pelvic region. I was also surprised to find that lightly touching my nipples was really stimulating for me.

Once a man learns to tune into his body and incorporate a sensual element into his sexual activity, he can then shift his attention back to his genitals and assume control of his ejaculatory timing with the stop/start technique.[2]

This technique is based on the same principle as a water faucet. Just as the force of water can be increased or reduced, men can use their hand to reduce or increase the flow of sexual stimulation they experience, and thereby learn to last longer. Learning this takes patience and practice. The first requirement is learning to recognize the "point of no return." This is the point when ejaculation feels inevitable, the moment when the prostate gland and seminal vesicles contract and empty seminal fluid into the urethra. Seconds later, wavelike contractions of the pelvic muscles propel the semen out of the penis.

The men in our study who had good ejaculatory control were acutely familiar with the feelings and sensations which preceded the "point of no return," when ejaculation was inevitable. As they began to experience these sensations, they stopped direct stimulation of the penis, turned off the spigot so to speak. Some men stopped manipulating the penis and just held it, while others began stroking other parts of their bodies. By refocusing their attention to the rest of their bodies, these men could prolong the period before orgasm. Each time they turned off the spigot, the accumulated sexual tension dissipated and thus delayed ejaculation. This does not mean that from a high pitch of sexual tension they dropped down to zero. What they were doing was merely abating the rapid buildup, slowing the flow. Once they began caressing their penis again, they could build up to an even higher level of sexual excitation.

Practice the stop/start technique until masturbation can be extended for fifteen minutes with, at most, two or three stops before ejaculation. Once this is comfortably accomplished, you then should repeat the process with a lubricated hand to approximate more closely the sensations of intercourse. After you are able to masturbate with a lubricant for fifteen minutes and only stop two or three times, the next step is to repeat this while fantasizing about

making love to a partner. Once this feels comfortable, you may
want to incorporate the stop/start technique into your lovemaking
with a partner.

If you are ready to try the stop/start technique with a partner,
explain the procedure to her first. Most women not only don't have
a problem experiencing an ebb and flow during sexual arousal but
actually enjoy stopping to cuddle, kiss, or play with parts of the
body other than the penis. The best position to use initially for intercourse is the female superior because it is more relaxing for the
man and muscle tension is built up less quickly. When you reach a
high level of arousal, let your partner know. She can help, at this
point, by slowing down the thrusting or stopping her movements altogether.

If she wants stimulation to continue because she is on the verge
of orgasm, not stopping would merely lead to a mutual release.[3]

THE JOYS OF MASTURBATION

Some men who were reexamining their attitudes toward masturbation went beyond appreciating it as an opportunity to develop
more skills as a lover or only as an alternative for an absent partner
or unrewarding sex. Going one step further, they felt that masturbation was an exciting, joyous, loving experience in its own right.

The beauty of masturbation for these men was that it allowed
them free rein to experience and explore their own orgasmic potential. As one man said, "You don't have to focus on anyone but yourself. You're free to devote all your attention to whatever stimulation
you choose. The key is that you have total control."

As Troy, a twenty-nine-year-old consultant, put it: "If you're in
bed with someone and they're not into what you want to do, you
can't do it. With masturbation, you're the director of the movie, so
you can do whatever you want. It's great."

With masturbation you write the script, direct the scenes, and
play the starring role. You're the only one who knows exactly how
best to do it. Dusty, a twenty-one-year-old student, put it this way:
"I'm in tune with my own feelings. I know what makes me feel
good, the little idiosyncrasies about my own body and what turns
me on. And it makes for a terrific orgasm."

The sense of privacy during autoeroticism freed Drew, a thirty-four-year-old bureaucrat, to do whatever he wanted without inhibition or fear of censure:

Sometimes masturbation is just a form of letting go of your normally conservative self. In the privacy of your room, when you're alone with your fantasies and physical feelings, you can do almost anything outrageous that you want to do, things that you may not do in a lot of other parts of your life. I think that might be why I'm having a little difficulty telling you everything—some of it just seems so private. Like you can walk around the room with an erection and just stick your penis anywhere you feel like. You can do funny things or anything you want because it's just you and your body. And while I don't think I'm very inhibited making love, I'm probably less inhibited alone.

The orgasm achieved during autoeroticism was described as so terrific that for some it rivaled those experienced with a partner. As Spike, a thirty-one-year-old investment banker pointed out, "I can have terrific climaxes with masturbation. Some are right up there with the best of heterosexual partner sex."

Then there were others, like Charles, a forty-five-year-old college professor, who claims that the intensity he reached during masturbation even surpassed that felt during intercourse. According to Charles, "There are times, given two bodies going at each other, when copulation can't quite rival the perfection you can achieve inside your own organism by going at it autonomously."

This is not to say that these men became advocates of solo sex exclusively. What their masturbatory sessions gave them was a renewed sense of their own bodies. Solo sex was no longer the stepchild of intercourse but stood on its own merits as a way to express their sexuality.

At times these men experienced masturbation as a celebration of their physical being. The feelings they expressed recalled the first line of Walt Whitman's poem "Song of Myself": "I celebrate myself, and sing myself." They had put behind them the shame and guilt stereotypically associated with masturbation and had come to view it instead as a way of appreciating their bodies' capacity for pleasure. One man said autoeroticism was his way to reaffirm his relationship with himself. Another described it as an instrument for reestablishing his virility. What these men shared was a rekindled sense of loving their physical beings. The difficulty in coming to these realizations was that most men had never been raised in an environment where it was acceptable to love their bodies. "I, like most men, was never taught to love myself," said Scott. "I did not grow up in the kind of an environment where I could love or respect my body for anything more than my physical strength. So, of course, what I focused on was developing my physical prowess—not loving my body for itself."

Eric, a forty-four-year-old administrator, discovered how wonderful and loving masturbation could be when a woman tenderly caressed him to orgasm. Afterward, he realized this was something he could do alone:

> When I was married, I did not want my wife to know that I masturbated so I was very quick about it and, as I reflect on it, fairly violent with myself. But after I was with a partner who masturbated me in a particularly loving way, I realized, "Gee, that's really nice." And I realized I could do that myself. Now, I'm much more loving, and masturbation is more enjoyable and much more pleasurable.

Most men reached this changed perception of masturbation over a period of years and through a variety of experiences. Those who held this enlightened attitude toward solo sex said it enriched their sexuality and enhanced their self-esteem.

Along with seeing masturbation as a form of self-celebration, many men came to view it as something akin to the sheer play of childhood. They considered maturbation an accessible, safe, free, fun, and rewarding form of recreation that needed no other justification. Some men found this difficult to admit without feeling less of a man. However, others, once they got over their inhibitions and fears, recalled how they were able to really enjoy their bodies and their orgasms by playing while masturbating. Such was the experience of Edward, a thirty-five-year-old college professor:

> Sometimes I enjoy acting like a kid and either watching myself come or taking aim at something I can hit. I've often hit myself in the head or eye or I've hit the wall behind me, so in that sense I can make it into a real game.

Larry, age thirty-eight, a minister and psychologist, fondly re-counted his masturbation experiences during childhood and told us how he had maintained the same playful attitude as an adult:

I've never put it into words, but some of my best memories of childhood were the days when I was sick at home. When I had some kind of a cold, but I wasn't really seriously sick, I had my world spread out on my bed—soldiers, cars, trucks, pillows. My mom wasn't hovering around me so I was alone, and there was nothing else to do but just play on my bed.

I think some of my very best masturbation experiences have the same flavor to them. I am alone. There is nothing I have to do or I want to do but spread all of my toys out on my bed. I'll turn on my TV-tape recorder and let fly for the next hour. I'll hold myself away from an orgasm and I'll get up to the edge and slip back. I'll find another picture, or I'll replay that scene on the tape, or I'll go get new batteries for my vibrator and then start all over again.

SEXUAL ACCOUTREMENTS

Many of those who acquired this new view of masturbation as grownup play used sexual accoutrements to enhance their experiences. They felt free to experiment with accoutrements without worrying about whether it was unmanly to do so. Some of the men we interviewed described the sexual toys they used when they played alone. What follows is a compilation of their personal preferences.

Lubricants

Lotions, creams, and oils were cited as the most common accoutrements used in sexual play. The choice of whether to use a lubricant seemed to be a matter of personal preference. Some disliked lubricants because they were too messy. "I'm no good at using cream," said one man, "my hands get too slippery." Others enjoyed using lubricants because they replicated the physical sensations of penetration. Men used baby oil, Vaseline Intensive Care Lotion, Unicure, Alpha Keri, or natural oils, such as almond, coconut, or olive oil.

Another treat some men enjoyed was masturbating with soap in the shower. It was not only convenient, but as Troy, age twenty-nine, points out, "The water gives you a warm overall body sensation. And right after ejaculation, the head of my penis is very sensitive, and the warm water makes it tingly and prolongs the effect a while longer."

Erotica

Other common props brought into the solo sexual experience were visual aids. Erotica, in the form of magazines, pictures, and films, were powerful sexual stimulants for many, providing the basic material upon which they could build delightful fantasies.

Some men gathered favorite pictures of beautiful women. Others had collections ranging from soft porn, like *Playboy*, to triple-X-rated hard-core pornographic material. In his bachelor days, Nathan, a forty-year-old administrator, had taken nude photographs of women he had known.

Over the years, I've developed a gallery of pictures of girls I have gone out with. As a part of my courting process, I would take nude pictures of them. As we got more involved, the pictures would get less discreet. By the age of thirty, I had developed a fairly large collection of girls I had dated at one time or another and by looking over the pictures could reminisce about ancient intercourses.

Modern technology has created a new class of accoutrements. A number of men had video systems or 8-mm projectors and kept an abundant supply of pornographic films on hand to show either before or during their solo sex sessions. One man even collected vintage pornofilms. Moviegoers said their favorite scenes from films were etched in their memories. During masturbation, they replayed the scenes, often with themselves in the starring role.

The power of the written word was a strong sexual catalyst for men who preferred to create their own mental image through reading erotica. A favorite for some were the letters in *Playboy, Forum* or others because they were ostensibly written by real people and it was therefore easier to fantasize about them. As sixty-two-year-old Lee explained:

I find *Penthouse* magazine or something like that to be stimulating, not because of the pictures, but because of the letters and the experiences people write about. The pictures are not really very exciting, they're almost too descriptive. I value my own imagination and I can use it more when it comes to the letters.

Others stated they liked such porno classics as *The Pearl,* which was written anonymously, or *My Life and Loves* by Frank Harris. And still others found that they were stimulated by books that weren't pornographic but contained beautifully written erotic scenes.

Mirrors

Initially prompted by curiosity, many men discovered that mirrors could be great masturbation enhancements. Larry, for instance, said he really enjoyed seeing what he looked like when he masturbated:

I didn't know what I looked like really, and so I was examining myself in front of a mirror and got a hard-on. I jerked off and came all over myself and watched it and it was terrific. For maybe six or seven months after that one of my favorite ways to jerk off was in front of the mirror. I liked that a lot.

Joseph, a thirty-four-year-old social worker, also enjoyed the stimulation of watching himself masturbate:

Sometimes I will take a full-length mirror, sit in front of it and masturbate. I like my erections. I really get off on them, so I take different views of myself. I like to watch my body move, and observe what I do when I have an orgasm. It's almost like watching someone else masturbate. Sometimes I will dance in front of the mirror. I like to swing my cock back and forth, and I fantasize that I'm dancing in front of a bunch of women. I really get off on that.

Clothing

Few men talked about using clothing as an accessory during masturbation. Two who said they did, however, found interesting ways to play with fabric. One man said he wrapped a silk tie

around his penis and testicles and then masturbated. Edward, a
thirty-eight-year-old divorced college professor, used his wife's soft
lingerie to masturbate with:

> Sometimes I have worn women's clothes, like nightgowns, to
> be able to have the feeling of the soft material. When I was
> married and my wife was out of town, I would sometimes wear
> her nightgown when I masturbated so I could have her smells
> and the feeling of her around me.

Receptacles

What was infinitely more popular than clothing for many men
was the excitement of ejaculating into an assortment of receptacles.
Some men who first masturbated as children by lying on top of a
pillow often enjoyed recreating that encompassing sensation as
adults during solo sex. Others chose washcloths, towels, and even
condoms as objects to ejaculate into.

To Larry, age thirty-eight, a condom is a toy:

> I like to jerk off with rubbers. I'd much rather come all over
> myself ultimately, but I like the feel of the rubber going on. I
> think that's the greatest.

Mel, a fifty-nine-year-old sales executive, likes rubbers because
they are efficient:

> I like to masturbate into something. You can put the condom
> on and it's a different feeling altogether. Also, then you don't
> have the bother of having to clean the whole goddamn mess
> up afterwards.

Leo, who is a fifty-four-year-old executive, masturbates with
props in a most creative way. He likes banana skins because they
simulate the sensation of being inside a vagina.

> I think people who really enjoy masturbating can find all kinds
> of unusual accoutrements. It has to do with how inventive you
> feel. For example, I've used banana skins for masturbation. I
> take the banana out, of course, and then wrap the banana skin
> around my penis and fold my hand around the outside. There
> are secretions inside the banana skin and it feels lubricated. I
> like it because I get more into thrusting my whole body than

just moving my hand back and forth. I use fantasy and imagine I'm inside a cunt or asshole.

Vibrators

While Leo was the only man who mentioned using banana skins as a sexual toy, a number of men said some of their most explosive orgasms came while using a vibrator on the tip or underside of their penises. We were surprised by the number of men who mentioned using vibrators while masturbating, since so many people consider them to be reserved for women. In fact, it was often a woman who introduced a man to the pleasures of being stimulated by a vibrator. Joseph, age thirty-four, learned from his girl friend:

I was introduced to the vibrator by an old girl friend and when I first tried it I almost went out of my head. It was too much for me, I couldn't deal with the intensity of it. But then by using it alone, I gradually got accustomed to it, and after some experimentation I really started to like it.

I take the vibrator and put it over the head of my penis and the cap fits right down over the top. If I use it down at the base or along the side, it doesn't work. There is not enough stimulation, or the right kind of stimulation for an orgasm. But when I put it on the head of my penis and stroke my penis very lightly at the same time, it isn't so intense. What I do is hold the vibrator in one hand and lightly masturbate with my other hand by going up and down, pulling the skin up and down, very gently. It's not a fast motion, not my typical masturbation motion at all. It's firm, but it's slow. And then, if it gets too intense, I'll stop and just let myself rest for a few seconds. Maybe I'll get into a fantasy or something like that and then I'll start again. I'll keep doing this until I have an orgasm.

Alan, age thirty-eight, bought a vibrator for his wife and found that it had an attachment that fit perfectly over his penis:

About three or four years ago, I bought a vibrator for my wife to use and one day out of curiosity I tried it myself and it was fantastic! There was an attachment that just fit over the tip of the penis, and I found that very stimulating. I got hard real quick. When I first started, putting it on high speed was a bit much. I've since grown accustomed to that intensity but also enjoy varying the speed. Now, by and large, I use it around the top of my penis or the underside of the head, although sometimes I like to go down the shaft, too.

If one feels good, another man said, two are even better:

I love using two vibrators. I don't use them both all the time, but when I do, I really have fun sticking a small one in my ass and at the same time rubbing my dick with another one. Usually what I'll do is lay my dick flat on my belly and gently rub the vibrator up and down the underside and right underneath the head. That feels great. And the one in the ass feels good too. My female partners used to enjoy it when I used two on them, but I found I enjoyed it as much as they did.

Clint, a forty-five-year-old management consultant, has a vibrator called the "Magic Wand." The magic it brought him was a steady stream of orgasms, without ever ejaculating.

I bought a "Magic Wand" vibrator for Natalie and I think I probably use it more than she does. The wand is about a foot long and it's got fast and slow speeds. The vibrating part is a little smaller than the size of a tennis ball. I use it on the underside of my penis and particularly on the underside up near the head. I use oil with it because otherwise the vibrator against my skin causes a terrible irritation. When I feel I'm getting close to orgasm I briefly take the vibrator away and just touch intermittently with it until I experience an orgasm. It's amazing—I have the muscular contractions, the general overall good feeling—everything is there except the seminal fluid. It's like multiple orgasms without an ejaculation. If I take the vibrator away at the very last moment, I can actually have about ten orgasms in a five-minute period. If I go all the way to ejaculation, then the session is all over.

FANTASY

Almost all of the men we talked with fantasized during masturbation. The rare exceptions were those men who focused on the physical sensations they experienced. Some men initiated their masturbatory sessions with fantasy and then focused on what they were physically feeling as they became more aroused.

The kinds of images men have vary. Some men have a quick fantasy image that flashes through their minds during masturbation:

It's usually the swing of a woman's buttocks that I've seen during the day, or maybe the exposure of her breast when she bends down.

Others piece together an entire scenario:

Sometimes I create a whole story out of someone I meet on the street where I fantasize that she comes over and then we have sex. It's a little more realistic, which makes it more exciting for me.

Some men only fantasize about their wives: "Every time I fantasize while masturbating," says Roger, age thirty-eight and a lawyer, "I'm thinking about making love with Alicia. It's like wishing. I'm pretending I'm doing it with her."

"I fantasize about having my wife sit on my face with her sexy lace underwear," said Gary, who is thirty-one.

Others, like Paxton, age thirty-three, say they fantasize about the kind of sexual play that isn't part of their usual repertoire during lovemaking: "I might fantasize about the things that I wonder about, or things I would like to try, that Candy and I have not made a regular part of our sexual practice, like rear entry or anal sex. Thinking about those things turns me on."

Another genre of fantasy involves flashbacks to a special partner —a particularly memorable lover or a person with whom they associate warm feelings:

I always think about someone who has given me a lot of sexual pleasure. I try to get a picture of what they look like and maybe I'll envision the two of us together again engaging in intercourse.

It's not only a current lover or a partner from the past who comes into men's minds as they masturbate. Some think about a familiar face on the subway or someone they've just spoken to casually. For one man, "it's the lady behind the bookstand or some other lady who appeals to me physically or a casual acquaintance who really turns me on. I conjure up the image of that person in my mind when I masturbate."

The more realistic the possibility, says forty-year-old Nathan, "the more I can develop the fantasy. I don't think I could have a particularly good masturbatory fantasy about a movie actress, but I can about the secretary at work or the lady next door or the girl at the 7-11 store."

Rob, a thirty-four-year-old newspaper editor, prefers more anonymous fantasy characters:

If I'm alone, I masturbate more frequently, sometimes several times a day. My girl friend is a business consultant and she flies out during the week so I really don't see her much. It has always been most exciting to build my fantasies around fictitious people, from twelve-year-old girls being examined by the doctor in gym class, to *Playboy* bunnies in whole elaborate scenes, complete with drugs, hot tubs, steam baths, and massage. Sometimes several women are involved, other times just one woman. I find those kinds of creative fantasies so much more intriguing and delightful than real-life memories. I close my eyes and I just go totally into a visual space as real for me as anything going on out here.

Some men explored themes in fantasy that they would ordinarily consider taboo. One man said:

My favorite fantasy is to be with two women who are making love. The dominant female really subjugates and seduces the other female, an innocent but lovely woman who eventually becomes as interested in making love to the dominant female as the other is in making love to her. Maybe I'm afraid to say it, but the "firm guidance" of the dominant one sort of borders on sadomasochism.

Several heterosexual men said that among their most vivid fantasies were ones in which they made love with other men:

I've never had a homosexual experience, but I have a lot of gay friends, and I've had quite a few passes made at me. So at times I fantasize about a couple of guys, but they're always people I know.

Whether a man imagined himself being loved by another man or playing with some sexual toy, the use of fantasy and accoutrements during sex directed men's energies during masturbation toward a single focus: experiencing bodily sensations and physical pleasure. These aids to lovemaking enhanced the experience, making it one of complete immersion. During *quality* solo sexual adventures, these men experienced a sense of play as well as a celebration of body.

Leo, for instance, can create any sensual setting he chooses when he wants to intensify his experience:

While masturbating, I'm touching myself and I'm fantasizing about being off on a warm beach somewhere, sometimes by myself, but more commonly it's with a woman. A fantasy can be about something that just happened to me in the last couple of days or a memory from the past. I might go back to some really beautiful times with a lover of mine. Sometimes my fantasies are stimulated by pictures or sounds. While it's mostly pictures, I've also drifted into fantasy by lying and listening to music and just feeling the pleasure. Sometimes the fantasy stops and I become so tuned into my own body I'm not aware of what I'm picturing, all I'm doing is feeling. It becomes a total body sensation. I'm totally into sex. My whole body becomes a sex instrument and I enjoy all the touches and I become completely focused on all of the great feelings.

Even men as free as happily married Leo—men who can create a wonderful, exciting, and intense sexual session for themselves—generally do not prefer masturbation over partner sex. Their first choice is usually a warm and intimate sexual relationship with a woman. Because of this, most men must, at some point in their lives, learn how to meet and initiate relationships with women. In the past, this has meant sharpening seduction skills. Today, however, other alternatives are available.

CHAPTER FIVE

FIRST ENCOUNTERS OF A CLOSE KIND

Men are often uneasy players in the game of love. Some find the game effortless and are used to winning; more fear rejection and abhor it. Some refuse to play at all. However, no matter how ambivalent they are, men realize that to meet a potential mate, an initial contact must be made. Yet, how comfortable a man is with the meeting and mating rites of courtship will often determine how he approaches the first encounter and how successful he will be. Here is how some of the men we interviewed feel about taking that first step:

- I love the excitement of spotting a good-looking girl at a party and leaving with her on my arm. I like to set it up so she chooses me over the competition.

- Every time I've walked up to ask a new woman to dance, I've had to give myself an internal pep talk. It takes a lot of courage, but it's something a man's got to do if he doesn't want to stand and watch on the sidelines.

- I've had it with women who expect me to make all the moves. Sometimes I want a woman who will come over to me first. It's flattering and it's also a relief.

- I don't care if I miss out on some opportunities. I'd rather let a relationship develop naturally. I'd rather respond because of the way I feel rather than because it's part of some grand seduction scheme.

Whatever part a man plays at the start of a relationship, he wants to win. And winning, according to the men we interviewed, doesn't just mean sexually seducing a woman. Ultimately, it means establishing an emotionally and sexually satisfying relationship. Traditionally, a man won by assuming the role of master seducer; he would mount a campaign to seduce an alluring, yet aloof heroine. But today, more and more men are veering away from this approach and are developing alternate seduction strategies. Some are doing so because they feel burdened by society's test of Real Manhood which means beating out the competition and successfully luring a seemingly unavailable woman to bed. Others adopt alternate methods of initiating relationships because they find their traditional he-man approach oppressive. For the men we interviewed, the most oppressive aspect of the aggressor role was that it left them continually exposed to the possibility of being rejected.

Men in this culture risk rejection at each and every turn as they get to know a woman they like. Society still expects the man to make the first move, to provide the impetus as well as the sustaining energy for launching a relationship. Traditional men wouldn't have it any other way. For instance, one man we interviewed enjoyed the role of initiator. He didn't see it as a burden, but as "a powerful role which gives you the opportunity to go after what you want—and often get it." Yet others hated the pressure of having to make the first move and continually risk being turned down. One man said, "I always feel I'm setting myself up emotionally for the big fall." Another says, "A man has to pass a test of one sort or another each step of the way. You ask: Should I open the door for her? Did I choose the right wine? Did I sit too close? Will I get invited in?"

How, then, do men cope with the ego-trouncing effects of rejection? In the following passage, Dan Greenburg, author of *Scoring: A Sexual Memoir*, recalls his early years and how he learned to accept the very real possibility of being rejected:

I happen to be a compulsive list-maker. I not only keep lists of the people I have to telephone or write or see, I also keep lists going back some twenty years or so . . . of every girl I have ever gone out with, . . . I have ever kissed good night, . . . I have ever necked with or petted with above the waist outside the clothes, . . . I have ever gotten to third base with, and every girl I have ever scored with.

The reason I made these lists to begin with was . . . to reassure myself at a glance that I was doing better with women than I actually was. If I was feeling particularly depressed about an inability to get a date with a girl I knew was the only girl for me at the moment, or if I had just bungled an evening by making a remarkably inept and sloppy pass, or if, more likely, I had painstakingly set the stage for a complex scenario of seduction and then not even made my move due to sheer cowardice—why, all I had to do was turn to my secret lists of dating statistics and see that I had managed to plant my lips successfully on those of an actual female person a total of 458 times or get my cupped hand onto a cashmere-sweatered breast a total of 113 times or snake my very own fingers under a skirt and to within four inches of an authentic, warm, slippery, white-pantied crotch on five separate and distinct occasions, and then I was able to relax.[1]

Men we interviewed, too, came up with stories of how they avoided feeling paralyzed when they were turned down by women. As an adolescent, Jonathan, age thirty-seven, devised statistical techniques to build up his self-confidence and convince himself that the numbers would eventually work in his favor:

I divided the world up numerically into two groups—males and females. The number of females is fifty percent of the population. And of those, about ten percent are eligible, and of that ten percent, ninety-nine percent are probably going to say no outright for various reasons, so I decided to just go for that 1 percent. I actually sat down with a world atlas and worked out the number when I was about fifteen years old. That computation helped because, even though I had had many no's from fifteen to seventeen, I knew sooner or later the odds would turn in my favor.

A lesson many men learned and one that women who are becoming more assertive have just begun to deal with is distinguishing a refusal from a personal rejection. These men learned to separate their feelings about their own desirability from a potential partner's positive or negative response to their overtures. Not personalizing a refusal enabled them to feel more confident and take more risks. "You have to be able to psyche yourself up to accept that somewhere along the line you're going to be rejected," said Jack, a thirty-eight-year-old engineer. "No man can be all things to all women because people either mesh or they don't mesh. Not every woman wants to jump into bed with every guy and vice versa. You have to expect some refusals because they *are* going to come."

Sixty-three-year-old Frank, a minister who has been separated ten years from a thirty-five-year marriage, revealed how he copes with a negative response:

Years ago, I used to play all the games—taking a woman out to dinner and everything and being disappointed when she didn't want me to go home with her. Now I just come out and ask, "Is it okay to stay the night?" If she says, "No," I say, "Okay." I don't feel it's a rejection, and I don't think I need to ask her if it's because I'm old, or because I'm fat, or anything like that. It's just the way it is.

The way a man comes to grips with the societal expectation that he be the initiator and therefore subject to rejection will determine the style or strategy of scoring he develops. The men we interviewed described a wide variety of seduction strategies. Each man had his unique style. However, we were able to distinguish four general seduction styles that reflected the degree to which a man accepted the macho philosophy.

A man who identified with the macho role and felt comfortable being the sexual seducer often developed what we call the *traditional strategy*. The traditional strategy was used by men who enjoyed determining the entire course of events—from making the first contact to sexual intercourse. Furthermore, this entire seduction process was carried out without the man ever openly acknowledging his goal. A *modified traditional approach* was used by men who still accepted responsibility for initiating sex but were more open about their intentions. They elicited a "go ahead" from their partners before pressing for sex. The men who did not want to play the aggressor role could take the *role reversal approach* by assuming a passive stance that was designed to encourage women to seduce them. And those men who were more interested in intimacy than sex decided to let the sexual relationship evolve naturally and used what we call the *no-role approach*.

TRADITIONAL SEDUCTION

Operating under the traditional strategy for Conrad, a fifty-seven-year-old widower, means "putting on a well-organized, systematic campaign that will lead to making love to the woman I've decided I want." Implicitly, a man who takes this approach views a desirable woman as a target. The goal is to pursue her and move from first base (the kiss) to home run (the bed) without letting her in on his intentions. He assumes that he has to sweep her off her feet to overcome her natural female resistance to doing that sort of thing. So he uses cunning, flattery, money, or whatever else he has at his disposal to lure her into his carefully spun web. Conrad admits:

> I exploit whatever strengths I have to impress a woman and because I can afford to take her to nice places, I find out as quickly as possible what she likes. If it's a symphony concert, I'll see that we get box seats. If it's dancing, I'll take her to the nicest place in town. It's bound to impress her. If she says she likes some particular flowers, I'll send them to her. I try to find out what she likes in literature and follow up in some way, for example, taking her to a movie based on a story she likes. What I do is make a studied effort to find out what she likes and what she doesn't like in order to make a big impression.

Scoring, using the traditional approach, requires absolute confidence. And even if a man doesn't feel particularly self-assured, he has to leave a woman with the impression that he is in order to be successful. Young, a twenty-four-year-old medical student, says he has overcome his shyness by emulating a friend who projected a self-assured macho image.

> When I was fifteen, I went to France where I met this American guy about my age who seemed to have a real easy time approaching women. The thing I noticed about him was that he was very aggressive. One of the key things he did was to use a lot of eye contact—to the point where women were forced to look away sometimes out of embarrassment. I real-

ized that for some reason women were attracted to this macho approach. So I imitated that, to a degree. I started picking up pointers from him. I realized that the most important thing is to act confident. So I started trying to act confident and I was immediately successful. Later on, in college, I had a roommate who was very handsome and a real nice guy. I just couldn't understand why women weren't going after him in droves. But he lacked confidence and initiative. He projected an image of a guy who didn't know what the hell he was doing. And women like to feel that the man knows what he's doing.

Others, like Jonathan, a thirty-seven-year-old history professor, had no problem approaching women because they genuinely felt self-assured:

I would just walk up and start talking to a woman, about anything, absolutely anything. I didn't run around with a lot of other guys, so I didn't have all the common lines that others used. I was just very open and honest. Then after I'd talk to the woman for a while, if she seemed interested or if I thought she was interesting, I would get her telephone number and address, put it in my little black book, and call her.

But most men felt they had to develop this ease in approaching women. It took Andrew, age thirty-four, a while after he separated from his wife to be able to strike up conversations with women he wanted to meet. What finally changed his attitude, he said, was realizing that:

Ninety-nine percent of the time a woman will be flattered if a man who is reasonably decent-looking comes up and says, "You seem nice," or "you look nice," or "I'd like to meet you." And women don't respond with rejection when they're flattered.

Here are some of the techniques Harry has used to meet women:

One of the prime places for me to meet women is on the bus going to and from work, and I'm getting pretty good at it. There were three women on the bus I wanted to meet. One day I just decided to stay on the bus and get off at this one woman's stop. So I passed my stop and I followed her off the bus and said, "Excuse me, I've seen you on the bus and I'd like to meet you." I felt really embarrassed, but she said, "Hi, my name is so-and-so. I'm flattered that you asked."

I met the next woman going home one day when the bus happened to be uncrowded. I just sat down behind her and kind of kiddingly said, "Gee, you don't ride on the M-17 any more in the morning." And she said, "No, I've been going in early." And I just made some silly comment like "Well, every-one on the bus has been asking about you and I said I'd report back if I found out what happened to you." So we started a conversation on that basis.

The third woman I wanted to meet usually got on the bus before I did, so it always ended up that she would have a seat in the front and I would be standing in the back, which made it impossible to start a conversation! So I just wrote out a note and as I got off the bus one morning I handed it to her. The note said, "I'd like to meet you but I haven't found a subtle way to do it. Would you call me at my office so we can arrange to get together some place other than the bus?" And she called me and we had lunch.

Letters and cards were common follow-ups used after meeting a woman. Conrad, a government bureaucrat, describes how carefully he laid the trap for a prospective lover—with a phone call followed by a letter and photograph:

I'm rather good at writing letters. I wrote a note once to a woman in the Midwest who was referred to me by a friend who knows my taste in women. First we had a lovely phone conversation, and then I wrote her a note and included a pho-tograph. She told me my note shook her up so much she cried for an hour after receiving it. She says she's carrying it around with my picture in her purse. In the letter I told her about all the things we could do if she were living here. I described in detail all the wonderful plays and symphonies we could attend. I made sure she understood how much more I would enjoy them if I was sharing them with her. I just made it sound as though my life would be richer if she were here with me. And it just got to her. We've been talking on the phone ever since. When we meet we'll pick some neutral site because it's very clear that when we get together it's going to be a terrific love-making session. And that'll be nice.

Unlike Conrad, some men were not as aware of their particular seduction strategy. Paul, age forty-two, says it took him several years of therapy to discover the unconscious seduction pattern he had developed in the years before his marriage. He discovered that his was the typical macho ploy of rescuing a somewhat vulnerable woman and playing upon her dependency needs until her feelings of gratitude eventually ripened into love:

Before I was married, my strategy was to find women who had some kind of weakness, either a problem in their life, some uncertainty, or some reason why they needed to depend on me. For example, I used to work in the personnel department of a large international company that hired a number of young, attractive women from all over the world. Some of them were just "lost" in Chicago and gladly turned to me for help and support. I also used the strategy of making myself needed in a situation where a woman had recently broken up with her boyfriend. I would initiate the relationship by offering to help. Then we would spend time together and I would be emotionally supportive and help her with her problems. From there sex would just naturally follow.

Another variation of the rescuer scenario is the man who plays out the Pygmalion story, taking on the role of an experienced man of the world who swoops in to transform an innocent, plain young girl into a self-assured and sexually aware woman. Nathan, now forty and married, fondly recalls how he adopted this strategy fifteen years earlier with the first virgin he ever enticed into bed:

This seduction probably took several months of planning before the vanquishment was attained. I was about twenty-six and she was in her early twenties and very unsure of herself. I would build up her self-image in so many ways—by telling her how nice she looked and even by going shopping with her for clothes. Eventually, in true Pygmalion style, I had transformed her appearance remarkably from that of a young professional-looking woman to a very sexy-looking young lady.

Finally, it was the process of overcoming her resistance without forcing her to do something that she didn't want to do that convinced her to be sexually involved with me. She was a devout Catholic and had had a variety of religious objections to premarital sex. We had spent months and months in foreplay, so that when intercourse happened, it was a culmination of endless hours of teasing each other and endless discussions about the relative merits and demerits of making love. But, ultimately, having sex had nothing to do with the intellectual process. It had to do with getting her so excited that neither one of us was discussing much of anything. We were just doing it!

Men intent on scoring must somehow manipulate the situation so that a woman is so swayed by passion that her resistance to sex is overcome. According to Warren Farrell, author of *The Liberated Man* and co-founder of the National Organization for Men, a man takes at least eighty-five different initiatives—beginning with touching a woman's hand and culminating in undressing her—before she is entirely willing. And each and every one of those steps is fraught with the possibility of rejection.

To sidestep the rejection, men trying to meet partners have to calculate their moves and carefully interpret the woman's reactions so they can elicit a positive response. Tom, age nineteen, says:

How a woman responds to my physical gestures will tell me if she's interested in more physical contact or not. So does her attitude and the feeling between us while we're talking. She has to seem really interested in me, or excited about being with me, because I'm certainly not going to press somebody who doesn't seem interested.

However, a physical gesture is not necessarily a signal for a full-fledged sexual overture. Charles, forty-five, says he initiates a series of subtle touches—casually caressing a woman's cheeks, stroking her hair, or brushing against her arms or legs—throughout the evening until finally he gets to another level that is understood to be sexual in its direction.

Some men suggested that massages, back rubs, and neck rubs were effective preludes to more overt sexual contact. It put the relationship on a more physically intimate basis and gave them a clearer indication of whether their partner would welcome further advances. Chuck, forty-three, and separated three years from his wife, recounts how one of his "most outstanding sexual experiences" began with a foot massage:

It occurred when a male friend of mine had a lady friend come from Georgia. I met them both and we went out for dinner. We talked and had a good time, and afterwards went back to his apartment and smoked a little grass. I remember lying on the floor, and she was sitting in the chair above me and there was nothing really sexual about it. We were just talking and I started massaging her foot. Then I massaged all of her. And that's how it started.

But the first kiss was acknowledged by most men as the most difficult step to take because it was so clearly sexual and left them most vulnerable to rejection. Young, age twenty-four, describes it as "the biggest leap between non-sex and sex":

The first kiss is always a special moment because you consciously have to decide to cross that boundary. I'm not exactly sure how it happens. I think it's just a kind of slow process. You start sitting closer and closer together until what you're talking about doesn't really matter anymore.

Spike, thirty-one, says, "Getting to that first kiss is so hard":

It's harder even than reaching in her pants. So I try to be funny, to put her at ease. I'm just not the type to say, "Hey, baby, what do you say we go into the bedroom?" I just can't do it. So I use humor instead. This is kind of corny, but I might say, "You have a spot on your cheek." And then, when I'm supposedly wiping it off, it's easy to kiss her. If she doesn't particularly respond, then I can keep my cover and jump up and get a paper towel.

Despite Spike's denial of being the kind of man who just sweeps women off their feet and into bed, his approach is definitely one that illustrates the traditional approach:

First we have dinner. I figure if they get nothing else from me, or if I get nothing else from them, at least our stomachs will be full. Then I usually try to get them back to my apartment and make them feel comfortable and relaxed. I always have logs in the fireplace already set up for a fire. I just have to light a match. Music is playing. A bottle of wine is chilled. Also, I have this couch. It's six feet long and very comfortable. To sit in it, you practically have to lie down. You're talking for ten, fifteen, twenty minutes, maybe you embrace, you kiss, you stroke, and then just swivel over, and you're already in a horizontal position. You don't have to go to the bedroom and break the mood. You can just make love on the couch.

MODIFIED TRADITIONAL

"I don't like being expected to play the Rock Hudson role to the hilt," says thirty-nine-year-old Alex. "I don't want to play opposite someone's Doris Day and have to 'wow' a woman into bed. It's not me." Alex is a somewhat traditional man who takes a modified traditional approach to meeting women. What distinguishes this approach from the strictly traditional seduction strategy is that at some point the man directly expresses his desire to have sex. He will orchestrate everything from the initial encounter to sustaining the chase—everything, that is, except luring the woman inconspicuously into bed. The man who takes the modified traditional approach doesn't want to assume responsibility for deciphering those last-minute sexual cues. He wants to know his partner is willing. He doesn't accept the macho role of having to overcome a woman's resistance to lovemaking. Alex, who is separated from a ten-year marriage, says he's become comfortable with this change in the scenario:

At some point in the relationship I will try to sound a woman out on her sexual values and attitudes so that I've got a pretty good idea as to whether our values are in agreement. Then, if I'm interested in her sexually, I will simply ask her point-blank whether or not she's interested in going to bed with me. I might say something like, "I would like to go to bed with you, how do you feel about that?" I will not play games after that point. If she's terribly uncomfortable with such a confrontive question, that's her problem. If she says no, for whatever reason, that's where the subject ends! I do not get into coercing her or suggesting that she's making a mistake. I mean, it's her loss, not mine.

Another man, who is married but has affairs on the side, says:

Sometime during the course of an evening you've got to lay it on the line. You've got to tell the lady, "Look, I'm attracted to you, I think you're attracted to me, and I would like to spend the rest of the evening with you." I don't believe in hyping someone with "I love you, let's go to bed." I think that's pure bullshit. I'm much more likely to say, "Look, I think you and I have had a very compatible evening. We've known each other for a while. Frankly, I would like to see the relationship take a slightly different turn and become something a little bit more exciting."

Taking the direct approach was a necessity born of circumstance for men such as Gilbert, a divorced thirty-four-year-old counselor, who became confined to a wheelchair following a car accident.

I'm confined to a wheelchair now, but I don't feel disabled. I'd give anything if I could get out of here, but at the same time it's not interfering with my relationships with women. I guess the reason why I'm successful with women is that they feel like they can talk to me about anything they're interested in. Then, when the relationship becomes more intimate, like, say, when she's sitting on my lap and we're getting carried away like any other normal couple, then I have to be honest and say, "I want more than just what we're having right now. But I don't know how you feel, so I want to check it out with you."

Being explicit about his sexual intentions also worked well for Burt, a divorced attorney, when a one-night stand was all he had in mind:

There are times when I'll meet a woman and I'm really only interested in sex, that's all. For example, I met a sexy-looking woman at a party and at one point she kind of had her arm around my shoulder so I just said, "Why don't you take me home?" And she said, "I'd like that." So we left.

Some of the men we interviewed were not interested in committed monogamous relationships. They were usually men who were recently separated and whose sole interest in women centered around sex, or men like Wayne, a twenty-three-year-old student, who didn't feel ready to commit himself to one woman and desired a variety of sexual experiences. These men felt it important to state their intentions directly to protect the woman from being hurt in case she wanted more. Wayne says when he's at a point with a woman when sex seems imminent, he tells her straight out what his sexual needs are and what limits he wants to put on their relationship:

> When we're sitting together and feeling relaxed or whatever, I start kissing them and telling them how attractive they are to me and how I would love to indulge in sex with them. Then I ask them how they feel about it. I'm not ready to get tied down, so I always ask them, "Would you be associating love with this?" Before I ever sleep with them, I always ask, "Does this mean I'm committed in any way?" Because if it does, I'm not ready for that. I don't just go jump between their legs. I tell them, "This is just a need I have, and I'd love to have it met by you. Let's come to some kind of agreement on what it's going to be." And if they tell me that they would feel stronger for me and wouldn't want to let me go, why then I don't do it. I say, "Guess we better not."

Other men felt that directly asking a woman to go to bed with them left them much too vulnerable. Rather than risk embarrassment by possibly being turned down, they advised taking a more indirect approach, which could still be interpreted as a possible entrée to sex, but because of its ambiguity still allowed the woman to tactfully avoid the issue. She could communicate her lack of interest by ignoring or making light of the sexual innuendo without having to come right out and say no. Some men used humor as a tactful way of communicating their interest while still leaving the decision up to her. Sixty-eight-year-old Don shared the following example:

> One woman came up here on business and I told her I'd be happy to have her stay at my apartment even though her company was paying all her expenses. She thought that was a good

idea. We spent the whole day working together and I guess we both had been thinking about sex. So when we got back home I said, "I have two guest rooms. One has me in it. It's your choice!"

ROLE REVERSAL

The two versions of the traditional seduction theme described so far place exclusive responsibility for the chase and the final capture in the hands of the man. Men are the pursuers, not the pursued. Yet many men said there were times they enjoyed playing the other role. They wanted the freedom to be passive or active, to seduce the woman or be seduced by her depending on the woman and the situation. Men who at times yielded their aggressor roles and allowed the woman to initiate sex utilized what we call the *role reversal* approach.

Men gave a number of reasons for being drawn to the role reversal approach to seduction. Some men were fed up with the pressure of the full-time initiator role. Others, like fifty-four-year-old Leo, wanted the opportunity to explore their softer side:

Being the initiator is really neat because it provides men with an opportunity to be very assertive and aggressive about their sexuality. The good part of that role is that you often get what you want because it's okay to initiate when you feel like it. But when you don't feel like doing the initiating—if you're feeling passive, tender, receptive, and nurturing, rather than assertive and aggressive—part of your sexuality gets cut off. Sometimes I want to be pursued, to be totally passive, and to receive sexual pleasure.

Still other men were turned on by a seductress who was willing to make the first move—and maybe even the last one. They wanted to be made love *to*. They were men who claimed they had a fuller sexual experience when they knew the woman was thoroughly interested. Furthermore, this seduction style eliminated the possibility of being rejected.

These men desired women who were willing to express their sexual desire directly, but many women in our society still find this difficult to do. They fear rejection even more so than most men. In addition, they have been brought to believe that nice girls don't do such things, that it is unbecoming and will turn their partners off. But Alex told us that neither he nor his friends are turned off by women who take the initiative. "Where are these women?" he asks about the forthright types who are described in women's magazines. "I'd love to meet them." He believes an assertive woman might be turned down by a man not because she made the first move, but more likely because he doesn't find her attractive or isn't in the mood for sex right then. This perspective was echoed by other men.

Says Basil, a twenty-one-year-old student, "I really enjoy when a woman plays aggressor. Sex is better, because you really know a woman is interested. Besides," he adds, "it's great to be seduced."

One reason George, age forty-seven, says his best sexual experiences occurred when women initiated was because he was relieved of any guilt or responsibility. He didn't have to wonder: "Should I push her? Does she want it? How far will she let me go?" Women who clearly communicate sexual interest, according to George, "make it easier for me to be most free sexually. In certain cases where I was the initiator," he adds, "I would feel guilty. On one occasion, I wasn't able to have an erection because, even though I think she wanted sex, I wasn't sure. I like a woman to make the initial contact so I know just where she stands."

Yet if women aren't accustomed to assuming what has traditionally been the male role, how can a man who prefers the role reversal approach encourage a woman to be more upfront? One way is to play what forty-two-year-old Valiant describes as "a waiting game." "I'd be the world's worst rapist," says Valiant, "because if a woman is not completely willing, I'm not interested. I'd rather wait for her to come round to me. Women are used to being put on the defense, so sometimes I put them on the offense. I just switch things around and kind of lay back until she is ready."

Jerry, a thirty-two-year-old scientist, also plays the waiting game. "I don't like the role of initiator," he says, "it puts too much of a burden on a man. I think it's nice to put the burden on a woman sometimes, so I try to subtly sow a seed so my partner will make the first move." These "seeds" are nonverbal messages such as warm physical gestures or conversations about something sexy or romantic. Then Jerry just waits.

In the following passage he describes how he set the groundwork with one woman friend in such a way that she was able to initiate sex later on. "We had become very close friends," Jerry says:

> But because she was going out with another guy, I never pressed for sex. However, over that period I made it very clear that I was interested but I wanted her to make up her own mind. One evening we were at the ocean together, at a beach house. Most of the other people had left early to drive back to the city when she literally dragged me into the bedroom and said, "Let's go." If I had pressed the issue it probably wouldn't have happened because of her involvement with the other guy.

John, a consultant, says the way he's managed to make a woman give him a second glance is to reverse the expectations:

> It's not essential I go to bed with a woman right away. Since most women these days seem to expect men to press for sex right at the start, if I can go out and have a good time with them and not try to "jump on their bones" the first time, it throws them off balance. Then they've lowered their guard and find me more appealing. They get kind of hooked at that point and eventually start coming on to me.

Billy, a thirty-one-year-old graduate student, has fun with the role reversal approach and says:

> It works amazingly well. I've even teased a couple of women by saying, "I really do want to see you, but one of the problems that I've been having lately is that after I go out for a few times with a woman she expects there to be sex. If there's none, she gets disappointed and ends the relationship. That really makes me feel uncomfortable, because it makes me think she isn't really interested in me as a person."
>
> If I meet somebody where I think the relationship might possibly be long-term, there's no need to rush into sex right away. So creating that kind of tension by making things a little uncertain is kind of nice. What I tend to do is take somebody home and maybe shake their hand and say, "I really enjoyed it. Thanks very much." I do this to exaggerate the reversal. To me, sex is probably going to happen anyway, so it doesn't mat-

ter if we play a bit in the beginning. It's nice to tease and, like
I said, it works!

Billy was in the driver's seat even while someone else appeared
to be driving, and that was the role reversal approach that men
seemed to be most comfortable with. In fact, several men told of
bold seductions planned and executed entirely by the woman that,
while fulfilling their fantasies, were not entirely comfortable in
reality.

Conrad, a middle-aged widower, is both intrigued and put off by
the forthright style of what he calls the "so-called new woman." He
was flattered by the attentions of one such woman, who, he says,
"clearly wanted me. I liked that, and I wanted to pursue it, but it
was also a bit disconcerting." He goes on to describe their third
date:

> I'm driving her home from dinner and she leans over and be-
> gins to unbutton my shirt. We'd both been drinking and she
> was feeling mellow. Then she unzipped my fly. Then she took
> my penis out of my trousers and began to stroke it. Now, I did
> not, during the first two dates, come on very strong myself, ex-
> cept that I made it clear I found her to be attractive. And I
> clearly saw this as another campaign that would hopefully lead
> to seduction, but I saw it as a long-term campaign. But this
> woman was coming on so aggressively on the third date that I
> didn't like it. I was surprised at my own reaction, because in
> my fantasies I thought it would be just delicious.

Reality intruded upon fantasy, because, as Conrad said, "this role
reversal shattered a pattern I'd been following all my life where I
make the selection and determine where and when the seduction
will take place." Conrad realized "this is rather rigid of me, but
when a woman comes on that strong, I guess it makes me wonder if
she'll take over in other areas of the relationship as well."

A similar reaction was expressed by Charles, a forty-five-year-old
college professor, after a stranger approached him and boldly put
the moves on him. The way she did it, Charles recounts, was to call
one night and say, "I've walked by your office a lot and seen you
and I'd like to meet you." Though he'd never met her, Charles says
she mentioned the name of a colleague. According to his colleague,

whom he called to find out more about her, she was an extraordinary woman—very smart, attractive, and nice. So Charles followed through:

I had her name, so I called her and said that I was coming over, if that was okay. And I went over for the evening. She turned out to be a very beautiful woman. I assumed we were getting to know each other, and so I drank some wine with her, talked to her, had a nice conversation. When I got up to leave, she came for me at the door. Physically. She put her hand on the door and stopped me. Then she put her arms around me and tried to kiss me. I felt just like I was in the position of a woman. Part of me almost thought about not reciprocating, because, although I found her attractive, I thought, "Gee, I'm just getting to know you." It was all reversed. But I thought, this must be how women feel sometimes, when they want you yet don't want you to make an advance too quickly. Anyway, we wound up in bed.

The men we interviewed wanted women to *share* some of the responsibility for starting up a relationship but were not comfortable with a total switch in roles. And they wanted women who expressed their sexual intentions to do so with taste, sophistication, and a touch of class. They wanted her to take a feminine approach and not pounce upon them caveman style. In this sense, they were really asking for nothing more than the same kind of tasteful manner women have desired from men.

Says fifty-two-year-old Bruce:

A balance has to be there. I don't want an overly assertive person or a person who is always reticent and has to be coaxed. There's a time and place. When it's the wrong time, it can be disturbing. But when the setting is right, it's great. I like a woman who recognizes the right time and place to be assertive and expresses herself sexually. It's important to maintain a balance and indicate some interest without overkill, so that there is some room in there for me to respond.

NO-ROLE APPROACH

"It's impossible not to get caught up in playing games to some extent in this culture," one man we interviewed told us. "Yet I try not to, because I don't like any falseness between me and someone I'm intimate with." He and others like him said they preferred to get to know a woman first and have sex develop naturally. Instead of planning some grand seduction, they wanted the lovemaking to evolve out of a mutual attraction and interest. These men said they did not want to assume a prescribed role in intiating sex. What they did want was to act on the basis of their feelings.

The freedom to choose the no-role approach obviously came about in part as a result of the sexual revolution. With women reexamining their role scripting and becoming sexually active at a younger age, and usually before marriage, many men no longer have to coax a woman into bed. After all, says author and sex therapist Bernie Zilbergeld, "Though some people talk about conquest, I wonder, what is there to conquer? I mean, not every single person is wanting to do it with you, but certainly somewhere on the block somebody's going to do it with you. So, in that sense, sex has become liberated."

Another writer on men's sex issues, Warren Farrell, described the dating scene today in terms of sexual supply and demand. He says:

One of the beautiful things about the last ten years is that the sexual supply has increased in relation to the sexual demand and the gap has narrowed. Before, when there was almost no supply, men were constantly going around having to demand, demand, demand. It's only been in the last three or four years that I have been able to refuse sexual experiences with women in any systematic way. It's only recently that I've really been able to be selective and to feel comfortable saying, "No, I don't feel like it tonight." Or, "I don't feel like it with you." Before that, if a reasonably attractive and intelligent woman offered herself to me, I would have jumped at the chance. Now men can afford to be more selective about the quality of the emotional experience. Also, as the supply of sexually available women starts matching the demand, men will be appreciating women for their intellect and the fullness of their emotional response, rather than pursuing them only for sex. They'll be having enough of it.

Perhaps this is already happening. The men we interviewed felt quantity was less of an issue than quality. These men were looking for deeper emotional involvements rather than mere "notches on a belt." Says Valiant, age forty-two:

Sex is not the most important thing to me. I'm not out collecting women. I could have had nine times as many as I've had, if that was what I was interested in. I'm interested in quality rather than quantity.

Ned, age thirty-four, agrees. He remembers a period in his life when:

I was screwing all over the city but I don't think I was really enjoying it that much. I'd characterize it by saying I was screwing more but enjoying it less. The thing I learned most from this is, if there isn't a relationship, if there isn't some real feeling, some caring, it's better to jack off than go to bed with someone. Otherwise I feel dirty and unclean, and pissed at myself for not saying no or getting out of it.

These men seemed to have gone through an evolution whereby they no longer felt driven to seduce every woman they encountered. Instead, they were looking for women they could be comfortable with, women they could talk to. They were primarily interested in intimacy. This is not to say they would never indulge in casual sex, but as we have previously stated, they said their best sex occurred in the context of a truly intimate relationship.

As a result, these men were moving away from the macho seduction strategies and toward a more natural flow of getting to know their partners. For thirty-six-year-old Jason, this change of attitude started to occur five or six years ago:

One day I realized that, although I had a nice job, a great car and apartment, and I was screwing my way through Philadelphia, something was missing. I didn't know quite what it was, so I got into therapy. I finally realized that what was missing from my life was intimacy. And while I'd been screwing my way up and down the coast—or trying to anyway—I'd never gotten any real satisfaction out of my sexual life. If I wanted a woman, I went after her as I would go after something in my business. I would design a strategy in my own mind based on what I knew about that person and I would go after her like I was going to sell a product. Now I go about it in a much different way. I go about it by not going about it. I let relationships ebb and flow much more naturally. The interesting thing about it is that as I became much more spontaneous and natural, I found that I didn't have to try as hard to find sexual partners. My sexual relationships got better; I enjoyed them more and the entire quality of my sexual life improved.

One reason Bernard, age twenty-nine, gives for having a more relaxed style of initiating sex now than during his teenage years is that it no longer has the singular importance it once did. As a result, he can "take things as they come." When he was young, however, Bernard says:

I used to have a very deliberate strategy. I proceeded almost by the numbers: I would wine them, dine them, and then try to couch my seduction efforts in a way that would allow me to save face if I were rejected. Today it's not quite so deliberate. As I get older, I find that sex has a more natural place in my relationships. If the other person is willing and interested, then the natural events just occur.

Thirty-eight-year-old Alan says he too has dropped the urgent focus on sex:

My strategy now, if you can call it a strategy, is to go out and have a nice time, and to just enjoy the woman's company. This often means that we won't have sex right away. First, I try to get to know her. Then, after three or four dates, *if* it starts to "click," we might have sex.

Whether sex came about as a natural link in a chain of getting-to-know-you events or was a planned ending to the first encounter, the men we interviewed shared a common desire for an intimate relationship. If the traditional scoring tactics led to a series of one-night stands, some men began to reconsider their approaches. Ultimately, they wanted a sense of security and closeness with a partner. Once they found this with a woman, perhaps even set up households together and married, another issue presented itself: how to keep a long-term sexual relationship alive and satisfying. After all, the excitement of the chase or the uncertainty of what is yet to come changes once a relationship is solidified. As newness settles into familiarity, couples want to be sure that the familiarity of their love-making won't settle into boredom. Increasingly, they are developing creative ways to keep their sex lives vital.

CHAPTER SIX

GOURMET LOVEMAKING

Sex started getting boring for fifty-nine-year-old Mel a couple of years ago. After thirty-four years of marriage, he says:

We had fallen into a clockwork-like routine with sex pretty much following the same pattern each time. Since it takes my wife much longer to have an orgasm, I would manually pleasure her, then would do it orally until she came. Then, I would enter her. By that time she would be completely wet, and within twenty or thirty seconds from the time I entered I would ejaculate. It got to be the same routine over and over. That's not how it was when we were first married when we would try out lots of different positions and routines.

Mel's complaint that his sex life had dwindled to a perfunctory release on Saturday night wasn't unusual. Lovemaking often suffers when, in the normal course of events, family and work obligations usurp the time and energy needed for intimate relationships. Some men complained that their sex lives had become routine and boring —meat and potatoes sex. Many wondered out loud whether it was even possible to extend the honeymoon relationship, with its romantic and loving feelings, for years after the marriage vows had been taken. The reality pointed out by one man was that "this may be an unattainable dream," with the fast pace of society and the divorce rate being what it is.

But others thought differently. Barring serious marital difficulties or overwhelming outside pressures, lovemaking, in their experience, still retained its vitality. These men did not perceive monogamy to be a restrictive state that eventually would strangle their sexual enjoyment. It wasn't necessary for them to repress their sexual needs by throwing themselves into their work or extramarital affairs. And they weren't about to stop searching for excitement, stimulation, and creativity in sex either. Instead, they sought to incorporate these aspects into their ongoing relationships. For the most part, this meant they had to reevaluate certain aspects of machismo.

According to traditional role scripting, the man is in charge of creating the romance only in the initial stages of the relationship. A truly masculine man is defined by his ability to attract and seduce women, by wining, dining, and courting them. Unfortunately, for most men, the courtship ends when some form of commitment is expressed in a relationship. Many men then see their familiar role of lover as no longer appropriate for their new status as husband or live-in boy friend. The time, energy, and money that were once devoted to courting and romancing the woman of their dreams now become irrelevant. Since sex is expected to be unplanned and completely spontaneous, they no longer focus on creating romantic moods which could lead to moments of intense sensuality.

Unlike their macho peers, the men who were successful at long-term gourmet sex understood that keeping their sex lives exciting required conscious effort and planning. They came to realize that, though spontaneity was desirable, it was not always possible. Planned sexual activities could be just as pleasurable and fulfilling—if not more so—than spontaneous sex, which usually occurred late at night when neither party was particularly energetic. Once they recognized this, they were willing to work toward creating more moments of passion, eroticism, and romance in their relationships. And these men unanimously agreed that their sexual relationships were revitalized and renewed by their efforts.

One fifty-year-old man reported:

I try to create a romantic environment now. At this point in my life it's one of the neatest things I do. I love it. I like to buy flowers and have candles around, and I like to have the food and wine just right. I even clean my house. Before Jenny came to spend the weekend I spent all day long getting ready. I enjoyed doing it. God, when I was a macho guy, I would never do that. It was just not the thing to do! But now I like to do it. I don't think I'm doing it for her nearly as much as I'm doing it for me. I like the process. And now, at this point in my life, I'm free enough to do it. It's just such a pleasure.

HAPPILY EVER AFTER

For the men who maintained vital sexual relationships, "happily ever after" was synonymous with keeping the romance alive. The essence of romance, for these men, was a feeling of specialness conveyed through words and actions. Sharing and recreating this feeling of specialness was one of the primary qualities that distinguished couples who enjoyed "gourmet lovemaking" from those whose sex life had become routine. Forty-eight-year-old Justin, a minister who has been happily married for twenty-three years, started each day by sharing a short morning prayer with his wife in which he silently thanks God for "handpicking his wife" for him.

For others, maintaining the feeling of a special bond meant consciously finding ways to maintain the intimacy. Thirty-four-year-old Ned agreed, and found that part of keeping the romance alive for him meant attending to the intimacy throughout the day:

It makes a big difference how we start off the day. If I wake up and I focus on all that has to get done and forget to give her a hug or make contact with her, it becomes an uphill battle. So I've learned to take a few minutes in the morning to give her a hug and talk about what I'm going to be doing and when I'm going to be back. It's like an investment. And if I call unexpectedly to say, "Hi, how are you doing," it's the icing on the cake. She just hums.

Sometimes the intimacy is fostered through developing a communication style that recreates the romance. Thirty-six-year-old Terry and his wife have developed a special "lovers' language" that evokes their original feelings of love.

When we start to feel sexual, we sometimes recapture a language that Glenna and I developed when we were going together. It's not exactly a baby-talk sort of thing, but it's a personalized communication that's been built up over fifteen years.

Some men, like twenty-seven-year-old Scott, created this sense of romantic intimacy by communicating nonverbally:

Sometimes it is awkward to physicalize your feelings for one another in public situations, such as cocktail parties, receptions, classes, whatever. But you can do a lot with your eyes— you can undress your wife with your eyes—and of course it makes her feel like a million dollars. And she can do the same thing to you. You can look across the room and lick your lips, or you can play with your tongue as though you're doing cunnilingus in the air, and no one knows what the hell is going on, but your wife suddenly becomes a queen at the cocktail party, in your own little private world. In this way you can communicate that you're dying to do it, and because of the circumstances you can't right now, but maybe later.

Whether verbal or nonverbal, couples often developed certain codes by which they expressed sexual interest. Common one-liners included: "Do you want to get lucky?" "Do you want to play around?" or "Let's not watch Johnny Carson tonight." One man would phone his wife during the day and say, "Let's not go out tonight. Let's just stay home. I can't wait to see you." Another man, whenever he found he could take a break during the day, would call his wife and ask, "Do you want to have a matinee?"

Often code innuendos developed from a particularly pleasurable sexual experience which not only emphasized the lovers' special bond, but also invoked the memory of that past pleasure. Fred, twenty-seven, referred to "prism time" for this reason:

We lived in a little room in Raleigh, and we had this small faceted crystal prism hanging in the window. At about four o'clock on a sunny day, the sun shone in and put prisms all over the wall. We called it "prism time." And that was the time we would lay down together. And we often had sex at that time because no one else was around then. So sometimes I'll just say, "It's prism time," or I'll say, "Honey, the prism's in here."

Bernard, twenty-nine, recalled an experience that has resulted in a code they use often to convey sexual interest:

> Once during a moment of spontaneous passion, I put some ice cream in her navel and then I licked it off. After that, every now and then, I'll call her up and ask, "Do you want to go for ice cream?"

Anticipation

Another key element in maintaining the romance in a sexual relationship is to build some sense of anticipation by planning for future sexual delights. As one man put it, "It's wonderful to know that one or both of you is busy planning for a special time to be lovers again. It's just fun to savor the idea, to anticipate all that pleasure." Another man, who has had to travel quite often, felt that having to spend time away was offset by anticipating his return home and how he would go about seducing his wife.

Silas, a fifty-four-year-old minister who has been married for thirty years, was aware of the necessity of planning ahead for gourmet lovemaking:

> I love planning ahead and looking forward to making love. Of course, you can't always plan an ideal situation or time. We all know that sometimes there are things that happen during the day which prevent you from meeting a scheduled affair, but usually, if you plan for it wisely enough, it can become a very wholesome reality especially if you're close enough to your mate to sort of suggest a time. Then both of you can begin to look forward to it. I think mental anticipation makes the sex better, especially if you try to be prepared physically as well by not getting too tired beforehand. That way you can give all your energy and feeling to each other.

A few men heightened their feelings of sexual anticipation by using some form of sexual abstinence. One man liked to enhance his sexual experiences by abstaining from sex for a few days or by abstaining from orgasm over a number of sexual experiences.

> I like going without sex for a while, like three, four, or five days in a row. It adds to the anticipation. Then I like to masturbate and not have an orgasm, or go for long periods of time

with a lot of sexual activity, and not have an orgasm. I just delay it and let it build. That really creates some peak experiences when I do come.

After nine years of marriage, Bowie and his wife have found a unique way of sustaining sexual anticipation, intensity, and romance. Theirs is a practice originally developed as a way of deepening their religious convictions:

Under Jewish law pertaining to family life, there's a two to two and a half week period of time, from the onset of a woman's period until a week after the conclusion of her period, when we abstain from sex. We have found that the period of abstinence greatly enhances the sex that follows. It's like having a honeymoon on a monthly basis.

SETTING THE SCENE

When sex did occur, the men we interviewed felt it important to put in the extra effort to set the scene in a particularly erotic or sensual way.

Gary, thirty-one, shared his version of setting the scene for romance after being married a few years:

I don't like just going to bed and fucking and going to sleep. I like planning for the sexual experience, like planning a lovely evening with a nice bottle of champagne, going out to dinner in a restaurant, or just having a nice meal at the house, and then going to our bedroom and doing some fantasy things. I like lighting some candles, or dressing up, or having my wife dress up in something really sexy, and then doing a lot of foreplay, a lot of teasing and playing and caressing, not immediately fucking. I need to talk and touch to make a transition from the active talking day into more of a touching and feeling experience. That transition to a sensual and sexual experience is real important to me.

To recreate a romantic atmosphere, some couples would plan a special evening out of the house. A typical scenario might include going to an intimate and romantic spot or a special restaurant where the mood was just right. Ned, thirty-four, who has been living with his girl friend for the past five years, shared one of the special evenings he arranged for his lover:

> I love doing romantic things for my girl friend. She is a John Denver nut. She loves John Denver. When he was here, I got first-class tickets for us to see him. I didn't tell her about them. I arranged for a big, humongous chauffeur-driven limousine to pick us up. We went out to dinner, saw the show, and came home. It was a fantastic evening. She was ecstatic.

Leo, fifty-four, recalled that for a period of eight months he and his wife-to-be were geographically separated. During that time the sexual intimacy was so intense that they now use that period as a model to recreate those feelings.

> When we were meeting cross country, we'd fly in and have forty-eight hours with no other agenda except us. We called it "island time" because it felt like being off on an island together. The whole focus was the other person and how much pleasure you could give. The feeling was enhanced because you were meeting after a separation, so it became a very special time. Now, in order to recreate that, we go away for at least one weekend out of a month. Or we create "island time" in our own home. When everybody else is gone, we don't answer phones or anything else. The total focus is the other person, how much fun we can have, how much pleasuring we can give, how much we can talk to each other without interruptions. I think it takes island time to keep your sex life intimate, special and, above all, highly charged.

Some of the men in our survey make dates with their partners as a way of planning for the private time necessary to recharge their romantic batteries. Silas explained that making romantic dates with his wife has always been an integral part of maintaining the romance in the thirty years of his marriage. The key to the success of these dates has been the amount of planning that he puts into them:

> I do most of the cooking in our house since both my wife and I work. I have more energy than she does. So when I want to

create a romantic evening I make sure the evening meal is all done and the house is clean. This usually happens on weekends, but whenever it is, I try to arrange it so that she does as little as possible and she knows this is a signal for a "date." Of course, she looks forward to it, too. She dresses in something that's sort of sexy while I may only have on a pair of shorts. There's the foreplay and tenderness that ends up making it a really enjoyable experience.

While planning was likely to ensure good sex, erotic experiences that just happened spontaneously often stood out as some of the most memorable. And while spontaneity could not be counted on, the men we interviewed advocated that whenever the mood hit and an unexpected moment availed itself, it should be seized. The bills should be dropped, the stove turned off, and the phone hastily removed from the hook so a brief moment could be stolen from the routine of life.

According to sixty-seven-year-old Clarence, sex anywhere and at any time creates the necessary diversity:

Why not have sex at the end of the day? Why not at the beginning of the day? Why not at dawn, when the birds are singing? Why not on the kitchen table? Why not on a couch? Why not on the floor? Why not on the rug? Sexual relations should not be just a bedtime occupation. Sometimes, the very worst time is at the end of the day when you're tired. But, on the other hand, it may be best at the end of the day, since sex is one of nature's best sleeping pills.

For thirty-six-year-old Jason, sex is often initiated as the result of a spontaneous gesture:

I guess the way I initiate sex is so spontaneous that there's no way to narrow it down. We might come home from work and be playing grab-ass and I might just throw her on the bed. As I throw her down on the bed, kidding around, I see her skirt fly up and I just might have the urge and reach down and pull her pants off and begin to have sex.

Many men, like sixty-six-year-old Gene, found that their relationships were more satisfying sexually when both partners were free enough to be spontaneous:

> If my wife is in the shower, then I'll get in the shower; if I happen to walk by the closet while she's undressing I'll give her a big hug. Sometimes I put my hand between her legs and say, "That's all mine." And she does the same thing to me. If I walk by with a bath towel, she'll reach out and give me a feel.

GOURMET TOUCHING

Whether the lovemaking was planned or spontaneous, men felt there was much they could do to enhance the experience. Both single and attached men found the quality of touching during sex often made the difference between ordinary sex and gourmet lovemaking. Touch can be one of the most important vehicles for expressing sexual feelings. For the men we interviewed, quality touching not only required a certain technical skill, but also an ability to sensually communicate caring feelings. Twenty-seven-year-old Lanny offered a specific example:

> Hands can be terribly communicative when you're making love to someone—especially if your partner is uncomfortable or nervous. The way you touch or hold someone can be very reassuring. When they get a little uncomfortable, you can just lay your hand on theirs and it can be very calming. It's also a way of showing them that you're thinking of more than just sex and getting into their pants. It's a way of letting the other person know that you care about them.

The quality that distinguished ordinary touching from gourmet touching for most of these men was the ability to convey loving feelings. Not only did the men want to convey these feelings by the way they caressed their partners, but they also valued lovers who had this same ability. As sixty-one-year-old Mark explained, when asked what gourmet touching meant to him:

> The skill with which people use their hands can vary enormously. There can be a way in which some people touch you that gives you a sense of being cherished. It feels like they're

cherishing every inch of your body. I can feel when their hands are connected to their heart as well as to their genitals by the way they touch me. I try to touch a partner with my hands or my mouth or my leg or my foot in such a way that both of our bodies are totally involved. When I'm touching her breast with my hand I try to do it in such a way that not only can she feel her breast being touched by my hand, but so she can almost feel what it feels like to be in my hand.

Many men who had this level of sensual communication in their relationships felt they could almost read their partner's body language and tune into precisely what caress their lover wanted. Roger described how this ability has helped him to become a gourmet lover:

Part of what I'm talking about is a sensitivity to reading where she's at, what she's feeling, and where she wants to go from there, instead of just looking at it from my own point of view. Instead of stopping because I'm bored with rubbing her back and want to touch her breast now, I try to read her body language to see if she's ready for that. And she tries to do the same for me.

The pressure of the touch administered was another important element of gourmet lovemaking. Many of the men we interviewed were more turned on by delicate soft caresses, while others favored more assertive passionate touching or even touching that bordered on being painful:

I was with a woman once who had very long fingernails and liked to use them. She left marks down my back that took weeks to heal. But I have to admit I liked it. There's something about this pain/ecstasy level that, when it's happening, it's not pain, it's ecstasy.

For most men, however, skillful sensual touching required variety. As one man explained it:

There needs to be different textures to sensual and erotic stimuli. You can't always use the same texture, just as you wouldn't use the same spice in every meal. Sometimes you're

gentle, sometimes you're rough, sometimes you suck lightly
with your lips, and other times you just reach out and grab.

Massage

Many of the men in our study enjoyed initiating intimate touching through massage. The massage did not have to develop into actual lovemaking but most often it did. In either case, the men enjoyed making the massage a truly romantic and sensual experience.

Mel, a fifty-nine-year-old sales executive, found that massage was
a wonderful prelude for gourmet lovemaking:

I used to get body massages from a masseuse, but that got to
be rather expensive. So we bought our own massage table,
which we set up right near our bed, and we massage one another regularly. My wife gives a very sensual massage. While
feigning a certain professionalism, she plays with my genitals
and stimulates me, and then she kisses the tip of my penis and
soon after begins oral sex, until the next thing I know we're
having intercourse on the table or we're hopping into bed.

Another man went on to share his specific massage technique:

I like to have both of us naked and position myself over her
buttocks so that my penis is lying in her crack, between her
cheeks. I get a massage oil or cream and start around the neck.
I love massaging around collarbones and necks. I love ears. I
love to run my tongue along the contours of the ear and kiss
underneath the ear. Then I work up and down the spine, using
a caressing pressure, or maybe scratch the back a little. Then I
begin kissing the spine; every once in a while I'll place a delicate kiss on the vertebrae while I work on the buttocks or on
the cheeks. I keep kissing lower and lower and eventually go
around the anal area and put my tongue in. Finally I move a
leg over and put myself in her vagina and I put my thumb in
her anus and we're having intercourse.

Many men preferred a sexual massage with oil or special creams
because of the slippery effect it had which heightened their tactile
sensations during lovemaking. As one man explained, "I love the
slippery, silky feeling you have when your bodies are all oiled up
and you make love!" Favorite oils were skin moisturizing creams,

natural oils like olive or almond oil, or special sexual products like
Kama Sutra oil. Some men even made their own massage oil by
adding to baby oil or olive oil concentrated scents purchased in
boutiques, drug stores, or health food stores.

Lovemaking

As the interviews continued, we became more curious as to how
men liked to be touched during lovemaking. We knew a lot about
women's preferences and we wondered if male sensitivities were
different, if certain parts of their bodies were more sensitive than
others.

Some men couldn't answer this question. As one forty-five-year-
old college professor said:

> I don't think I have any erogenous zones outside of my penis,
> as far as I can tell. I don't know whether any other men do, but
> I doubt it!

Traditionally, men have been perceived as the givers of sensual
and sexual pleasure, not the recipients. According to the macho
script, a man's pleasure comes from seducing the woman. He
focuses on her pleasure. The enjoyment of his ejaculation is a fore-
gone conclusion. Consequently, many men are totally unaware of
the potential pleasure that areas of their body, other than their genitals, have to offer them.

The men we interviewed who had already come to this understanding were beginning to explore the pleasure potential of the
whole body—not just their genitals. Although everyone's body is
different and touching that excites one person may be relatively un-
stimulating for another, general patterns of enjoyment did emerge.

Facial caresses applied by their lover's fingertips or mouths were
extremely stimulating for most men. A number of men also found
that it was really nice to have their ears caressed by a wet tongue:

> At first I hated having someone blow in my ear, especially if
> they followed it up by sticking their tongue in it. I just thought
> that was horrible, but after a while I began to be more open to
> the sensualness of it. Now it gets me kind of primed up and
> turned on. But when a sexual partner asks me what really turns
> me on, I still feel a little silly saying, "Just blow in my ear."

Like women, some men found their nipples and breasts particularly responsive. Barry, sixty-seven, married sixteen years, said:

> I don't know how many men have discovered how sensitive their own nipples are, but my nipples are extremely sensitive and I love to have them stroked or sucked while we are making love, so I told my wife and she does it.

Men spoke of enjoying caresses on their lower chests, abdomen, the small of their back, inner thighs, and the back of their knees. Even the bottom of their feet and their toes contained sensitive nerve endings that could be stimulated during lovemaking. Scott, twenty-seven, enjoys having his wife stroke his stomach as he begins to ejaculate:

> My wife strokes my stomach as I'm coming. Those muscles seem to start the ejaculatory system going for me. And it's a tremendous turn-on to have her knead my stomach as I'm coming.

Some men were also discriminating about the specific ways they liked to have their genitals touched. These men wanted their genitals to be caressed just as lovingly as their faces, mouths, ears, or nipples:

> There's a feeling of being accepted more with a partner who is not only willing to touch my penis, but who really enjoys it. I think that is one of the more erotic things for me.

Men went on to detail how they liked to have their genitals stroked. Some liked their penis to be held firmly and/or tightly while their lover rhythmically stroked the shaft. As the penis became engorged, many men preferred a change in pressure, whereas the exact rhythm varied from man to man. While many of the men we interviewed were too embarrassed to give us a precise description of how they like their genitals stroked, Ron, a twenty-four-year-old medical student, felt comfortable describing his unique preferences in detail:

> If a woman knows how to use her hands, that's really good. When she's coming up the shaft of the penis, I don't like her to go over that rim, around the head of the penis, because that's

irritating. I like her to stay under the rim. But a lot of women think that the head of the penis is very erotic. I appreciate it if the woman wants to tease me by stimulating the head while doing something with the rest of the penis. But stimulating the head of the penis *alone* does not give me an erection or orgasm. Also, a lot of women think that the way to help a man with an erection is to pull on the penis. But I don't like to have my penis pulled on. What works for me is to actually constrict the vessels near the base of the penis, which stops the blood from leaving it. So a woman should stroke with more pressure going down and very little pressure coming up, just enough to hold the penis in place. In order to have an orgasm, I need to be stimulated near the base and with motions going down instead of coming up.

SEXUAL ACCOUTREMENTS

One of the questions we posed to our interviewees was whether they ever used any sexual accoutrements, in other words, anything other than their own bodies, to enhance their lovemaking. A common response was that using accoutrements was unnatural, unnecessary, and, by implication, unmanly. This was expressed by seventy-year-old Riley, who believed that men shouldn't need any accoutrements:

I have a contemptuous feeling about those things. I think they're crutches, and I think anybody who's in touch with the real energy doesn't need things like that. He doesn't need tricks, and he doesn't need tools.

However, most of the men, particularly those in their twenties and thirties who were brought up in a culture of greater sexual permissiveness, were much more open to experimentation. They did not feel that using accoutrements was unnatural, and they did not seem threatened if pleasure was derived from something other than their own bodies. Twenty-seven-year-old Raymond expressed these feelings aptly:

Be willing to try new things, certainly not things that scare you out of your wits, but be willing to fantasize, and to be playful.

If your lover suggests something that doesn't just shock you, like wanting to pee on you or something, then give it a shot. And take sex as play, not as a means of proving yourself. Don't treat it like work. You don't have to be a big achiever, and all that macho stuff, during sex.

In keeping with this philosophy, some men referred to accoutrements as toys that could keep a sexual relationship alive for years. Thirty-seven-year-old John went so far as to keep his "toys" in a trunk and believed that a well-stocked trunk was a boon to any relationship.

The accoutrements men talked about ranged from light-dimmers to handcuffs, depending on the types of erotic atmosphere they wanted to produce. Since many men were extremely aroused by visual stimulation, items that enhanced the visual image of their partner were mentioned over and over again. This meant that the quality of light in the room was an important factor.

Like most men, Charles, a forty-five-year-old professor, wanted to have enough light to see his partner but felt that too much light was actually a turn-off:

There is the old Jewish prohibition against light and even D. H. Lawrence said it's only good in the dark, so maybe I'm perverted. But I like genitals and I prefer seeing them. I like soft lighting from different angles rather than stark light, which tends to be a little intimidating.

Subtle lighting was created by leaving a light on in the closet or bathroom or by using a dim light near the bed. One man used a small night-light just below the edge of the bed. Others favored more dramatic lights like strobe, black or colored light bulbs to create the kind of low visibility but erotic atmosphere they preferred for quality lovemaking. Candlelight was another favorite since it provided sufficient visibility while creating a romantic atmosphere. Men also seemed to enjoy placing candles near the bed or in the bathroom for a sensual and dramatic effect.

Another favorite sexual accoutrement mentioned in conjunction with soft lights and candles was mirrors. One man in his twenties said:

On occasions I've used mirrors to expose different positions.

One time I had mirrors on my ceiling and around all of the walls. Like in *Playboy* or *Penthouse,* the excitement of seeing the organs adds to the sexual experience.

Some men found that new female partners were sometimes initially uncomfortable with bedroom mirrors that were obviously sexual in nature. So one man solved this problem by putting a mirror on a sliding closet door and would wait until the relationship was far enough along to suggest sliding the door to the right place, or he would just leave the door there unless she complained.

Colognes both for themselves and for their partner were suggested to heighten the pleasures of smell. A few men enjoyed dusting their partners with scented powder during foreplay. Some used baby powder, but a number of men mentioned Kama Sutra powder, which came with a sensuous feather duster.

Using various foods was another way men enhanced their lovemaking. Whipped cream, for example, was mentioned by a number of men. According to thirty-eight-year-old Jack:

Get a can of Reddi-wip and put as much as you would like over the other person's body wherever you would like and just start eating and licking. It is very, very sensual. It was funny. One time it was the only thing we bought at the store and I remember the cashier giving us some sly winks, so somebody else must have had the idea too.

Many men preferred to use whipped cream as a "topping" for oral sex. John, thirty-seven:

By placing whipped cream on the erect penis, the woman can eat the cream off and perform oral sex at the same time. It can also be used on the vagina. But you have to plan ahead for that sort of activity, unless, of course, you happen to be in the kitchen.

Gary, thirty-two, combined his love of desserts with gourmet sex by covering his lover with whipped cream topped with cinnamon and chocolate chips. Others substituted strawberry syrup or chocolate syrup for whipped cream even though this often meant having to change the sheets afterwards because of the sticky mess. And apparently it's true that "everyone loves Sara Lee"—at least it was true for thirty-one-year-old Billy, an unmarried graduate student, who said:

I really like Sara Lee cheesecake. I like putting it on breasts and various other parts. Then I just lick and eat it off.

Some men chose various foods as sexual enhancements because of the tastes and textures, while other men suggested ice because of its temperature. John explained that the low temperature of the ice, when applied to intimate parts of the body, produced stimulating sensations:

If you place a glass full of small pieces of ice near the bed, you can insert a piece in the vagina with your mouth. A half to a third of a normal ice cube is more than enough—you just want to drop the temperature of the walls of the vagina, not give her frostbite. Then I penetrate her immediately after. The vagina becomes very cold because of the ice and since the penis is very warm, the temperature difference makes it quite stimulating to both of us. The sensation lasts for only about thirty seconds but it can be repeated a number of times during the evening. It helps to put a towel over the bed to keep it from getting wet.

Another man described a special turn-on that occurred at a motel where his partner used ice in an extremely provocative way:

The first time she did it, she told me not to go away because she wanted to show me something. Meanwhile, she put on her dress and went down the hall and brought back this bucket of ice. I had no damn idea what she intended to do with it, but she said, "Trust me." I guess that was part of the turn-on too, because I had to lie there wondering what the hell she was going to do with that bucket of ice. Then she put a piece in her mouth and I wondered if she was just going to sit there and eat ice. But she chewed it up a little and then performed fellatio with ice in her mouth. She called it "fire and ice" and it was a real turn-on.

A large percentage of men mentioned using drugs occasionally for enhancement of their gourmet sexual experiences. The drugs used included alcohol, marijuana, cocaine, LSD, and amyl nitrate. Although habitual use of any of these substances was, in most instances, denied, their occasional use seemed rather widespread.

Alcohol was actually the least favorite drug used to enhance lovemaking by the men we interviewed. While a small amount of alcohol created a mellow glow, it was easy to misjudge and imbibe too much, which could create erection problems.

Marijuana, on the other hand, was the most popular drug used by men to enhance the pleasures of sex. Although only a few men were habitually using marijuana, many were comfortable occasionally using it as an aphrodisiac.

As sixty-seven-year-old Barry explained, the main sexual advantage to smoking pot was to magnify the physical sensations:

A little pot makes a difference. If I'm high on grass, then the physical sensations become magnified enormously.

When forty-three-year-old Chuck smoked grass he found that the sexual energy between him and his partner seemed to flow on and on and on:

Sex on grass is an incredible experience. In one day I've had intercourse up to about seven times. I had seven ejaculations.

Amyl nitrate, or poppers, are used by cardiac patients to stimulate the heart. Because it dilates the capillaries, it produces a rush. Some men reported that if used early in the arousal process amyl nitrate interfered with erection, but if used at the moment of climax the rush produced intensified the experience of orgasm. While considered physically harmful as a recreational drug, it was nevertheless used by a few men. Jerry, a thirty-two-year-old bachelor scientist, was careful to prepare his partner for the experience:

When we're in the middle of intercourse we both inhale it, then it becomes a very intense physical thing. It intensifies the orgasm maybe ten or twenty times. The end result is usually that both of us reach orgasm at about the same time. It seems like it's going on forever. I think your partner should know what to expect, though, so it's a good idea for her to inhale it a couple of times before sex so she's not afraid.

Cocaine received mixed reviews. Some men found that it inhibited their erections. As one man said, "Sometimes I get so speedy and my thoughts start coming so fast that my energy gets directed to this and that and, before I know it, I've lost my erection."

For other men, cocaine had just the opposite effect. These men found that the occasional use of coke transformed the lovemaking to a sensual flow of sexual energy. Such was the case for forty-three-year-old David:

> What coke does is slow down that driving action. It makes sexual feelings more generalized and less frantic. Sex has a softness, like a blue-light feeling. So your body becomes more receptive and the energy becomes less directed. Now that may be a drawback for some men who feel that an erection is where it's at. However, I like sexual play regardless of the erection. If for some reason the erection goes for a while, it will come back if I continue playing. Meanwhile, I can start over or move the focus to some other part of the body: work on the neck for a while, kiss. I like to spend two or three hours making love. I like to have one orgasm and then take a rest and have another one. Coke just helps to do that. It makes sex a more general state.

Several men had some gourmet sexual applications for the use of cocaine. One man suggested rimming the anus with coke before anal sex because of its numbing effect. Putting cocaine on either the top of a woman's clitoris or the head of a man's penis was suggested because of the tingly sensations it produced once the area was aroused.

Some men suggested a legal substitute for cocaine called "Tiger Balm," a Chinese herbal mix found in health food stores or oriental markets. Like cocaine, it gives a cool, soothing, and even somewhat numbing sensation if rubbed on the penis, and it does not interfere with the firmness of the erection.

LSD or acid was used by a number of men on rare occasions, for a very specific experience. Because it is such a mind-altering drug, these men were extremely cautious about setting up the proper conditions before indulging themselves. As thirty-one-year-old Billy explained:

The less control I have, the more vulnerable I feel; the more vulnerable I feel, the more I need to trust the person I'm with. Since acid diminishes the sense of control I feel, I'm very careful who I take it with.

Being in a safe environment with trusted friends was crucial to all the men who used acid as an enhancement for sex. Also, since LSD commonly lasts at least eight hours, with intense hallucinations in the beginning, most men advised having sex after the drug had peaked.

One man described an intense and pleasurable hallucination while having sex on LSD:

It was like I was in one of those department stores, where a mirror is in front of you and a mirror is behind you and you get an infinite number of images. It was just like I was surrounded by an infinite loop of pussies that I was eating. It was just incredible. There were millions of me, and all of them were feeding into this giant funnel. It was fantastic.

All in all, the most commonly mentioned sexual accoutrement was the vibrator. Men who used vibrators generally used them mostly for the woman's pleasure. However, some men were threatened by the woman's enjoyment of the vibrator. As one man explained, "It feels like I'm being replaced by a machine." But most men, like John, a thirty-seven-year-old divorced shipping consultant, had the opposite philosophy:

I have found that some women are able to achieve a more intense orgasm by using a vibrator, whether it's during penetration or without penetration. For whatever reason, the orgasm seems to be more intense than through regular intercourse. The thought that a machine may be doing better than they are may be very scary to some men. But I don't think it is anything to worry about. The two experiences are not really the same. The personal interplay just isn't there with the machine. The woman I'm with right now uses a vibrator fairly regularly in our sexual encounters, either in the beginning or the middle of the experience. It varies from time to time, but we can continue making love afterwards, and I find it's very nice. I like the fact that she's not inhibited to use it in front of me, so that

I can be there when she's having such an intense orgasm, even if I'm not penetrating her at the time.

A few men were open to experimenting with vibrators during intercourse for their own pleasure. Some of these men found that they ended up enjoying the vibrator as much as their female partners. Such was the case for thirty-four-year-old Dean and his wife:

I really like to incorporate the vibrator into sex. I don't like to use it directly on my own genitals but I like the feeling of being inside Beth when she uses it on her clitoris. The vibration is transmitted to my penis, plus there is an intense throbbing. We keep the vibrator next to the bed and sometimes I'll just reach over and turn it on and at other times Beth will. I think we probably use it about sixty or seventy percent of the time we make love.

Some men talked about using dildoes. Dildoes are stiff, phallic-shaped objects that are primarily used for vaginal or anal stimulation. Some dildoes are also vibrators. They come in a variety of colors, shapes, and sizes. Size was an important consideration because, as one man said, "I look for a dildoe that seems to be a comfortable size for insertion into the anus, since many people find large objects in the anus painful." Another man, when thinking of using a dildoe for vaginal intercourse, chose a size larger than an ordinary penis because, as he said, "I think there's some element of fantasy involved in using a dildoe."

John used dildoes with his girl friend in the following ways:

Dildoes are certainly useful in foreplay. They can also be used to combine oral sex and genital penetration for the female. If a woman has had the fantasy of being with two men, I can use the dildoe as well as my own penis to act that out for her.

A few heterosexual men occasionally used cock rings for sexual variety. Cock rings are rings made out of different materials that encircle the penis at the base so that, in its engorged state, the blood is trapped, and the penis remains hard longer. A cock ring of a flexible material was preferred because of dangers involved in squeezing the penis too tightly.

Thirty-eight-year-old Larry, married for fifteen years, liked the sensations produced by a cock ring:

I love my cock ring. It's fun to jerk off with, and it's fun to fuck with, too. It really tightens the skin in my scrotum and makes it hypersensitive, so when Sheila is going down on me, she can get both balls in her mouth at the same time. Also, it's made of rubber so it has a little stretch to it.

Clothing was also used to arouse sexual desire. And while some men found nudity the ultimate turn-on, the majority found a scantily clothed body much more arousing.

Forty-year-old Sam said:

Nudity doesn't turn me on half as much as brief nudity. I think that once all the clothes are off, the mystery is resolved. Brief clothing, to me, is much more sexual than total nudity.

For twenty-seven-year-old Jim, the mystique of a partially clothed body was explained by what he termed the "wrapper syndrome":

I think part of it's the whole wrapper syndrome. Presents that are wrapped are a lot more fun to get than presents that are not wrapped, even if it's the same present.

The erotic quality of brief clothing for women almost always involved some type of lingerie. Stockings, garter belts, and high heels were especially favored. Chuck, forty-three, told us:

I'm really turned on by garter belts and no underwear. I love to lay on the floor while my wife does the dishes, and look up her dress.

Others were aroused by scanty clothing because it usually was a sign of their partner's sexual interest. Richard, age fifty-three, said:

I don't get turned on by the elegant long black things. They don't do much for me. But when she's got something short, where I can see her legs, and see her curves, and when she walks around dressed like that specifically to be sexy, it works. It's not so much what she's doing as her intention to be sexy that turns me on.

Gary liked the sensual feel of sexy lingerie, and ended up buying his wife a whole sexual wardrobe:

I like my wife to wear silky things. I just got her a present of a camisole and some underpants, which I think are real sexy. They're kind of baggy, but you can get your hands up in them. And I like things that feel nice to rub against. She has really beautiful long legs and I like rubbing my cheek against her legs and going right up to her crotch and just biting into her, you know, just gently and teasing. I like that.

Another chief attraction of sexy lingerie was that it made the woman extremely accessible to her partner. Most men were turned on by this. Spike went so far as to have a silky Chinese robe handy for his current lover:

I bought a Chinese robe for someone who's long gone. It's very nice. So now, if someone stays, I always give it to her to wear, because it gets cold here and some people feel uncomfortable walking around totally naked. This way she doesn't have to walk around naked, and yet the robe is still sexy. She can just slide it up and make love with it on. Or, since it opens right down the front, I can kiss her anywhere I want to, just by opening it up.

Crotchless panties were also a great favorite because they provocatively displayed a woman's genitals and at the same time offered easy access. One man said:

I've been known to buy panties with a slit right in the cunt. And she has been known to buy drawers for me with openings so that my penis would hang out. We both like to turn each other on. It's not just the woman who has a body. A man has a body too!

As Gary explained:

I've got this sexy old-fashioned bathing suit which my wife got for me. I don't particularly like it all that much, but she loves it, so I put it on. She thinks it's a tremendous turn-on, and I want to turn her on.

Gary enjoyed the provocative role so much that once he danced and stripped for his wife while wearing the underwear she liked:

Once I danced for her, I just did this very sexy striptease, and she loved it. It was wonderful. I did this very seductive teasing. I'd come right up to her and kind of rub my leg against her shoulder or her face. It just seemed to drive her wild.

A few men were even turned on by wearing women's underwear themselves. Joseph, age thirty-four, remembered enjoying wearing women's panties:

Once I put some woman's panties on and had her pull them off me. I liked the feeling of the satin. They don't make men's stuff like that. But I could never wear them, really. I mean, I'd be turned on all the time.

A few men found traditional street clothes more arousing than brief lingerie.

Such was the case for forty-eight-year-old Justin:

There are times when I feel turned on by my wife when she is fully dressed. She might come in from the office wearing a suit. She looks so feminine. I think the quality of the cloth blends in with the softness of her body and it gets to me. But it has to be a dress or skirt—not jeans or pants—for me to enjoy having sex with her when she's fully dressed. Then I can just pull up her skirt and then pull down her panties. It allows for sex in circumstances that would be impossible if she were wearing slacks.

Clothing, or the absence thereof, was one of sixty-one-year-old Roy's most cherished erotic memories:

The biggest turn-on I had was when my ex-wife and I went out one night to the bar at Maxwell's Plum. She didn't have a damned thing on under her coat. *Nothin'!* She was wild. She just thought it was great, and the turn-on for me was fantastic.

Having a partner dress up in sexy or scanty clothing was one kind of turn-on. Helping her remove that clothing was another. As one man said, "The act of disrobing her is so exciting. I don't know why. Maybe because there's something almost taboo about it, or maybe because it gets into my rape fantasies." As eighty-eight-year-old Russ remembered:

> Standing up in my living room and undressing my wife was one of the most outstanding sexual experiences I remember. Of course, we would then go to bed. We wouldn't make love standing up, but the slow undressing and lovemaking before was wonderful.

Sometimes men enjoyed the more passionate act of ripping off their partner's clothes as a prelude to sex. One man, while having it as a fantasy, never wanted to act it out. "I don't do it because I'm too conservative. I think about the price!" Others, like Brad, age fifty-two, resolved that problem by saving old clothes or using inexpensive T-shirts:

> A T-shirt is easy to rip off. It's a symbolic thing. I think it makes a woman feel that here's a guy who has such uncontrollable feelings that he wants to rip my clothes off before fucking. This happened spontaneously when I was really mad and since then I've let it happen some more. It is certainly something I would like to continue as other forms of lovemaking become routine.

EROTICA

The erotica used by the men in our study included books, pictures, and movies. Many men enjoyed using any or all of these forms of erotica as an occasional stimulant prior to or during sex, and some of the men's partners enjoyed the erotic material as well. John liked his girl friend to occasionally read an erotic book prior to lovemaking to enhance the experience that followed.

> If a partner of mine wishes to read a pornographic book while taking a bath before getting in bed, this may enhance the experience. She might even want to emulate what happened in the book by role playing. Books are a very good aid if you're lacking in imagination. Any typical sex book off the bookshelves goes through the full gamut of positions, places, and different things you can do. So if you can't think them up yourself, you can let someone else do it for you.

Albert, age forty-two, felt that using pornographic pictures not only stimulated his arousal, but also helped him fantasize during sex:

I like to have porn magazines around, particularly if I'm not really turned on and my partner wants to have sex with me. Then it's real helpful for me to have pictures to look at. It gets me going, and it gives me something to fantasize about, too, when I'm having sex.

Many men enjoyed "at home" erotic movies as a stimulant for gourmet lovemaking. Some even enjoyed going out to an X-rated or triple-X-rated movie alone or with their partner. Thirty-six-year-old Jason and his wife found that an occasional erotic film stimulated their sex life:

We know that when we come home after a pornographic movie we are going to have sex. After all, you couldn't watch that kind of movie for a couple of hours and come home and not do anything about it.

John owned his own projector and liked to keep a variety of films on hand so that his lovers could choose the theme that enticed them most at the moment.

I have a collection of pornographic movies that we can view prior to or even during the sexual act. You can obtain them at your local pornographic bookstore—just walk in and pick them off the shelf. I keep a variety on hand, two females and one male, two males, two females, racial mixtures of the partners, so most partners can find something that turns them on.

FANTASY

Many of the men we interviewed preferred their own imagination to the images produced by others. These men primarily used fantasy in three different ways. Some men fantasized privately before, during, or after lovemaking to increase their sexual arousal and enjoyment. Some shared their sexual fantasies aloud with their lover or spouse, while others agreed beforehand, with their partner, to act out particular fantasies.

In the past, macho men felt that sharing or acting out fantasies was childish, unnecessary, and definitely unmanly. However, some of the men we interviewed found that sharing fantasies with their partners provided fun, variety, and excitement and at the same time created greater intimacy. These men were reclaiming the childish parts of themselves that enjoyed fantasy and role playing.

Sharing or acting out fantasies, according to sixty-seven-year-old Barry, a professor, is also a creative way of expressing sides of your personality that don't ordinarily get expressed:

My own fantasy life is extremely rich, extremely varied, and in fantasy I've seen myself in many different roles. For example, I enjoyed being the master with this young woman who wanted to be my slave. But I would have been just as happy being the slave and having her as the master.

I'm really showing my trust in you now by telling you this. I've seen myself in both the dominant and submissive roles. I've seen myself being a man with a woman as well as with another man. And I've even seen myself in the role of a woman with a man or another woman as a partner. They're all parts of me, but twenty years ago I wouldn't have allowed this into my consciousness. And I think there are many men, and undoubtedly many women too, who won't permit themselves to have such thoughts.

Fifty-three-year-old Richard sometimes fantasizes that he is a woman when he makes love to his wife. This fantasy actually helps him to be a more assertive lover:

I love to imagine I have breasts, and sometimes I imagine I'm a woman and I'm making love to another woman. Somehow this seems to free me to be assertive in a certain way. I carry this concept in my head that the man is sort of cool, while the woman is the passionate one. But if I fantasize that I'm a woman, then it's all right for me to be all over her, kissing her a lot, and things like that rather than just being cool and holding back.

Many men felt that their fantasies, which were just another way to focus on sexual feelings and maintain arousal, were private and they did not want to share them with their lovers. Some thought these fantasies might be painful and bewildering for their partners, since they involved being sexual with another person. As one man said, "My wife would be crushed if she knew that sometimes I fantasize about someone else, even though they don't mean anything to me. To her, it would be like adultery in the heart."

Some men experimented with actually sharing their sexual fantasies with their partners. Not only was this experience sexually stimulating but it also often increased the level of intimacy in the relationship. However, Edward, a thirty-five-year-old divorcé, had some negative experiences sharing fantasies when there was insufficient trust and openness in the relationship:

I need a nonjudgmental atmosphere where it's okay to have thoughts without worrying about being laughed at. I have one bad memory of a sexual experience. I was screwing this woman and I was saying something to her in the passion of the moment when she said, "How romantic!" in a sarcastic tone. I was instantly flaccid after that. I mean, it's exactly the kind of ball-cutting thing I don't want to have to worry about.

But when he was in a safe and secure relationship, Edward used many fantasy images to create an erotic ambiance:

One of my favorite fantasies is to imagine the woman in a swing. I see her swinging very slowly toward me with her legs spread apart so that by the time she reaches me my head is level with her crotch. I hold her there for a while and eat her and then slowly push her back. She swings back to me again very slowly and all during the time we both have the pleasure of contemplating what will happen when we make contact again.

Paxton and his wife titillate each other by making up erotic stories. His wife sometimes merges the story with reality by arousing him with the same touch being used by the main character in the tale:

A thing that we do together sometimes is tell stories. The most recent one was Candy telling me about how I am in the woods when I meet this attractive lady. At the same time that Candy is stroking me, she describes this lady and what she does to me in great detail. Candy then becomes the lady and touches me in the way she is describing.

Larry and his wife sometimes relive the memory of the first time they made love with a third person to warm themselves up for sex.

Sometimes we'll use fantasy to start us off. After a particularly neat day, around three or four in the afternoon, when both of us are just randy, one of us will start it. We'll talk about the first time we opened up our sexual relationship to others. We'll recall that experience and fantasize that together while we make love.

Some men wanted to carry their fantasies further and act out these scenarios. One man called this "sexual fantasy tripping" and said that it was an important part of his sexual relationship with his wife. The men who enjoyed acting out fantasies felt that having good communication was the key to successfully introducing fantasy into their relationships. As Sam explained:

If I can sense that a person's open to exploring their sexual fantasies, I would let them know I like fantasy tripping sexually. If the communication is open, we can say, "Yes, I think I'd like to try that fantasy," or "No, I can't get into that fantasy," without feeling rejected or as if there's something wrong with us because we cannot get into each other's fantasy. The fact is, some people like chocolate ice cream, some people like vanilla. I think sexual fantasies operate the same way. Not liking it does not place a moral evaluation or judgment on a particular fantasy.

According to Edward, keeping the lines of communication open ensures that both people will continue on the same wavelength:

If we're acting out some fantasy or roles, perhaps we will decide in advance who is to initiate the sexual activity and how it's to be done. For example, we might decide that I'm not to initiate any kind of sexual activity, I'm just supposed to be teased. Or it might be decided that I'm supposed to initiate all the sexual activity and I'm to do it in a rough, aggressive way. Sometimes the best-laid plans fall apart on the spur of the moment. And sometimes, depending on the intimacy and flowingness of the relationship, the fantasy can be unrehearsed and spontaneous. I think in really creative sex the fantasies can take off in any direction at any given moment if people are really communicating. One person will pick up on what the other person's into and just go with it. I find that the most exciting.

The sexual themes that men enjoyed acting out ranged from simple scenarios such as the boss seducing his secretary, to action-packed dramas of burglars breaking in and raping the woman of the house. Clarence, age sixty-seven, initiated sharing highly romantic sexual fantasies on his wedding night:

We got married right in the middle of the Depression and had less than a hundred dollars to get started on. So my gift to my wife for our wedding was a spotlight and a big red velvet cloth for us to lie on. We initiated what we called "love dramatics." We would use the spotlight with various colors as we acted out our love drama. I always did the initiating. But she loved to read out loud, so we'd find a love scene, a short story from Shakespeare, for example, and we'd act it out as part of our foreplay. I've always been incurably romantic in that sense.

Other men were turned on by fantasies that brought back erotic memories of their childhood. For twenty-seven-year-old Raymond that meant asking his wife to act "bratty":

A lot of my sexual fantasies are about girls who are around thirteen to fifteen. That age just really turns me on. I told Rhoda about that a long time ago. So sometimes she'll act like a little bratty thirteen-year-old, or she'll even wear oversized T-shirts like a little kid would wear. I love it. I find it so seductive.

However, the most common fantasy theme that was acted out was meeting someone for the first time, picking them up and seducing them. Joseph, age thirty-four, enjoyed this theme because it gave him the freedom to take on different personalities:

Sometimes I'll pretend she's picked me up in a bar and she doesn't know me. We come home together and then play the scene out. That usually leads to really lustful, passionate sex.

When we're into the role, we play it out totally and I often take on a very different personality from the way I usually am.

Paul, a thirty-three-year-old schoolteacher, tries to find out what a woman's favorite sexual fantasy is and then sets up that situation for her:

Barbara was a classmate of mine at the University. We spent about two or three weeks together in summer school in a psychology class. And she was very, very responsive to me and I was more than responsive to her. She was also engaged, unfortunately. But over the period of our summer sessions, we had several lunches together. Over those weeks, I was able to figure out her major fantasy in terms of a sexual encounter. So one day I invited her to my little "condominium in the sky," where I had prepared a pleasant picnic, complete with a bottle of champagne and sophisticated things to eat, like very extraordinary cheeses and sliced mango arranged beautifully on a plate. The fact that I had done all of this was a sort of role reversal that gave her the freedom to adopt a different role for herself.

So we had a drink and then went outside and had this lunch under a mimosa tree, which happened to be shedding flowers at the time. We were sitting there and talking and getting very, very close mentally. In fact, we talked a lot about her feelings about getting married, especially since she had a three-o'clock rehearsal for her wedding, which was the following day. This was our last chance for a picnic before hubby came on the scene.

Afterwards we went up to my apartment. I think I simply said, "Would you like to take a bubble bath?" and she said, "I'll draw the bath." So there was that immediate "yes" on both sides. She had this fantasy of being picked up out of the bubble bath, wrapped in a great big terry cloth towel, and carried into the bedroom and made love to. So that's what I did and, even though she was dripping wet and her hair was a mess, it was a nice way to culminate the relationship. Since she was married the next day, that was the first and last time we had sex together.

Alan was surprised when his wife spontaneously initiated his favorite "Mrs. Robinson" fantasy:

We had had an extremely romantic dinner at a fantastic restaurant when we were in Chicago visiting her mother. We didn't want to go back to her mother's, so she suggested stopping at a motel. We got to the motel and had to check in without any baggage. It was so obvious. I even considered what name to put down. Anyway, she had a big purse that almost looked like a small piece of luggage, so I carried it in. Then she started this fantasy. She sent me out to get ice, and when I got back we immediately got into this dialogue. She was the single person in from out of town on business and I was the college kid working part-time earning some money as a bellhop. In the process, she got really turned on to me and seduced me. Meanwhile, I always wanted an older woman to come in from out of town and take advantage of me, so it was my fantasy too.

I remember laying down on the bed and, without taking her eyes off of me, she did a real seductive strip. She just took her clothes off, one by one, and then proceeded to take my clothes off. She began kissing me on the lips and then she kissed me all the way down my body until she went down on me. It was absolutely dynamite! I loved it! When I think about my sexual experiences, that's one of the highlights.

Edward, a college professor, once got a birthday card from an ex-student that initiated a seduction fantasy:

This woman gave me a birthday card that read, "I may not be the best birthday gift in the world, but I'm the easiest to unwrap." The card was a coupon she had made up. The coupon read, "Fantasies unlimited—coupon redeemable for an evening spent fulfilling a fantasy. This offer expires January 21, so act soon." So I thought about what sort of fantasy I was interested in and struck up an arrangement. Since I felt that she was more interested in me than I was in her, I was a little circumspect about how to accept the offer without encouraging her. So I waited awhile before accepting and then made it clear that if she could do this in the spirit of pure play, then I was interested. Otherwise not. She said she could, so we did.

The fantasy was that I wanted to be dominated and she was a woman who fit quite naturally into that role. She was an assertive, strong-willed person. I wanted her to dress somewhat elegantly in a dress and heels and then just do whatever seemed right to her. I wanted her to control the sexual flow. She was a playful and creative person, so I didn't feel I needed to be any more specific, and I was right.

Sometimes fantasy themes of domination included bondage. The bondage experiences related were playful and consisted of erotic teasing while one person was temporarily helpless. These were not sadomasochistic situations in which pain was inflicted. Many men liked the dominant role of being sexually powerful with a "helpless woman" in their games of bondage. Other men preferred the helpless role. However, since bondage requires one person to tie up the other, initiating bondage so that each person, particularly the woman, is comfortable can require some delicate negotiations. John gave some practical advice for men contemplating bondage with a lover or spouse:

Don't hurt anyone, obviously. You don't want to scare someone or mar them. You also don't have to become a boy scout to learn special knots. Just a light wrapping is required to make her seem helpless—and it's only the appearance of being bound that's necessary, since she has agreed to it and is not going to try to get away. Besides, at the end, usually the woman likes to have her hands unconstrained so that she is a lot freer to move and achieve orgasm. Sometimes women can achieve orgasm while bound up, but most I've known needed freedom to move.

Once trust is achieved between the two people, you can do almost anything you want because you don't have to worry about getting physically hurt or being forced to do something that you don't want to do. I want her to enjoy it as much as I do. If she's unhappy about the bondage, then I'm certainly not going to enjoy it either.

For thirty-four-year-old Joseph, tying up his girl friend was erotic, not only because he felt especially powerful but because he could more easily observe all her reactions to his sexual advances:

I played one game where I blindfolded the woman I was with, tied her in a chair, stripped her down, then did all these sexual things to her until we eventually wound up making love. While we were doing this, I really got into looking at her. Because she was blindfolded, I could just watch her carefully.

Many men enjoyed the submissive role of being tied down as much as or more than the dominant one. The primary attraction seemed to be the feeling of helplessness, a sexual feeling they did not ordinarily have. One man enjoyed being tied up and sexually teased by watching his girl friend undress and then masturbate:

Many of the fantasies I enjoy involve a certain kind of passivity on my part. I enjoy being teased, especially a certain kind of uninhibited, lustful teasing when I'm tied up. I like to watch a woman undress herself and masturbate, especially when she is hot and completely uninhibited while I'm tied up and can't do anything about it. The first time I was ever tied up or did any bondage at all was a very liberating and terribly exciting experience. I felt dirty and naughty doing it and I liked it. It was the first time I was able to feel so helplessly passive and to have a woman be so overtly teasing and seductive, so I found that enormously exciting. She tied me up to the headboard of the hotel bed and my feet were tied alongside the bed. I was naked and she was wearing a dress. She lay down in front of me with her head toward the foot of the bed and spread her legs so I could watch her play with herself. Eventually she took her clothes off and put on various other costumes like teddies and long nightgowns. It was the first time for the two of us; so it had the excitement of something novel as well as the thrill of discovery. In some ways it's like going to Baskin-Robbins and tasting all the flavors of ice cream. We tried almost everything. And while we were a little self-conscious through it all, we were very comfortable with each other, so as we did it more and more frequently, the self-consciousness disappeared.

PLACES

The most comfortable place to have sex for most men was in the privacy of their own homes. They enjoyed having sex in a place where they felt relaxed and had access to such creature comforts as music, food, and soft lights. As Bruce explained:

> With few exceptions, I am most comfortable having sex at home. My house is ideal and has everything from a pool to drinks, food, and music. I've been collecting art for the last ten or twelve years, so it's an arty, comfortable setting that makes me feel good.

Most men agreed that the bedroom was the most comfortable place for sex. Fifty-three-year-old Greg explained why:

> For the last thirteen or fourteen years I've noticed that if we're going to make love, I prefer to do it in a bed. I don't want to do it in the car, in the corner of a saloon, or on the floor of an office. I want it in bed. At my age I want the comfort of a bed.

Some men, particularly those who were unattached, felt it was important to create a sensual atmosphere in the bedroom. Sam accomplished this by buying sensual sheets:

> I find certain materials very sensual and erotic—especially silk and satin. So I've purchased bed coverings that you can spread out and have sex on. This way, your entire body is exposed to the feel of the silk or satin.

One man even went so far as to create the master bachelor pad where his bed was literally the center of operations:

> Everything works from the bed. If I want music, I flick a switch. If I want lights, I can adjust them any way I want. A master control module controls them all, including the TV. The bed is the heart of the house. It's so comfortable and can accommodate three people.

Others designed or bought special beds that they found more conducive to gourmet lovemaking. For Joshua, age twenty-eight, this meant buying a waterbed:

I have a waterbed and it's much nicer than a regular bed. It's much more comfortable. In addition, it's easier to roll over in a waterbed and if your arm or leg gets caught underneath, it doesn't get crushed the way it does in a regular bed.

Fred preferred a Japanese futon for lovemaking because he could take it to any room in the house:

I have this Japanese mattress that rolls up and I can easily just pick it up and plop it down in the living room, in front of the fireplace, or anywhere else, for that matter.

Some men created variety in their lovemaking by using different pieces of furniture. They made love on the couch, in a chair, on the kitchen table or even under it! They also enjoyed sex in different rooms, such as the den, living room, or kitchen. One man was in the process of remodeling his house and said, "It takes a lot of time and energy to complete a portion of it, but every time a room is finished, we celebrate by having sex in that part of the house."

The bathroom was mentioned over and over again as a favorite spot to have sex. Most men thought of the bathroom as a room where intimacy could flourish. As one man said, "It's great fun to take a shower together. Showering with someone is a sexual experience. Just the experience of washing someone and being washed is so intimate."

Steve, age twenty-seven, added a mirror to his shower and a bar to hold on to so that sex could be more exciting:

One of my favorite places to have sex is in the shower. So, being a designer, I've put in a full-length mirror and a dance bar so you can hang on the bar and not slip and break your neck!

A favorite place to create gourmet lovemaking experiences was in motels and hotels. For many men, this brought back courtship memories. Others found that sex in a motel or hotel suggested a vacation atmosphere where there weren't any responsibilities. Ben, age thirty-five, chose a motel that had been specifically designed for having sex:

I remember once we were traveling around and we were in Monterey in the afternoon. We went down and bought some avocados and cracked crab and by evening found ourselves in Sacramento. There was a porno motel there, so we checked in. We were the only couple to stay all night. It was sort of a business place. It was pretty kinky for me, eating cracked crab and avocados with mirrors all over in this room that had porn on the TV set.

Some men had sex in their offices or in restrooms. One even had sex in the balcony of a church! Tom, a nineteen-year-old student, had sex in his college darkroom:

I was really horny one night and I was working in this basically one-person darkroom. There was this girl who I was not at all interested in having an emotional relationship with, but who I was turned on by, so I called her up on the pretext of borrowing something from her. I asked her to bring it down and I pointedly invited her to come down to the darkroom. When she arrived I started playing with her, and made it clear through hints and joking that I was interested in sex. She was all for it too. The darkroom is a great place to do it because people don't just walk into a darkroom. There is a little safety light on outside that means "Don't come in here because you'll ruin all my pictures." So we were assured that nobody would come in. And the yellow and red safety lights were nice and low.

Men also enjoyed having sex in all types of moving vehicles: buses, trains, sailboats, and even planes. However, all in all, the most popular vehicle for sex was a car. Some men felt that having sex in a car was a turn-on because it was reminiscent of their teenage days when "parking" was the thing to do and the car one of the few places where they could safely have sex. Thirty-seven-year-old John, for example, still enjoyed occasionally going for a drive and then parking and making love!

A number of other men also enjoyed being aroused while driving their car. As Ron explained:

One of my favorite things is getting a blow job while I'm driving. She was blowing me once just as we were coming into a city. I remember, we were right near a stoplight and there was traffic all around. I was braking and clutching just as I was about to come.

Billy occasionally enjoyed arousing his girl friend while taking a trip in the car:

Once my girl friend was driving and I started rubbing her crotch. I just watched her, the way her body moved and squirmed and the way a flush came over her face while she was trying to drive. That was really nice.

Other men found that the possibility of being watched added to the intensity of the sexual experience. This was true for John, who remembered having sex on a bus:

I did it once on a bus going to Montana. It wasn't easy. It was a long bus ride and most of it was at night. I struck up an acquaintanceship with a young lady on the bus and after sitting and talking together for many hours, we found a blanket and lay down on the long seat at the back of the bus. The male-dominant position was the most comfortable since the seat wasn't wide enough to do a lot of twisting and turning, and we didn't want her head bobbing up and down.

Some men were enamored of having sex outside and found that basking in the beauty of nature provided natural and varied settings for gourmet lovemaking experiences. Thirty-year-old Kenneth and his wife enjoyed making love surrounded by the majesty of nature:

Making love in the woods, on a blanket in the middle of nowhere, was wonderful. It was about forty degrees so we didn't take all our clothes off. We seemed to stay warm naturally, though. Making love under the crisp blue sky where there are birds and trees and no people gives you a sense of life all around you. The heightened awareness from having sex in that environment makes it a very enjoyable situation.

Often men who enjoyed outdoor sports used those settings for some exciting sex. Clarence, age sixty-seven, a college professor,

recalled how he and his first wife enjoyed making love while mountain climbing:

> Among other things, I was a mountain climber, and my wife
> and I climbed together. Obviously we had to celebrate our
> climb, and we'd have intercourse on top of the mountain. For
> many years, we'd take the children and each summer we'd go
> to the Adirondacks to climb. Carlene and I would find ways of
> having time for ourselves, and we would have intercourse by a
> mountain stream or somewhere else that was beautiful. We
> learned to associate sex with anything that we enjoyed. Our sex
> life fit into the enjoyment of climbing a mountain, or of camp-
> ing, of the out-of-doors, of music, colors, sounds, odors, in-
> cense.

Twenty-year-old Peter explained that he and his wife-to-be had a
special hideaway in the country, which was the setting for many romantic memories:

> There's a special place out of doors that we have. In fact, the
> story about this place is devilishly romantic. When I was eigh-
> teen and she was thirty, we had this really passionate love
> affair. Anyway, while we were having this torrid, wonderful
> affair, she was living with somebody else so we saw each other
> on the sly. We had this secret place where we'd go, that's very
> hard to find because you can't see it from the road or trails. It's
> a kind of closed-in, sheltered place and there's a little brook
> and a really beautiful big tree. We'd meet there at certain
> times and spread out a blanket and have a picnic or make love.
> Anyway, one day we were both reading one of my favorite au-
> thors, Dorothy Sayers, who wrote about a place called Tall-
> boys. So I went into town and got a beautiful little brass
> plaque, and had it engraved with the word "Tallboys," and
> then the date, 1978 with a dash, and no ending date. I took it
> down to our place and carved a little section of bark off the
> tree and nailed the plaque into the tree. It's still there, this little
> brass plaque that says "Tallboys."

A number of men enjoyed the sensuality of the sun, sand, and
surf while making love at the beach. Some went so far as to make

love not only in the water but underwater. Gary, thirty-one, re-called:

I like spontaneous sexual experiences. I remember one time I made love with a woman I taught how to scuba dive. One day we were in the Caribbean, and I took her thirty feet underwater and we looked at each other and we suddenly felt like making love. So we took our bathing suits off, left our scuba tanks on, pressed our face masks up against each other so that everything became pitch black, and we screwed our heads off. And it was wonderful. Then we put our bathing suits back on, separated our faces, and looked over and there was this line of fish looking at us, wondering what the hell we were doing. I just started cracking up laughing so hard I almost choked.

Spike, a single thirty-one-year-old investment banker, remembered a time when he and his girl friend made love on what they thought was a deserted beach:

We thought we were on a very deserted beach. Then after eating each other and fucking for a good forty-five minutes, we got up and there were people all over the place. There were people playing Frisbee around us and guys walking their dogs. I was flabbergasted.

POSITIONS

A major way many men spiced up their sexual relationships was by incorporating a variety of intercourse positions into their lovemaking repertoires. Although they used a wide range of positions, some were more favored than others.

The standard missionary position, with the woman on the bottom and the man on top, was by far the favorite choice of most of the men we interviewed. Many chose this position because it allowed for more intimate contact with their partners. As thirty-four-year-old Ned explained:

We've experimented a lot. For a time we used to throw *The Joy of Sex* on the bed and say, "Okay, we'll do whatever is on the page it opens to." But my favorite is still the missionary position. There's more body contact. I can feel her breasts against my chest, and it allows me to put my arms completely around her.

The missionary position had other benefits. Some men found they had more maneuverability in this position and so could be more active. Other men favored this position because it allowed for deeper penetration, especially if a pillow were placed under the woman's backside or her legs were raised above his shoulders.

Other variations on the position included having the woman lie near the edge of the bed while the man stood or knelt beside the bed. Several men mentioned occasionally adapting the basic missionary position by having intercourse between the woman's breasts rather than in her vagina. One man gave a detailed description of what made this exciting:

I like to fuck a woman between her breasts. I like a woman with quite large breasts—they have to be big enough for it to be enjoyable. By pushing her breasts toward each other, a valley is created. Then she lubricates this with her saliva or some sort of massage oil, or maybe just the saliva that's on my cock after she's gone down on me. While she holds her breasts together, I like to mount her and start rhythmically plowing between them. It's even nicer if there's a pillow underneath her head and her mouth is propped up so that I can go between her breasts and right into her mouth.

The second favorite intercourse position among the men we talked with was the man on bottom with the woman on top. Many men, like thirty-four-year-old Joseph, chose this position when they wanted to assume a more passive stance:

If I'm feeling more passive, I like to be on the bottom. It's a totally different feeling than being on the top. On the bottom I'm actually receiving energy. I'm taking it in and I'm more into the other person and their energy. The energy is on the person that's making love with me. I'm definitely not as active or aggressive.

Men who were free enough of their macho scripts to use this position liked the feeling of the woman being in control. They liked assertive, active sex partners. As one man said, "I like her on top almost better sometimes, because then she has to do most of the work."

A number of men favored the man-on-bottom position because of the face-to-face contact, which afforded exciting visual stimulation. Such was the case for thirty-eight-year-old Roger:

I like it a lot when she's on top of me because then I can see her whole body, and I like the way she looks. I like to see her face. I like to see her breasts and her stomach, and I like to reach around and touch her butt, which I can do in this position.

However, the most practical feature of the man-on-bottom position was that men felt they had more control over their ejaculation. Fred, twenty-seven, explained:

I like for her to be on top because I have both hands free to feel her entire body. It helps me to relax and kind of draw out my stimulation. If I'm on top, like most of the male members of the animal kingdom, it's over in a minute or less, depending on how excited I am and how long it has been since we had sex last. When she's on top I can take my time and draw it out a little more, which is much more satisfying for me. She likes it too, because she gets more stimulation that way. We usually have simultaneous orgasms when we can take our time.

Rear entry, with the man entering from behind, was third on the list of preferred intercourse positions. The most typical stance for this position was the woman on her knees and the man entering from behind. This position was a favorite for a variety of reasons. Some men enjoyed rear entry because they felt more powerful in that position. As thirty-one-year-old Gary explained:

I like having sex doggie style. I think it's ancestral. All the other hominids do it that way. I also think I associate a position of dominance with it, a sense of being in control.

Some men felt that rear entry provided a different kind of tightness that increased stimulation or that stimulated a different part of their penis than other positions. "It rubs more on the bottom, along the urethra, when I enter from behind," said one man.

Others preferred rear entry because it offered a different visual experience that was extremely stimulating. As one man noted:

> I am very much of an ass man. I love beautiful asses, and rear entry gives me a very nice view of hers.

Twenty-four-year-old Young liked this position because he felt freer to fantasize since he couldn't see her face. He also had a special technique that he described to us:

> I like rear entry with her lying on her stomach and me on her back. But I find that some women are just built differently, so when that position doesn't work, I put a pillow under her belly.

Many men had their own favorite variations on the basic rear entry position. Larry, who at thirty-eight has been married fifteen years, often enjoys rear entry when he and his wife are lying on their sides, one behind the other:

> I would say most of the time we sleep in spoons, her on her side curled up and me behind her curled up. Well, that's a real neat position for initiating sex, especially with the nightgowns she wears, which expose her genitals. It's not that unusual for me to wake up horny as hell in the middle of the night, and I can easily just slip into her and very gently wake her up. It's soft and gentle. It's not a highly impassioned high-driving fuck.

Some men preferred the side position with both partners facing each other. John, thirty-seven, said:

> I get a lot of pleasure from being able to view my partner, to physically see her. Normally, the best position for that is the side position. I guess if I had to choose one position that I would do for the rest of my life, that would be it.

Another position that was also frequently mentioned was the lateral or scissors position. Again, the key attraction to this position seemed to be that men could see more of their partner's body during intercourse:

> If there is any one position that I prefer it would be where both of us are on our sides, and she has one leg under me and

one leg over me, with me at a ninety-degree angle to her. This way, I can watch the penetration. I can see her legs, her crotch, her thighs, her hips, her belly, while we're humping and pumping. To see her whole body fucking, being fucked, being turned on, is really beautiful for me.

Some men occasionally enjoyed having intercourse while standing upright. Sometimes both partners would be standing and at other times the man would be standing while his partner might be seated on the edge of the bed. Forty-three-year-old David described the merits of having sex while standing up:

I like the standing fucking position, if it fits right, because there is more mobility. You can control your thrusts, and that turns out to be really pleasurable.

Others liked to be seated and have their partner sit on their lap during intercourse. One man explains exactly how this position works for him:

Sometimes I like to sit on the bed and have my partner sit on my lap and wrap her legs around my back as I hold her. That way I can control it so that I don't slip out, because when the sex gets started, it can get kind of wild and you've got to have a lot of control.

Since the men we interviewed understood the need for variety in gourmet lovemaking, many had a wide range of positions in their sexual repertoires. They found that changing their sequence of positions helped to keep their lovemaking fresh and interesting.

SELF-STIMULATION WITH A PARTNER

Many of the men we interviewed found watching their partner masturbate very exciting. As one man explained:

When I'm making love to someone, I get so self-absorbed, particularly just before I come, that I kind of blank out. So sometimes it's nice to just be able to watch somebody else—to see their face, their eyes, their body as they get turned on. It's especially exciting to watch them come.

Larry, age thirty-eight, who has been married for fifteen years, concurred. For him, watching his wife masturbate is always an enjoyable treat:

We might be in bed reading, or watching the end of the news, when I'll start to feel the jerking of the bed as she slips into her first orgasm—and I won't even have known she was touching herself. It's a beautiful way she has of telling me that she's turned on and of initiating sexual contact. All I have to do is turn my head and I can watch and I like that a lot.

While watching the woman masturbate was almost a universal turn-on, most men responded to the taboos of self-stimulation by feeling awkward or embarrassed about touching themselves in front of their partner. Those open to sexual exploration, however, who could overcome their inhibitions, found masturbating during lovemaking to be a highly charged sexual experience.

Billy was turned on by the exhibitionistic quality of masturbating in front of his partner:

I like the exhibitionistic part of having somebody watching me, and then looking up and seeing how excited they're getting. Sometimes I'll "talk dirty" and tell them what I'm feeling and what I'd like to be doing to them. Some women will read porn to me while I'm masturbating. Occasionally when somebody sees me getting more and more excited, they'll bend down and give me a lick. Some women get so turned on watching that they start masturbating themselves.

Another man said:

Sometimes I like to feel like I'm some sort of a sexual god or something. So sometimes Rhoda will lie on the floor and I'll stand above her and masturbate. I really enjoy feeling powerful, and she likes that too.

Some men discovered that masturbating with a partner, as an alternative to intercourse, added variety to their lovemaking. As thirty-four-year-old Dean explained:

I think one of the best things that happened sexually in our marriage over the years was getting comfortable with masturbation. Masturbating next to each other really opens things up a lot. Intercourse doesn't have to be the whole focus, even though we're still very conventional in the sense that that's probably the thing we are most likely to do if we have a sexual experience. But there'll be times when we take a bath together or something and just start masturbating in the bathtub. It allows for a range of different sexual activities.

Self-stimulation also provided a way of being sexual and intimate when only one person was interested. This was true for twenty-seven-year-old Raymond, who was recently married:

Masturbating with her is so wonderful because any time I want to make love, it's available. That way if she feels tired, I don't feel like I'm going to be intruding on her, because all she has to do is just lie there and watch. She can even go to sleep if she wants. But she doesn't, luckily. So it's real nice and I like feeling that free.

Thirty-six-year-old Jason found that, when he and his girl friend were physically separated, mutual masturbation "long distance" was a way to still be intimate:

While my girl friend is a thousand miles away, we masturbate over the phone together, which is a very wonderful experience. Sometimes we get on the phone late at night and we talk about how nice sex used to be with each other and how much we enjoyed it and we masturbate.

For many men, masturbating with a partner was a breakthrough in the relationship and in understanding the opposite sex. As David explained:

Women have always been very mysterious to me. So about two years ago I was making love to a girl that I was fond of and I said to her, "You know, I have never watched a woman masturbate." And she said, "You know, I have never watched a man masturbate." So we watched each other. The openness of it and the fact that we were doing this thing that is somewhat forbidden made it very exciting. It also helped us both a lot in our relationship with each other as well as our relationships with other men and other women. Most people don't talk about it, so you don't know that this part feels much better than that part, or if you do it this way, it will feel better.

Thirty-eight-year-old Alan, who has been separated for two years, recently masturbated in front of a partner for the first time and told us how he went about it:

I never had the nerve to masturbate with my wife, but I masturbated in front of a woman a couple of weeks ago. I was real uncomfortable about it. It was our first experience in bed together, too. I just started talking to her about it and I realized I had always wanted to do it but had never been able to. I just said to her, "I want to do it with you and I'm nervous as hell." Meanwhile, I found out she had never seen a stag film before. So we watched a stag film, and I pulled out my vibrator, and stripped, and I actually did it—I masturbated—and I was so embarrassed. I was afraid I wouldn't get hard. But she got so excited that she started doing something to arouse herself, and I started doing myself again. Then she was kissing me and touching me and I didn't want to masturbate anymore. I wanted to be inside her, so I told her that and she said, "Fine," so we had sex. I was really proud of the fact that I could get past my uncomfortableness and my embarrassment and masturbate in front of a woman. My fantasy had become reality. It was like I did it and she got excited and it led to all this other neat stuff. It was a real positive experience for me.

ORAL SEX

Almost without exception, the men we interviewed enjoyed both cunnilingus and fellatio. Cunnilingus was mentioned over and over again as a primary staple of gourmet lovemaking. Since it was clear that for a lot of women cunnilingus was one of the best ways to achieve orgasm, being proficient at cunnilingus was considered an important requirement of a gourmet lover. Men realized that the more pleasure they gave the woman, the more interested and active she would be in pleasuring them. However, the main reason that men seemed so turned on by cunnilingus was that they loved the physical experience itself. As Joseph, age thirty-four, explained:

I really like to go down on a woman. I love it. I could do it for hours and hours and hours. I love that sense of pushing, of thrusting. I'd like to crawl right up through her vagina and into her womb. If there was a wall to put my feet against, I would probably do that.

Men loved the sense of power they felt seeing their partner's response to their caresses. As thirty-six-year-old Michael explained:

I love the softness, the warmth, and the moisture, which is a direct reaction to what I'm doing, so that's terribly exciting. A woman responding to the way I touch her genitals is one of the biggest turn-ons as far as I'm concerned.

Twenty-seven-year-old Scott teases his wife about how much he loves her "orgasmic juices":

She always tastes great. She doesn't douche or anything like that; there's just something very special about the way she tastes and smells. I love the taste of the orgasmic fluid, too. God, if you could only bottle that and drink it. It's a dessert for me. We call it "honey from the crotch of God," because it's so special.

Men loved fellatio as much as, if not more than, cunnilingus. In fact, men's major sexual complaint revolved around fellatio: that their partners did not like it, would not do it, or were not proficient at it. Although these men had a wide range of individual preferences as to the way they liked to have their penis orally stimulated, they had some basic suggestions for how gourmet oral sex should be done.

In general, men were stimulated by a partner who could create arousing friction by the way she applied pressure to the penis with her mouth. Lanny suggested:

At some point it's important to talk with your partner about what you like about oral sex, or any kind of sex for that matter. As for me, I don't like getting teeth all over my penis. A lot of women don't realize that when they're giving a blow job they're scraping you. Now of course some men like that, they find it very erotic and it heightens their experience, whereas for me, it just hurts. So I tell a partner to put her lips over her teeth. Also, I think it's much better to have her tongue wrapped around the penis and to create a little bit of suction so that the sides of her mouth are touching the penis as well. That way there's contact all the way around, and her mouth is like a little vagina.

Other men, like twenty-four-year-old Young, preferred rougher stimulation:

I like a little bit of rough handling occasionally. It's a fine line, because it can be too rough and it can hurt. But being overly gentle with the penis can be real boring sometimes. I have even occasionally suggested that a woman brush it with her teeth, very lightly, but some women are afraid they'll do it too hard.

One man advised the use of hands as well as mouth during oral sex to simulate vaginal stimulation:

My secretary asked me to explain how to blow her husband, so I did. The secret is to use your hand as an extension of your mouth. As your mouth moves up, your hand follows, and it's all lubricated. So it feels like the penis never leaves your mouth; your mouth and hand are like one big vagina. Then I like my partner to play with my balls with the other hand. And I go absolutely berserk; I mean, I just start screaming and yelling. I love it.

The midline of the penis, which is a ridge that runs along the underside of the penis extending from the head down to and surrounding the anal opening, is composed of highly sensitive tissue. As one man put it, "the underside of the penis is definitely the joy side." Another man said he particularly liked it when his wife caressed the midline or underside of his penis with her tongue while his penis was in her mouth. Still another preferred to be teased by having his partner break the contact with her mouth and lightly lick him from the tip of the midline down to the bottom.

Larry suggested still another technique that really heightened oral sex for him:

During oral sex, I like to have a woman put two fingers at the base of the penis, one on the front side and one on the back side and pull the skin down, not painfully, just lightly. To me that makes the sensations more intense. I also seem to engorge more and my penis gets larger when that happens. It's a real exquisite feeling when done by someone who knows what they're doing.

Bernard's girl friend had a special technique for oral lovemaking:

She combines a very sensual kind of rhythmic technique with her mouth that is wet and soft with a special kind of caressing with her hands and body. She outlines my body, my sides, and my back with her hands. She'll take her legs or her feet and rub them up and down my thighs. She uses every part of her body to touch me while we're having oral sex.

ANAL SEX

Incorporating the anal area into sex was a gourmet delicacy engaged in by many of the men we interviewed. Men enjoyed using their partner's anus for intercourse as well as having their own anus stimulated by their partner's finger during foreplay and intercourse. Anal intercourse and anal stimulation seemed to be enjoyed for both physical and psychological reasons. Physically, the opening to the anus was particularly pleasurable for some men, as was deeper internal stimulation, which massaged the prostate. One man felt that anal stimulation made him more aware of what was happening inside him—particularly the contracting of the prostate—during orgasm. Entering a partner's anus was enjoyed because of the tighter fit it provided.

Psychologically, anal sex touched off different emotions depending on whether the man was on the giving or receiving end of the anal stimulation. Thirty-one-year-old Billy enjoyed anal intercourse because it brought out a sense of male territoriality and dominance for him:

I find anal sex really attractive at times, because it brings out those male dominant feelings. It reminds me of when I used to play football, and at the fifty-yard line I could feel what territory meant. There was almost a growling and an anger that, dammit, this was *my* land. Don't step on it! And those feelings are brought out when I'm having anal sex with somebody.

Men who assumed the passive role often enjoyed anal penetration because they experienced it as an act of submission—of giving oneself up to another person. Joseph, a thirty-four-year-old social worker who is divorced and living alone, felt this way:

I had a real aversion to any kind of anal penetration for most of my life, but within the last year and a half or so, I've gotten to the point where I like to be penetrated. I really like the feeling. It's a sense of giving myself up. It's a different type of sharing. A woman can grab a hold of my penis and she can jack me off, and that's external. It may be intimate, but my experience is that it's truly more intimate to have a woman go inside me and stimulate me.

Charles, age forty-five, who is four years into his second marriage, also equates anal sex with a special intimacy:

We probably don't have anal intercourse more than once in twenty-five times or so. But when we do, there is this funny kind of intimacy to it. It isn't something you do with everybody. You have to know somebody well. By the time a man and a woman have anal intercourse, there's some kind of special confidence and trust between them that's hard to explain. The vast majority of times when my wife and I are fucking, I feel like we're very intimate, and certainly when my arousal is at its peak I'm feeling very tender toward her. But I notice that the few times that I seem to gravitate toward anal sex, I've had this extraordinary feeling of closeness to her.

In order not to experience anal sex as painful, certain preparation is necessary. The key elements mentioned as necessary for initiating a positive first experience with anal sex were creating a bond of trust and an atmosphere where the woman can be totally relaxed.

John had initiated several women into the delights of anal sex and passed along this advice:

A proper mental attitude has to be established first, so I don't think it's something that should be sprung on your partner. You can bring it up, but not jump right into it, unless she's had experience with anal sex. I think the key to successful anal intercourse is technique. It's something that must be approached slowly, with care, patience, and K-Y jelly. A lubricant should definitely be used. Certainly a position where the female can relax is essential. I think probably the most successful position I've found is the side position. The woman lies on her side while the man sits up so it's more of a half-rear entry, half-side entry position. If she's lying on her left side, I would straddle her left leg which is the bottom leg and her right leg would be thrown over my right leg. That way she is not using a lot of strength to hold herself up in any position. Also, you can reach her clitoris and manually stimulate her in this position. The second best position is when the woman is on her back with her legs raised. Then you can have her put her legs so they are resting on your shoulders. In these positions, the woman can relax, which makes penetration easier.

Various other positions were suggested:

I had anal sex in the shower once, with the woman just bending over, as if she were touching her toes, and another time with my partner standing up with her hands against the wall and her tush sticking out.

Erik said:

I was introduced to anal sex by lying on my back with my partner astride me and that has been the most pleasurable position for me. I've since tried it in the missionary position and with rear entry, but I like my partner astride me the best because of the visual aspect that position provides.

TALKING

Having partners who talk or make noises during lovemaking was a turn-on for most men because it indicated that their lovers were enjoying themselves. As one man said, "Unless both of us are enjoying the experience, it's not a turn-on for me. I don't really fulfill myself with someone who is just going through the motions."

Making noises during intercourse is generally seen as a feminine trait. The stereotype of the macho man is someone who is in complete control and silently orchestrates the lovemaking. However, many men are rethinking this traditional masculine image. As forty-three-year-old David explained:

It turns me on a lot when my partner is noisy, but women are much nosier than men. You don't find very many noisy men who will groan and moan and completely let go on a verbal level. There's some embarrassment about letting go that much and I'm just learning how to do it, how to moan and groan and even say things as I feel them.

Some of the men were free enough of their traditional scripting to verbalize their feelings of passion. Some even liked to "talk dirty" during sex. Others, like Billy, a thirty-one-year-old bachelor, preferred women who would talk dirty to them:

I like any kind of very specific gutter language. Sometimes I'll model it for women by telling them aloud what I'm doing or what I would like to do. Having her beg for sex is also nice. If she says, "Please," she gets a little reinforcement and then I might pull back some more and say, "Please what?" or "I beg your pardon?" to make her get more specific about what she wants me to do to her to turn her on.

Others, like thirty-four-year-old Drew, preferred more romantic love talk because they felt it enhanced the intimacy of the experience:

I like to repeat somebody's name. Then you are not only relating to the body but also to the personality. So I find that a big turn-on. I also like being able to say things like "You're beautiful, your neck is beautiful, your arms are beautiful, your ass is beautiful" or "I love the way your body feels." It's not so much that I like talking about sex, I like the romanticism of opening up and saying, "I love your eyes" or "I love to look at you in this light."

ORGASM

Most men rarely think about enhancing the quality of their climax, particularly since machismo emphasizes how many times you score rather than the quality of the experience. However, a number of the men we interviewed were concerned about the quality of their lovemaking in general and the quality of their orgasms in particular. They agreed that all orgasms were not the same.

Even though a man ejaculates, his climax may be concentrated in his genital area rather than in his whole body. Also, not all releases or ejaculations are accompanied by orgasm and not all orgasms are accompanied by ejaculation. And while most men felt their first orgasm of the night was better than the second or third, and that, in general, orgasms were better when sex was frequent rather than when there were long intervals between experiences, other patterns were individual. The quality of a man's orgasm could vary from time to time and from experience to experience. And many of these men wanted to receive more pleasure by expanding their orgasmic repertoire.

For some, a quickie was totally satisfying. Thirty-two-year-old Vince recalled:

> We were on our tenth wedding anniversary trip and it had been one of those very hectic days. We had theater tickets and we were running late, so my mind was on taking a shower and getting there on time. Just as I got out of the shower, and even before I started drying myself, Jane shouted from the other room that she bet we couldn't have sex in two to three minutes and still make the theater. It was an exciting challenge and we did it! It was a great evening—great sex and great theater.

However, most men equated gourmet orgasm with prolonging the pleasure not only for their partners, but also for themselves. The essence of prolonging the sexual pleasure for many men centered around holding back their ejaculation. Ned, age thirty-four, prolonged the pleasure by withdrawing just before climax:

> I like to stop before climax. I like to stop and just pull out, and maybe talk or eat a little something and start again; and then stop and talk and eat some more. I love prolonging it, not rushing it.

For seventy-two-year-old Alvin, a retired chaplain, one of his most exciting sexual memories as a young man was meeting a woman who taught him how to prolong the pleasure through extended foreplay:

> My partner and I met and we knew from the beginning we were going to have a wonderful time. We had dinner and shortly afterward we went to a room, a beautiful place, and undressed each other. We were finally naked; this was the first white woman I'd been with, and she was beautiful. Then we very slowly caressed each other. I was swept off my feet. She asked me if she could kiss my prick. I'd always wanted a woman to do that, but it had never happened before. And she did it beautifully. Then I felt I should do something in return. So without asking, I positioned myself where I could return the compliment. I kissed her pussy and again it was a first. I thoroughly enjoyed it. Finally we decided to just kiss, and this went on for two or three hours without ejaculation or orgasm. We'd get to a point where we'd stop, not because I wanted to but because she knew when to stop. Finally we both made love and I had at least two or three intense orgasms, which amazed me because I didn't think it was possible. And it was all her doing—she knew more than I did, and I told her so.

Some men experienced multiple orgasms—several orgasms within a relatively short period of time—on a regular basis. The few men who had this ability, like forty-year-old Nathan, felt the secret was to have an incomplete ejaculation the first time:

> In order to have multiple orgasms, the idea is to not have a complete ejaculation the first go-around. You might have two, three, or four of them if you give some forethought to holding back on the climax in that first ejaculation. I can decide when I don't want to have a complete ejaculation, because this process is controlled by my thoughts. Then I can generally have another sexual experience in another half hour's time. This varies according to when I have had my last intercourse or masturbation experience. When I have been starved for sex for a matter of a week or two, then my capacity to control my body is almost nil. If I have masturbated the night before or if I have had intercourse the night before or the morning before, then I

am able to master my body a great deal more and actually plan out how many times I want to have an ejaculation.

A number of men felt that la crème de la crème of gourmet lovemaking was simultaneous orgasm. To many of them the simultaneous explosion of the two people was the ultimate in orgasmic fusion. The intensity of both people craving that release with the same level of passion while teetering on the edge was a powerful energy connection. Such was the case for Gary:

My best orgasms happen when my wife and I come together. I get myself and my wife to a place of being very close to coming, and then just kind of postpone it for fifteen minutes, or twenty minutes, or even an hour sometimes. I used to do it by thinking about my penis not coming. Now I do it by breathing. I just take a few deep breaths and relax. Instead of trying to hold it back, I exhale a little bit, take a few deep breaths, and just keep myself right at that very edge. And it's wonderful, because when she's right at that edge also, it's a high, intense, almost spiritual feeling. There's this whole energy exchange happening all along the fronts of our bodies and especially where our bodies are meeting—our mouths, our heads, our necks, our throats, our hearts, our bellies. It's an amazing incredible connection. Then usually one of us begins to come, and the other one spontaneously comes also.

For the first time in his life, thirty-nine-year-old Alex was experiencing a sexual relationship where simultaneous orgasms occurred naturally and frequently. In trying to reconstruct and analyze why and how this happened, he came to the following conclusions:

As we move along at each stage in the lovemaking, we proceed at the same pace. We know when the foreplay ends and we get down to the serious business. There's no discussion of that, it just happens smoothly. We're picking up on physical clues from each other. Mostly she's reading my body because she's got better control over her orgasm than I have over mine. She seems to pick up on a certain tensing in my body as I approach orgasm and she times her release perfectly. I've never had so many simultaneous orgasms in my entire life. As a matter of fact, I didn't think it was possible before, and that's what intrigues me so much about it.

AFTERWARD

Contrary to the old macho scenario where the man satisfies himself, rolls off his partner, and falls asleep, many of the men we interviewed wanted to extend the intimacy after intercourse. As fifty-year-old Chris explained:

Sex doesn't just end with the climax, it's the caring and the holding and the closeness afterward that really ties it together. If you just roll right over and go to sleep, that's no good. I don't like that.

Forty-three-year-old David agreed:

The biggest turn-off is when somebody loses their interest the minute they come and immediately turns into this business-like person who puts their clothes on. It is like being in a whorehouse. And to me that is very sad. Afterward I like to hold my partner and take a warm washcloth and wipe her dry. The Japanese women do that, and I think the cleaning up is a very nice part of the ritual.

The men we interviewed wanted intimacy *and* exciting sex. They sought this by being innovative and, at the same time, sensitive to their partner's needs. However, changing established patterns of lovemaking involves more than the man alone. It takes the cooperation of both partners. And the same is true of working through sexual problems or misunderstandings. Making these changes requires good communication skills. Many of the men we interviewed felt that developing these skills was an important goal and worked toward it, even though the process was often difficult and awkward. How they went about establishing good communication is the subject of the following chapter.

CHAPTER SEVEN

LETTING YOUR PARTNER KNOW

They sit across the lunch counter from each other, Woody Allen and Diane Keaton, in the final scene of Allen's Academy Award-winning film *Annie Hall*. He plays Alvy, the intellectual Jewish New Yorker, and she is Annie, the beautiful yet bewildered WASP from the Midwest. Nostalgically they reminisce about their bittersweet affair, which has long since ended. As we watch these two sophisticates, who are unable to reconcile their differences and keep their relationship alive, Alvy speaks his innermost thoughts in the following voice-over:

> I realized what a terrific person she was, and how much fun it was just knowing her. And I thought of that old joke: You know, this guy goes to a psychiatrist and says, "Doc, my brother's crazy. He thinks he's a chicken." And the doctor says, "Well, why don't you turn him in?" And the guy says, "I would but I need the eggs" . . . Well, I guess that is pretty much how I feel about relationships. You know, they're totally irrational and crazy and absurd, but, I guess we keep goin' through it because most of us need the eggs.[1]

Although we can't agree fully with Woody Allen that relationships are "totally irrational and crazy and absurd," we certainly can't dispute his point that most of us need the "eggs." The men we spoke with reiterated this point in interview after interview. What was most important to them was the quality of their intimate relationships, because the benefits—those eggs—the caring and sharing, gave their lives meaning and a sense of security.

But establishing and maintaining that intimacy is not an easy task. Two people—Alvy and Annie, for instance—can reach out to each other in the expectation of love and fulfillment and still emerge empty-handed. The greatest obstacle to intimacy is the difficulty in negotiating differences that exist between two people, and this includes sexual differences. Building and maintaining a close relationship requires a willingness on the part of each person to accept, compromise, and mesh their distinct likes, dislikes, beliefs, and perceptions. The fundamental key to attaining this end is being able to communicate effectively.

Even couples whose relationship is built on a solid foundation, and who share similar values and interests, have minor and perhaps major irritations or problems that affect the normal course of their lives together. Minor differences such as deciding the best method for washing dishes, or which friends to invite for dinner, can erupt into major confrontations and spill over into the sexual aspects of a relationship if a couple can't communicate effectively.

Effective communication is a two-way street. It means being able to clearly express your thoughts, feelings, and opinions and, in turn, being able to listen to your partner's reactions and perceptions with an open mind. One man said that for him it is "a willingness to risk putting his foot in his mouth." For another it means "tearing down my walls of self-protection and making myself more vulnerable in order to strengthen my relationship." Whatever your personal definition is, successful communication results in understanding—understanding your partner's point of view and having that understanding reciprocated—rather than blaming each other or trying to prove the other wrong. Such mutual understanding is a basic prerequisite to problem solving.

However, when the issues are of a sexual nature, communication is infinitely more difficult—primarily because so many cultural stigmas prevent an open discussion of sexuality. Since sex has become a topic for more open discussion only recently, we are all struggling to some degree with the effects of deep-seated taboos that have been engrained since childhood. And since most of our parents spoke about sex in hushed tones, if at all, rarely were we exposed to any role models for talking about sex.

Roger, a thirty-eight-year-old lawyer, says he and his wife were "raised to be fairly inhibited about sex," which is why they find it much more difficult to "sit and talk about it than to just do it." He goes on to say, "No wonder it's not easy for us to say things like 'I like it when you put your tongue here,' 'Suck me a little harder,' or 'Your touch is too forceful and it hurts.'"

Few of us have had practice using phrases such as Roger's. Furthermore, sexual language differs between men and women and even from individual to individual. If one partner feels put off by the language used by the other, more attention will be focused on the words used than the feelings the other attempts to convey. Consequently, it is often necessary first to arrive at some mutually agreed-upon sexual vocabulary before communicating about specific issues. For instance, one man told us, "It was hard for my wife and me to talk about sex right from the start. She would use words like 'snuggle' and that didn't turn me on. I would use words like 'fuck' and that really turned her off. It actually took awhile before we could decide on a sexual vocabulary that worked for both of us."

What makes it difficult for men in particular to discuss their sexual preferences and reactions is machismo. The assumption here is that men shouldn't have any special sexual needs. After all, everything and anything is a turn-on for a macho man. And he's not supposed to need any information from his partner, either. He should already know all about being the consummate lover. So for a man with sexual problems, or anxieties about pleasing his partner, it's often embarrassing to seek out information or ask for guidance. According to Ben, age thirty-five:

What stops men from communicating about sex is a fear of making a fool of themselves. They're afraid of making themselves vulnerable because they're supposed to be the tough ones. They're supposed to be the ones whose feelings shouldn't get hurt. But of course they do.

Even Verner, age forty, a sophisticated and successful screenwriter, was too embarrassed to ask his partner for the specific physical caresses that would give him more sexual pleasure:

A lot of women are very passive. They don't do anything and I'm not the kind of guy to say, "Hey, would you grab hold of my stick and put me in third gear?" Instead, my mind goes,

"Oh, she doesn't seem to know what to do. She isn't going to turn me on." That upsets me, but I don't say anything because I am too embarrassed. I would like to think that people just automatically know what the other wants. However, I realize that this is not true. Sometimes you have to sit down with someone before sex and say, "You know, I like a finger inserted in my asshole and a twisting of my muff."

As one man ironically summed it up, "With the repressed way most of us were brought up, the crazy expectations put on men, plus all the fears men have anyway, sometimes it's easier to just fuck than to talk about it!"

Basil, a twenty-one-year-old student, for instance, preferred to suffer in silence with a new partner rather than tell her he'd prefer a different kissing technique:

I remember this one girl who would keep her teeth quite close together when we kissed, and that hurt a little. But I don't think I ever said anything about it because we didn't get to know each other well enough for me to say anything.

And behind the bravado, some men are just plain shy. As one man confessed: "I tend to be kind of timid about saying exactly what I want."

The overwhelming majority of the men we interviewed said it took time and sometimes more than an occasional struggle to develop good sexual communication with their partners. Yet, in rare instances, some struck up an immediate sexual rapport that needed no verbal guidance. Right from the start, they say, sex was perfect.

John, a thirty-seven-year-old divorced shipping consultant, describes a "one-in-a-million shot" where he and a new date "were perfectly in tune":

We'd gone out to dinner somewhere and had come back to my place. It was winter. We lit a fire, had some wine, and at that point started foreplay. We made love several times in front of the fire during the evening. I was quite taken aback by the fact that we were so in tune with each other. I seemed to do all the things that she liked, without needing to communicate. Normally, in my relationships, there has to be a conversation about what is preferred and what isn't. But for some reason, everything came up roses. I couldn't do anything wrong and it was just a one-in-a-million shot where two people were perfectly in tune. I guess that's probably what really makes that evening such a special memory. Although we'd only seen each other once prior to that, it was as if we'd been lovers for a long time.

For some men, that sense of instant intimacy and a perfect sexual fit carried over into a lengthier relationship. Dan, a thirty-one-year-old physician, describes his marriage as having that quality right from the start:

It seemed like our bodies fit each other. We didn't have to say things like "Could you move your thigh a little to the left?" or anything like that. It was like our bodies were manufactured by the same company so everything fit together just beautifully. Even the kissing and the holding and touching were perfect.

For most of us, however, an easy sexual rapport is not effortless. Our sexual natures are as varied and unique as our fingerprints. Edward, a thirty-five-year-old college professor, captures the experience of many when he says:

No two people like to be touched in exactly the same way. That's never happened in my experience. And it's only through a certain kind of verbal interaction that the subtleties of one person's desires will ever be understood.

Deciphering such differences is considered the man's job, and many men we interviewed felt oppressed with this role of sexual mind reader. They couldn't intuit what a woman felt or wanted, yet often they were expected to. This expectation created a sense of frustration for men, who would have preferred direct feedback from their partners. Edgar, twenty-seven, expressed his own frustration as he described how difficult it was to find the right "combination" for each lover:

You have a man and a woman. And the woman's like a safe. The man's outside with this big tumbler and he's trying to find out what the right combination is. Eventually he finally discovers it, but when he changes partners and tries the combination again, it doesn't work. You feel like yelling, "You changed the combination!" because she's different from the lady next door or across the street. Everyone's got different preferences and you have to find out what "special combination" works for each woman. And that can be tough!

Given the fact that everyone's sexual patterns differ and that most people can't read their partner's mind, sexual communication becomes paramount to a thriving sexual relationship—and to a healthy overall relationship. This point was driven home in a most painful way to thirty-seven-year-old George whose first seven-year marriage ended in divorce. "Throughout it," he says,

> I didn't recognize that we weren't communicating. I didn't express myself very well and neither did my wife. She must have been very unhappy because when she reached a point where she was able to communicate, she asked for a divorce.

For George, as with the forty-four men in our survey who had suffered a separation or divorce, it took the breakdown of a relationship to motivate them to look inward and ask the painful question, "What went wrong?" For most, the answer was a failure to communicate. George says the divorce prompted him to go into therapy to figure out what had gone awry in his relationship. The journey was a painful one, and George says, "While I would not have preferred it this way, I learned a lot from the divorce in terms of what I wanted in my next relationship and how important it was to communicate."

RECIPE FOR GOOD SEXUAL COMMUNICATION

Every man we talked with shared what he considered to be an essential ingredient for good sexual communication. The most important factors mentioned were trust, honesty, a healthy attitude toward sex, the ability to listen, and the willingness to say no when appropriate. And while it's rare to find a relationship that contains all the suggested ingredients, we felt it useful to have an ideal to aim for. That way, when communication breaks down or is less than adequate, it may be easier to determine which ingredient is missing.

Trust

"Trust" was the word that came up over and over when we asked men what they needed most to willingly expose themselves and open up to their partner. They wanted a nonjudgmental environment with a partner who liked, cared for, or loved them. This gave them the emotional security they needed to express their sexual desires and respond to their partner's. "A woman who really cares," says Verner, "encourages me to respond similarly":

There are women I have been with who seem to ask me what I want in a way that is not threatening to me. I can tell by the way these women approach me that they really care and want me to be happy too. Knowing this helps me to indicate what I want. It is important to me that a woman shows me some concern and attentiveness, and I try to do the same.

Some men said they could let down their defenses and be with a partner once they were assured that she really cared and could accept all sides of their masculinity. As one man says, "To the world at large, I've always tried to be like the guys who write to *Penthouse*—but that's not what I'm really like inside. Inside, there's a lot of little boy in me, and he really wants to be reassured." He says he's more likely to expose this anxious part of himself and "let that little boy out sometimes" with a woman who shows him that she really cares.

Having a firm foundation of friendship provided the emotional cushion of trust that twenty-seven-year-old Raymond had at the start of his second marriage. Over time, he says, their sexual communication has deepened, although "in the beginning, communication was never a real big heavy kind of thing":

With Rhoda I feel a lot like we're just friends. So our sex has been more like the sex that I have with friends. Although it's gotten to be a lot more than that, too. We'd always talk to each other, and ask each other what we liked. And as we came to trust each other more, we'd each start risking a little more, in terms of saying what we wanted the other person to do.

Roger, a thirty-eight-year-old lawyer, says his wife encouraged him over the years to express his sexual preferences. Now, he says,

"I can open up and not be embarrassed or ashamed to ask for whatever I want sexually." Her judgment-free attitude made him feel close enough to freely make suggestions, without fearing criticism or ridicule.

Attitudes

Ideally, sex should be a natural and essential part of life that can fulfill some of our biological, physical, emotional, and recreational needs. When couples feel that sex is a natural part of their relationship, they are able to communicate about sex more easily. For instance, thirty-six-year-old Michael says:

> If the relationship is one in which both partners feel that the act of sex is a normal, wholesome activity, then there's no problem talking about it and saying things like "I like this" or "I don't like that." It just feels very natural to say things like that.

Yet, from societal messages we've received since our earliest years, it's not uncommon for some people to think of sex as bad, nasty, or sinful. People who have such attitudes are likely to dismiss certain sexual ideas or actions their partner may want to suggest. Communication becomes thwarted, because one partner already feels criticized and negatively judged by the other. To keep open the lines of communication, it's essential to be openminded about the different preferences and attitudes that exist. But withholding judgment on your partner's preferences doesn't mean you have to alter your own tastes. You needn't engage in acts that are incompatible with your own values. But, to build intimacy within a relationship, it is important to refrain from labeling those desires of your partner that are different from your own as immoral, unnatural, perverted, or weird. Making strong judgmental comments such as these can have a devastating effect on fledgling communication efforts. Instead, try to listen to your partner carefully, and remember: There are many different ways to express your sexuality. After all, Baskin-Robbins makes thirty-one varieties of ice cream —enough to suit most individual tastes.

Listening

Once you've built a foundation of trust and have an accepting attitude toward each other—and toward sex—the next ingredient needed in creating a genuine rapport between lovers is learning to listen. Suspending judgment while concentrating on your partner's viewpoint is crucial to real communication. Although this seems obvious and simple, it is actually one of the most difficult things to accomplish.

Men, because of their role scripts, have even more difficulty listening effectively than women. Warren Farrell, author of *The Liberated Male*, says that the business world often teaches men to listen poorly. Successful men, he says, listen with only part of their mind; the other part is busy finding fault with an opposing person's argument and formulating rebuttals to impress the boss or other important people. This does not work at home, however, because it's not what his lover needs or wants to hear.

In addition, men are taught to be problem solvers. Presented with problems at work, most men feel it's their responsibility to figure them out. Many take this role home with them at the end of the day. Rather than simply talking out a problem or expressing their feelings, which women are more able to do, men approach a problem as something requiring solution. They often seek out facts and alternatives instead of providing compassion and attentiveness. Some men say they actually feel helpless when they sit and passively listen.

Trained as a journalist to listen and to respond with questions, not solutions, thirty-six-year-old Jason believes these skills have helped his personal relationships. He says:

> I've always tried to make my partner as comfortable as possible when talking about sex by listening carefully. I guess because my major was in journalism I've always been able to listen very well and ask a lot of good questions to help the other person clarify what they're trying to say. I can sit and listen to someone for hours and just keep asking questions. I've always been hit with the response that "Oh, you're so easy to talk to." And if people can talk freely to me on other subjects, communicating about sex comes easily too.

Listening carefully is a way to really understand a partner's point of view. And since two viewpoints always exist when two people are involved in any exchange, it is absolutely essential to understand a partner's perspective to communicate fully. Otherwise, conversations can degenerate into "finger-pointing" sessions. Stuart comments: "If you're looking for a way to make your partner wrong, you can find it. In the final analysis, it's the finger-pointing that kills communication. Because when you point the finger, the other person becomes the crazy one and then, of course, they don't want to say anything more." Blaming each other adds fuel to the already-burning fire, settles nothing, and often snuffs out any useful communication. Yet, if a partner's point of view can be seen and understood, it can facilitate compromise.

Honesty

Without honesty, the entire communication process is threatened. It is essential for people who are trying to concentrate on expressing their thoughts, feelings, and perceptions to be as honest as possible in order to keep the entire foundation of trust from crumbling.

Many men told us how difficult it is for them always to say what they were really feeling in their intimate relationships. The issue, for some, was not knowing how to be tactful or delicate in telling a partner something potentially painful. Surviving in the business world, they said, often means learning to concentrate on the facts, learning to make difficult decisions, even to be cutthroat at times. Consequently, men often learn to give feedback in a blunt, brutally honest fashion. As a result, the most prevalent reason men gave for holding back their true feelings was their fear of hurting their partners and ultimately having their partners reject them. Even if they believed intellectually that honesty was indeed the best policy, emotionally it was difficult for them to carry it out.

Dusty, a twenty-one-year-old graduate student, was on guard with his true feelings, until he recognized that it hurt more to withhold the painful truth than to reveal it:

> For a long time I've had a problem being honest with women. I used to worry that if I told them the truth I would hurt them or they would think less of me and not want to be with me. I used to go to any lengths to avoid telling them what I felt. But finally I realized it hurt them more in the long run because everyone discovers the truth eventually. So I began saying what I really feel.

Holding back on true feelings can create rather than solve problems. Most of us can remember times when we avoided the truth and our partners could sense a discrepancy between our spoken words and our unspoken feelings. If our dishonesty was discovered later on, the resulting breach of trust may have made a much more devastating and longer-lasting impact than if we had been honest from the start.

Some men concealed their true feelings to the degree that they preferred to fake orgasm rather than let their partner know they were not sexually interested. Frankly, we had not previously been aware that men *could* fake orgasm. However, enough men we interviewed told us they had done so, at least a couple of times in their lives, to convince us that it was indeed possible. The men who had faked orgasm felt that their behavior was justified, in that they were protecting not only their own ego but also their partner's. Fifty-two-year-old Jim, for instance, said he would rather fake an orgasm than let his partner down or run the risk of appearing less than a man in her eyes. "To think that I was less than the world's greatest lover would probably break my heart," says Jim, not entirely joking. "So in a case where I'm trying but for some reason I can't climax, a little moaning and groaning does the trick. Nobody's the wiser for it and my partner says, 'Oh, you're fantastic,' and 'Gee, you made me feel super.'"

Forty-year-old Alfred maintains that, in certain situations, faking orgasm is absolutely "the only gentlemanly thing to do." He told us about one of those occasions:

I met an attractive young lady in a bar and asked her to dance. We became friendly, and during the course of the evening I asked her if she would like to spend the night with me. She laughed and said she couldn't make it but would like to know where I would be during the week. I told her, even though I was going to be a couple of hundred miles away. The rest of the evening was very pleasant and we parted company amicably.

Two or three days later I was in this other city at a restaurant and I got a call at dinner from the hotel manager saying that someone had come to see me and was waiting in my room. When I called the hotel, I recognized her voice and asked her what she was doing there. She answered, "I wanted to see you." Boy, was I flattered! She had driven two hundred miles just to see me. She said she was starved, so I dropped off the people I was with, picked her up from the hotel, and returned to the restaurant. Later that night, when we got back to the hotel, I started to make some sexual overtures toward her and finally said, "Come on, let's get into bed." That's when this twenty-two-year-old lady reached in and removed her teeth! It turned out that she had been in a severe car accident a couple of years earlier. Well, talk about the erection dying—it did. And although I maintained somewhat of an erection, I finally just gasped and groaned and created my own version of an orgasm and said, "Okay, let's go to sleep."

Certainly, there are situations in which faking orgasm might be the least offensive and most socially graceful course of action. However, the major reason most men faked orgasm was to conceal their macho vulnerabilities. With sex roles continuing to shift and more women initiating sex, men are finding themselves in uncharted waters. No longer are they the sole sexual initiators who determine when and where sex will take place. Since a macho man is still expected to be ever ready for sex, men are beginning to find themselves in the uncomfortable position of being pursued by women when sex is not foremost on their minds. Consequently, men who don't find their partners sexually attractive or who are not particularly aroused at the moment are put in the age-old woman's role of faking or having to learn to say no.

Saying No

When sexual honesty is an integral part of a relationship, ideally the door is open for both men and women to acknowledge when they want sex, as well as when they don't. Mel, a fifty-nine-year-old sales executive who has been married for thirty-four years, believes:

Part of being honest is giving permission to the other person to not have sex when they don't want to, to say when they're aroused and when they're not aroused. Before, when I had trouble being honest, I would fake it, or use all sorts of stupid devices or excuses, whereas now my wife and I are able to say when we want sex and when we don't want it, and that has really helped to make our whole sexual relationship better.

Interestingly enough, while men were reluctant to turn down sex with their partners, they appreciated women who were honest with them. Rather than attempting to make love to a woman who was somewhat resistant or hesitant, they preferred not to make love at all and, instead, to wait for the right moment or the right partner so that the lovemaking would be enthusiastic and mutually satisfying.

Stanley, age sixty-five, says he's glad his wife has finally learned to be honest when she doesn't want to have sex:

Until recently, my wife would never say to me, "Leave me alone, I'm not in the mood." She would never verbalize those feelings. Instead, she would submit, regardless of how she felt. And, frankly, I prefer her telling me, because I can feel when she's really "not there" when we're having sex, and that's not enjoyable to me.

Women felt similarly, according to those we interviewed for *Shared Intimacies*. They said they preferred men to be straightforward and say no when they didn't want to make love, rather than going ahead half-heartedly and possibly experiencing erection problems or participating in sex that felt almost perfunctory.

Yet men aren't accustomed to saying no. Tradition has the female declining a male's advances, not the other way around. He-men make all the moves, try to score, and seduce an unwilling woman into bed. When the roles are reversed, and a woman starts to express her sexual needs, a man can have a difficult time turning her down. Ned, a thirty-four-year-old graduate student would rarely refuse his live-in mate of five years. As a result, he says:

I'd overreact and resent it. I did everything from going to a movie I didn't want to see to having sex when I wasn't interested. Sometimes I didn't even ejaculate. I'd have an erection but all the feelings would be blocked. I felt like I was off somewhere else thinking about how I was going to write this paper and all the while I'd be making sounds like I was involved, but I really wasn't.

I felt that in order to break through the block and feel more sexual feelings, I had to be more willing to risk, to say, "No, I don't want to." For a while, when I was practicing saying, "No, I just want to hold you and be close," when I really didn't feel sexual, she would go off the wall. She'd be angry. She'd cry and feel totally rejected. But I feel I have a right to say no when I don't feel sexual. She feels perfectly fine saying no, and I'm expected to still be loving and to cuddle. So I stuck to my guns and when I wasn't feeling sexual I would tell her so. Of course, I had to learn to say no in a nicer way. I used to say it real nasty like, "Hell, no." So I've had to learn how to say it with more caring and then let her take responsibility for her reaction. If she's into her garbage around it, that's something for her to deal with. But now she's worked through it, and it's great.

When I take those kinds of risks and stick with them, I get this special sensation in my stomach. The closest I can come to describing it is the feelings I had the night before Christmas as a kid: there is anticipation, excitement, and the feeling of being alive instead of not feeling anything at all.

DEVELOPING A GOOD SEXUAL COMMUNICATION SYSTEM

Yet it's true that most people have difficulty talking about sex. In both new and old relationships, it can be awkward and embarrassing to broach a topic that has historically been considered taboo. Hence, most people find that even when the right ingredients are all present, they are more inhibited than they'd like to be when it comes to initiating a discussion about sex. So how does one go about breaking an old pattern and opening the lines of sexual communication? Succinctly stated: very slowly!

It is important to remember that it takes time to transform habits that have developed over a period of years. Basically, change is scary for most of us. We resist change primarily because we cannot be certain of the outcome. Even if our current situation is miserable, at least it is "familiarly" miserable. We need time to make gradual changes, try out new behaviors and become comfortable with them.

When unresolved anger and resentment have mounted up over the years, you may encounter difficulty making changes on your own. Couples sometimes need professional assistance—a certified marriage counselor, family therapist, or sex therapist—to rectify these old hurts and resentments before caring communication can be restored.

Seeking the services of a qualified professional is not a sign of personal inadequacy. Most sexual problems are based on poor communication, inadequate information, learned negative attitudes, and lack of emotional support for trying out new behaviors. The entire counseling process is confidential and any decision to share your experiences with friends or family is entirely up to you. Even if too much damage has been done to keep the relationship intact, therapy can help you develop the kind of communication skills that will enhance future relationships.

The majority of couples, however, do not seek the services of a therapist to resolve problems. Over the years they figure out their own ways of developing and improving upon their sexual communication skills. Unfortunately, the problem-solving techniques that took years to develop are rarely shared with others. That's why we asked our interviewees to tell us about how they learned to communicate with their partners about sex.

Some men we talked with continued to find communicating effectively to be a problem and could offer no solutions. In fact, a few of the interviews turned into therapy sessions as we discussed the difficulties they wrestled with. For example, one seventy-six-year-old man had had a prostate operation and, as a result, had difficulty maintaining a firm erection. Prior to his operation, he and his wife had never had any sexual problems so they had had no experience discussing sex. Consequently, both of them felt awkward talking about the effect of the operation on their sex life. And now, five years after the operation, they rarely have sex.

Many other men in our sample, however, felt they had established open sexual communication in their intimate relationships and were eager to share their discoveries with us. Through them, we collected a potpourri of ideas on how to transform sexual communication.

Getting Started

If your tongue feels thick and your stomach queasy when you broach the subject of sex with your partner, don't think you are alone. Even couples with years of marriage behind them say it's difficult to express their innermost needs and desires. Winston, a psychologist who has been happily married fifteen years, considers sex "a very loaded issue" because it involves opening up the possibility of getting turned down:

Even after fifteen years, it still hurts my feelings if I ask Pearl to make love and she doesn't want to. I tell her not to take my reaction very seriously, so it doesn't upset her. But I still struggle with that sometimes.

To make it easier on themselves to talk about such a sensitive subject, many men had devised indirect methods to lead into discussions about sex. They chose to communicate a preference or address a problem by indirect means so the subject wouldn't be intimidating or threatening to their partners. Getting started that way helped establish a bond of trust and a basis for a continuing sexual dialogue.

One indirect way Dan, thirty-one, shared information with his sexually inexperienced wife was to joke about sex:

I might be telling a dirty joke and my wife wouldn't understand it. So in the process of explaining it to her, we had to discuss specific sexual activities and behaviors. She was a neophyte in the sexual world, and her questions helped to initiate very detailed conversations.

Gus, a lawyer who had been married for six years, would use issues raised in articles, books, and TV shows, and by their friends, to talk in third-person terms about his and his wife's sexual needs or inhibitions. Because his wife was uncomfortable with certain areas of sexuality, Gus felt the distance created by depersonalizing these discussions made her less defensive and him more understanding:

Having these open discussions has helped me to tolerate and accept my wife's sexual hangups because through the conversation it becomes clear that she knows she has a hangup and she's trying to deal with it. She is not saying that problems don't exist or, "If you were kinder, or softer, or more understanding then I wouldn't be like this." It's clear that she's not trying to put the blame on me, and that makes me more accepting of her.

For Todd, the security he felt in his marriage made him comfortable enough to talk about the sexual aspects of previous relationships. This gave him and his wife an opening to discuss *their* sexual relationship and provided them with useful information about the other's likes and dislikes:

We both had sexual experiences before we met and were always able to talk about them. Sex was never a taboo subject with us. I knew all the guys that Sara went to bed with and she knew about a lot of the girls that I had had intercourse with. Through these discussions, we got to know each other better, we learned each other's preferences, what we liked and didn't like.

One man found using sexual quizzes or questionnaires that appear in popular magazines particularly useful for initiating a discussion about specific sexual activities such as oral sex, anal sex, or masturbation. He said:

I think those questions are wonderful. You don't have to sit there and say, "What do you think about oral sex?" Somebody's already written it down, and the question is right there in front of you.

Gary, a thirty-one-year-old writer, and several other men, suggested a rating system for communicating about sexual desire:

We used to share numbers on a scale from one to ten to let each other know how turned on we were. Ten means I'm so hot that if we don't go to bed and fuck, I'm liable to rip your clothes off. Zero means forget it, I have no interest whatsoever. Three means if you can get it up you can have it.

Dennis, sixty-seven, found a way to make communication fun by using a card game called "The Love Game." Although the game was bought commercially, creative and industrious couples could easily make their own set:

I had a deck of cards that was designed for people with sexual problems. A stack of communication cards instructed you to do things like tell your husband three things that you like best about sex, or ask your wife what was the best time she ever had sexually, and so on. Then a second set of cards told you to tickle your partner with feathers or blow in their ear. A third deck got down to more specific petting techniques and positions for intercourse. I played the game with my wife and, while it sounds terribly stilted and contrived, it turned out to be a big turn-on. I was surprised at how well it worked because I was so skeptical. It was just amazing. I've even used it on occasion with some clients. Some of them like it and some don't.*

Another way to exchange feelings about sex was suggested by a woman who wrote to us after *Shared Intimacies* was published. She and her husband each read separate copies of the book, underlined passages they found particularly meaningful, and then traded books. She wrote, "We were shocked to discover, after fifteen years of marriage, what we didn't know about each other. My husband asked why I hadn't talked to him about these things, and I had to admit, 'I just didn't know what words to use.'" A number of books on sexuality such as *Total Sex*, by Herbert and Roberta Otto, can serve the same purpose. The idea is just to generate a discussion about a variety of sexual subjects.

But some people who tended to take an indirect approach in talking about sexual issues found at times they weren't getting the point across. They needed to adopt a more direct method of communicating. And then there were others who never felt comfortable mincing words. A straightforward approach was the style they took most of the time.

Regardless of the approach used, the men we talked with suggested thinking beforehand about a setting that would be conducive to discussing such an intimate topic as sexuality. Some said it was best to choose a nonsexual environment where they could talk privately and at length, away from their ordinary daily routines. A quiet walk, a dinner out, or a daytime car trip were some specific suggestions they made for setting the scene. Others liked to talk in bed.

* Contact *Uniquity* for new age sex and communication games: 215 Fourth Street, P.O. Box 6, Galt, California 95632.

Regardless of the setting, once discussion begins, don't get side-tracked. The men we interviewed said unless you concentrate on the subject at hand, outside distractions or anxieties can steer you away from the pressing issue.

Alan, a thirty-eight-year-old administrator, described how, with some careful planning, he avoids these possibilities:

I like to block out a part of the evening and have an agreement that we're going to talk about sex. I don't expect it to be real easy or comfortable at first, although eventually it can get to be that way. I also think it's very important to try to separate sex from the other things that might be going on in the relationship. For example, saying, "Well, when you came home I wanted to talk, but then you did this and I got turned off," is a way of avoiding the subject. You can always find things to distract you from the discussion if you want to.

No matter which method you choose to start your discussion on sex, when you get into the thick of things, remember not to blame and to be as specific as possible. Be sure to communicate details. Clearly indicate the techniques you want your partner to try, for example, "I like it when you put your tongue in my mouth when we kiss," or "I like you to bite me a little harder," or "My penis is most sensitive here."

Getting down to specifics is difficult for many people. If you have trouble thinking about what to say, here are a few questions you might want your partner to answer. For example, ask her: What are the things you like about making love to me? What things would you like me to do more of? Or less of? Then ask, How do you like the following areas of your body to be touched—face, neck, breasts/chest, arms, hands, legs, feet, genitals, back, buttocks, etc.?

Dan, a thirty-one-year-old physician, is able to get very detailed with his wife about his sexual preferences. "Explaining to her what feels best for me and asking for that same information from her is a lot better than waiting for those magnificent orgasms to just somehow happen," Dan points out. He describes how he communicates his needs to his wife in a sexual setting and how he asks for hers in exchange:

I would manipulate her clitoris and then her vaginal walls and ask which felt better or if it hurt. When I was sucking her breasts, I'd ask if she enjoyed that. If we were doing mutual masturbation, I'd tell her what makes me feel good. I'd explain to her how my penis works, that there's a certain point on my penis that feels really good and how that correlates with her clitoris.

Bringing up sexual issues doesn't really have to turn into an intense Big Talk. It's even possible to have fun telling your partner what you like in bed and asking her what she prefers. Wayne, twenty-three, discovered that the verbal exchange could be a playful turn-on:

This human sexuality class I'm taking is definitely a plus to my sex life. I used to play it by ear. If I were making love to a lady and she was relaxed, then I would know that she wanted it slow and easy, and if she tensed up and started grabbing me, then I'd kind of give it to her fast. But that class taught me to just say what I want, ask for what I want. I tell her that my balls are my most sensitive part, and I like head, or whatever. I ask her, "What do you like?" Talking has definitely made sex better for me. It used to be that when I'd start having sex, everything was silent, but now it's like any recreational activity. When you're having fun, you don't just sit there. If you're playing a game of hockey, you're not just quiet. You talk. So that's what we do, we just talk about this and that and it really turns me on.

Erik, forty-four, says hearing his wife's verbal responses adds an erotic dimension to his lovemaking:

I want feedback on how I am doing and how she's doing. I want to know whether something feels good to her. So, while her physical response tells me something, I like hearing the words, too. It's arousing to me, especially in foreplay. I enjoy hearing that she likes my body or that my hair is soft, and I like it when she says, "Wow, that was fantastic."

Critical Feedback
As long as it's the good news that is being shared, communicating sexual feelings can be fairly easy. The tough part for most people

comes when it is time to express criticism. There may be aspects of your partner's lovemaking style that displease you and things you'd like to see changed. But how do you go about suggesting those changes? People are sensitive about their sexual performance. No one likes to be criticized. So discussions are often postponed as you tiptoe around.

But unless you can communicate your feelings to your partner, they can end up interfering with the sexual experience. Ron, age twenty-four and single, described the following situation in which not talking about sex brought the whole sexual encounter to a premature and abrupt halt:

> I've had partners who will be in an uncomfortable position and sometimes I'm not aware of it and they won't say anything until it's gotten to the point where they can't stand it anymore. Then they want to stop altogether.

Eventually, sexual displeasure can gnaw away at you and build into frustration or resentment. However, while it makes perfect sense to just tell your partner your feelings directly, most people find this difficult. Negative feedback is often received as an assault, especially for men who equate their sexual prowess and proficiency with their masculinity. Since one unspoken definition of a virile man is that he satisfies his woman, any information to the contrary can diminish his masculine ego. And it's not enough to know he's fulfilled his lover in the past. The macho man feels put to the test every time he makes love. The only feedback he wants to hear is applause. But when applause isn't forthcoming, how can criticism be given so that it doesn't jeopardize a man's sense of worth as a sexual being? The men we interviewed had some suggestions as to how to soften the blow of a critical comment.

Men again referred to the importance of the quality of the relationship. Above all, men needed to feel that their partner cared. And when critical feedback was conveyed in a loving and respectful way, men were more able to hear their partner's comments without feeling hurt, angry, or rejected.

There were a number of ways that men felt the caring could be conveyed: the verbal message could be softened through a particular tone of voice or endearment; feedback could be given positively rather than negatively; the right moment for expressing these feelings needed to be chosen carefully; and information could be given nonverbally.

Tone of Voice

Many men told us how important a gentle tone of voice was in conveying critical comments. A softened tone lessened the impact and made the message sound caring and nonjudgmental. As one man put it: "I guess it's more the tone of voice than anything that lessens the impact of criticism—using a very soft tone when saying 'don't do that' or 'this feels uncomfortable' really helps." Others said they were also reassured when their partners preceded a request with an endearment, for instance, "Sweetheart, could you please be more gentle?" or "Honey, don't stop now."

Verbal requests that aren't softened with endearments or a gentle tone can come across like instructions being barked. And Verner, forty, says these harsh sexual pointers ruin his sexual experience. "Sometimes," he says,

> women have asked me to do things and they sound like "Simon says, 'Do this,'" "Simon says, 'Do that.'" I have been very put off. It's like the co-pilot in a 747 who is giving instructions, "Flaps up, landing gear down," etc. I have been with women who have been really militant about giving instructions, particularly women who are feminists. And I feel violated or something because of the way they do it. It becomes a verbal and very conscious dialogue with a lot of instructions and compliances to instructions rather than pleasure, and I get nervous and begin to feel like sex is really a burden.

In addition to a caring tone of voice, "I" statements can be very helpful when dissatisfacton is being conveyed. As the name implies, "I" statements are messages that are expressed in the first person: "I am turned off by this" or "I'd like you to pleasure me longer," instead of second-person statements like, "You turn me off" or "You don't stimulate me enough." The first assumes responsibility for your feelings and reactions, whereas the second blames your partner. When you use "I" statements, you are simply stating how you feel rather than judging who is right or who is wrong.

Knowing what you want so you can use "I" statements, however, is sometimes hard for a man. "My training and upbringing as a man has taught me to be the dutiful one—the caretaker—but not to know what it is that *I* want," said thirty-seven-year-old Leif:

> I've always had a sense of what I wanted my partners to be—a Playboy bunny or something—and when they didn't fit that image, I was always disappointed. Now I've had to learn to change my focus and be specific about what I want in sex, what really feels good to me, instead of some abstract notion of how *she* ought to be.

Accentuate the Positive

Another way men suggested communicating sensitive issues without assaulting their ego was, as the Cole Porter song goes, "to accentuate the positive, eliminate the negative." By presenting information in positive, constructive terms, rather than negative, destructive ones, the underlying message that comes across is, "I like you," "I like our sex together, even though we might have to make some changes." Blunt, critical, negative words imply, "Sex with you is lousy," "You're an inadequate lover," "I don't want to continue the relationship." To avoid giving the latter impression, some men told us they only spoke to their partners about the positive aspects of their sex lives. They hoped that by omitting criticism and reinforcing the positive they would encourage their partners to do more of those things they liked. Sixty-seven-year-old Dennis tells his partners:

> "That feels good," or "Do that," but in a positive way rather than saying, "Ouch!" "Don't," or "You hurt me." Those aren't good signals. So I try to do it by emphasizing the positive and overlooking the parts I don't like.

Seth, a thirty-six-year-old lawyer, agrees:

> I think it's possible to make suggestions by saying "such and such really felt best," rather than describing the other things that are not very good or very enjoyable. Sometimes I seek information in the same way. After having made love, I may ask a partner which part of it she liked best. The implication is that everything was pretty good, but there were some parts that were better than others.

Another man told us that it was easier to talk about sex with his wife when they began with those sexual experiences that were mutually pleasing and then went on to discuss things that might need to be changed. That way, a positive tone was set for the discussion and, in addition, some of the specific ingredients that contributed to their best sexual experiences could be defined.

Some men felt it was possible to hear direct feedback and still not feel inadequate or rejected as long as it was clear that their partner didn't want them to stop, only to try something different. Vince felt that constructive sexual communication should point out new sexual possibilities:

> Certainly nobody's been more critical and up front with me than my wife has been in terms of saying, "I don't like this" or "I wish you'd really cut that out." However, it very seldom comes across to me as a put-down. The big key is if the person says their complaint in a way that invites their partner to keep up what they're doing but to try something different. Instead of conveying the notion that "you're shitty at it and I don't want you to do anything but stop!" it's important to say, "I don't want you to stop the whole thing. I want you to do this instead," or "This is how you can do it better."

Timing

Many men we interviewed believed that an important element in successfully communicating sexual information was selecting the right moment. With few exceptions, most men said they preferred not to talk to their partners about sexual problem areas while making love. They felt that this kind of discussion during lovemaking interrupted the rhythm and hampered spontaneity.

Bernard, a twenty-nine-year-old management analyst, says giving or receiving critical feedback during intercourse puts a damper on the lovemaking:

> I would communicate negative information afterwards or sometimes beforehand, but rarely during, because I think that destroys the moment. I would characterize good sex, enjoyable sex, as something spontaneous, something you don't consciously evaluate. I think a partner feels that when you take time to ferret out what's good and what's bad, it becomes more

logical and objective and less emotional and warm. This can cause a partner to withdraw some of their enthusiasm.

But talking about the positive things as they occurred was considered sexually enhancing by some men. "I've felt that it's better to reinforce the sexual act with good things when they're happening," said Jason, age thirty-six, "but I've found it better to discuss negative things at some other time." However, some men, like thirty-seven-year-old Todd, felt that any verbalization during sex, positive or negative, detracted from the experience:

I don't like to talk or be talked to during sex. I don't like someone to tell me, "Move this way, do this, do that," because I think sex is fundamentally a silent act. Lovemaking, to me, is a spontaneous and nonverbal emotional experience.

Alex, thirty-nine, is also reluctant to talk about sex while he's in the middle of it:

I don't want to put my partner on the defensive or make her feel awkward or negative about what's happening. I've had experiences where I have said something to my partner like "Why don't you try this" or "This feels good" and it's had a negative effect on the sexual experience. So I gave up communicating during sex.

When it is important enough to Alex to mention something to his partner, he waits until after the lovemaking:

I wait until the experience is over to talk about it. I've said, "Hey, by the way, I'm not particularly crazy about too much anal stimulation," or "I like it when you touch the tip of my penis," or "I like it when you fondle my testicles," or "There's a certain spot that you sometimes touch that I really like."

Many men like Alex found the intimacy of the afterglow, when both partners felt loved and cared for, more conducive to discussing sex. So they waited until intercourse was over before they brought up sexual issues. And there were others, like Art, a thirty-four-year-old physician, who preferred to discuss sex only when they were totally removed from it, "maybe a while later, the next morning, maybe over dinner or at some other time, but not while having sex or even right afterward."

Clearly, different approaches work for different people, depending on their individual needs and vulnerabilities. As a consequence, the ultimate decision about when to raise these issues rests with the couples involved. John, thirty-seven, had no hard-and-fast rules but shared the following commonsense advice:

> I think the urgency of the matter dictates when I communicate. If there's something that is completely turning me off, that would ruin the experience for both of us, I would certainly say something then and there, regardless of what we were doing. The experience would be wrecked anyway. So it's better that I say something rather than just end it. However, I think that correcting someone during the act can create defensive walls. It might make them feel inadequate. If it's something that is mildly unpleasurable to me that is likely to pass or is not going to affect me that much, then I would probably wait until after we're finished and we're quiet and then we would have a talk. Then I can give some explanation and still show affection while talking, which can reassure them.

Nonverbal Communication

Verbal communication by itself had certain drawbacks. Some men felt that talking alone was inadequate for really communicating specific sexual techniques. In these cases, men found it helpful to show their partner as well as to tell them. Joseph, age thirty-four, for instance, said:

> It's taken me awhile to teach Paula how to masturbate me. In the beginning it didn't make any difference how she jacked me off. The fact that she was doing it was enough. After that, it got to the point where I could not have an orgasm while she was doing it. She would be too rough, and would bend my cock back too far. She knew she wasn't doing it right and she felt bad about it. Finally she started asking me questions about how I liked to be touched and I tried to explain. But when she tried to do it she still couldn't, so then I started showing her. I'd put my hand over her hand as she stroked my cock and tell her, "This feels good, this feels really good, this doesn't feel so

good, this hurts." I told her I don't like just a steady rhythm. I like variations and differences in speed. She finally got a feel for what was good for me. Taking her hand and showing her as well as giving her instructions on what felt good and what didn't did the trick.

In addition to sometimes being inadequate, verbal communication can be overdone. Many men felt you could overtalk and overintellectualize the romance away. Raymond, twenty-seven, addresses some of the limitations of verbal communication:

You can beat something to death verbally. It's sort of like eating too much or doing anything too much. In small doses it's fine, but in large doses, it can be problematic.

And some men, like Dean, age thirty-four, resented feeling compelled by social pressure to verbalize their sexual feelings all the time and with every partner:

I went through a phase, as part of being liberated, when it was important to talk. I thought that I had to be assertive sexually, that I had to show my partner what I want and ask for what I want sexually. Before sex I would have an upfront discussion of the sexual agenda, especially with a new partner but even with an old partner. I remember some very awkward experiences trying to do this, so I've come to the personal conclusion that overcommunicating is essentially a sexual turn-off to everyone. More recently, I just try to enjoy what we're doing rather than constantly asserting myself. Now I think it's more important for me to be sensitive, to rely on more nonverbal, implicit body language to get my message across to my partner and to be sensitive to her bodily signals as well.

Like Dean, many men expressed their needs through nonverbal signals. Some men we interviewed shared with us examples of the signals they exchanged with partners during lovemaking. One said he pays attention to his partner's physical responses or the sounds she makes to see whether she's reacting pleasurably or not. He watches her face to see whether she's enjoying his caresses. Another uses his hands to communicate. "I let my partner know with my hands if she's moving in the right direction. I might use pressure on her shoulders and her neck to direct her," he told us.

The most familiar and commonly expressed method of silently communicating a sexual preference to a partner was the Golden Rule: Do unto others as you would have them do unto you.

Jim, a twenty-seven-year-old single medical student, said:

If I like something to be done, I do it to her. For example, I like being kissed around the ear and neck, so I'll do that to her to let her see how it feels. I like it, so maybe she'll like it. And if she likes it, maybe sometime down the road she'll do it back to me.

Unfortunately, the nonverbal example set during lovemaking doesn't always produce the desired results. Sometimes nonverbal cues can be confusing and body language can be misinterpreted, and at other times the groping and gesturing can be just plain annoying. Alex, age thirty-nine, had experienced these drawbacks of nonverbal communication:

Sometimes the reaction of my partner when she is particularly enjoying something is very similar to her reaction when she is being irritated by something, and I have had the experience of watching a woman react physically and not being sure whether or not she's turning away in pleasure or displeasure. For example, sometimes the pleasure seems to be so intense that she needs to close her legs to kind of shut it off for a little while. That's exactly the same kind of reaction she would use if I were irritating her, and so I don't always know what her reaction means. Sometimes I get very confused and I don't know what the hell I'm supposed to be doing.

There are other times when I'm stimulating my partner orally and she seems to want penetration, but rather than saying, "I'd like you to enter me," there seems to be a lot of frantic pulling and gesturing and tugging to bring my head up and position my body. It's perfectly obvious what she wants, but I resent her doing it that way. I would rather she say, "I'd like you to enter me right now" or "That's enough of that," instead of making some jerky physical movement.

When nonverbal signals worked, verbal messages weren't necessary. And when they didn't, most men were practical, and talked about the problems they thought were affecting the sexual relationship. Edward, age thirty-five, like most other men, used a combination of both approaches:

First I will try nonverbally to indicate that I want a change if I'm not liking the way I'm being touched. I might move my body to a more appropriate position. If the person does not understand my message, then I'll try to express verbally what I want in a way that keeps her from feeling badly about any discomfort I may have experienced.

Ultimately, the particular method chosen for communicating was less important than making certain that a sense of caring was expressed when critical feedback was being given. Knowing they were genuinely cared for by their partner helped men to distinguish between information and a judgment about their sexual adequacy. Feeling loved and accepted enabled them to concentrate on solving the mechanical problems of sex. As Larry put it:

Sometimes I mix love and sex up together and I won't say something I'm really feeling for fear my wife will think I don't love her or that she won't love me if I express my real feelings. These fears can kill the communication right there. When I can separate sex from love and say what is on my mind, I'm more likely to be able to get my needs met in the relationship.

Ultimately, enhanced sexual communication is just one aspect of good communication in a relationship. As one man said:

Before, working out issues in my emotional relationships and dealing with sex were two separate things, but now they go hand in hand. With the relationships I've had lately, they've all melted together. We communicate about everything. It's super.

But the process of learning to communicate is not easy and can not be expected to happen overnight. You may need to experiment with a variety of communication methods before you find one that works. And even then it may take awhile before your partner can assimilate and effectively utilize the information. Terry, age thirty-six, who has been married for fifteen years, found this to be true in his marriage:

> I like to have my testicles rubbed gently. But Glenna would handle my penis fairly roughly and she would handle my testicles the same way. I would say, "Would you hold my testicles, touch my testicles?" Then she would go at them with so much enthusiasm that it was really painful. This took some time and some painful experiences to change. And even after lots of communication, it's still not easy for her to be as gentle as I would like.

However, it is good to know that the process does get easier the more you do it. According to thirty-four-year-old Art:

> I was afraid to discuss sex, but once I started to talk about it, and talked about it enough, I realized there was nothing to be afraid of. I realized there was nothing to worry about or to be prudish about. I think I just got used to it after some practice. And Melanie became more receptive to talking about it and hearing about it too. And the more willing we were to talk about it, the less afraid we were that it might change our relationship, our sex life, or our commitment to each other. And the less we feared these things, the better the communication became.

But no matter how effectively you learn to communicate, it is essential to keep your expectations realistic. Your partner can never possibly be all things to you at all times. No one is perfect. If the expectation is one of perfection, it is only likely to lead to disappointment. As Bennett realistically summed it up:

> You can't expect the other person to be and do exactly what you want when you want it. Sometimes we expect too much. If I have a really good sexual experience with a partner, not every time, but one every three or four times, that's doing damn well.

Also, it is important to keep in mind that two people make up a relationship and the needs of both must be taken into account when changes are being made. Sometimes one person is ready to move more quickly or in a different direction than the other. Therefore the desired changes may not develop according to a preconceived timetable. When this happens, it is essential to remember to relax and allow for the time required. Thus, it may be necessary at times to back off for a while. Sometimes, if pressured to make too many changes too quickly, a partner may resist making any changes at all. This was the case with Paxton, who has been married eleven years:

A source of conflict between us was an expressed wish on my part to try out some new things sexually. But Candy felt I was pressuring her. So I backed off. And since then, in the last year or two, she has been the one to initiate some different positions and new things. I think that my giving her more room to express herself decreased the pressure or whatever she was experiencing and has really paid off for both of us in the long run.

Most of the men we interviewed agreed that altering patterns in their relationship was often difficult and took time. Yet, as Paxton pointed out, this long-term effort paid off by opening up the lines of communication and, ultimately, produced more of the sexual satisfaction both partners wanted. Even if surmounting obstacles to communication was difficult, men we interviewed agreed with the assessment of Alvy, in Woody Allen's *Annie Hall:* "I guess we keep goin' through it because most of us need the eggs." The men we interviewed weren't content, however, to "keep goin' through" the same old nonproductive communication patterns. Instead they decided to "work through" those patterns and develop better communication in their relationships. When the lines of communication are open, they told us, there's more warmth, intimacy, and security. The relationship becomes a richer partnership. And even the eggs taste better.

CHAPTER EIGHT

WHAT TO DO ABOUT SEXUAL PROBLEMS

Finally he met her. Brian was twenty-five and already had had a number of sexual partners, but nobody he was willing to take home to Mother. When he met Jacque, he says, he immediately began imagining what sex with her would be like. At the outset he didn't press for sexual involvement because she was someone special. "I wanted her to know I really cared about her, that I wasn't just trying to get in her pants. Yet, when the night was right and we finally made it together, I came so quickly she probably never even got a chance to feel me inside."

The anticipation and the subsequent disappointment of Brian's first premature ejaculation turned out to be an ongoing sexual problem. During the first two months after he met Jacque, each time they got together and made love, the same thing happened. He would worry about ejaculating too quickly, the anxiety would build, and his worries would come true. It became a self-fulfilling prophecy. By the time the third month rolled around, they had stopped seeing each other altogether.

Eventually, Brian, now thirty, was able to look back and acknowledge that his inability to accept a suddenly malfunctioning penis had caused him to make all sorts of excuses. He stopped being interested in sex, and soon after he stopped calling Jacque. The problem resolved itself when, a few months later, he slept with an old girl friend and everything worked out fine.

During the interview, Brian came to realize how strongly some of the he-man scripts had influenced his behavior. "If you asked me if I was a macho guy," Brian told us, "I would have said, 'No way.

Not me!' Yet obviously on a gut level I felt disappointed in myself for not being able to perform. Although intellectually I know it's impossible to always be able to get it up, I still felt, deep down, that something was wrong with me." Even if he had understood what was going on, Brian said he still wouldn't have known how to handle it. In his mind, Jacque was disappointed and considered him a failure. How could he open up and talk to her about his fears? He wasn't about to turn to his male friends for advice, since they rarely talked about their problems, especially those dealing with sex. Besides, men who ejaculate prematurely tend to see themselves in a negative light. As Brian said, "You see Burt Reynolds up there on the screen and you know he makes his women happy. Show me an acceptable male star who loses at love. You can't," he complained. "Society rewards winners and laughs at losers. And in my mind a man who has a sexual problem is a loser."

Lacking positive role models, Brian was hesitant at the onset of the interview to talk about his sexual problems. So was almost every other man we interviewed. Everything was great, they wanted us to believe. In contrast to the women we interviewed for *Shared Intimacies*—who readily admitted having had sexual difficulties—most men initially dismissed our queston "Have you ever had any sexual problems and, if so, how did you solve them?" Typically they answered with a quick denial or said their problems were trivial or had been solved long ago. Unlike women, who in this culture are almost expected to have sexual problems or difficulties that require assistance, men hesitate labeling any difficulty a "problem," for fear of being judged inadequate. Some of the men we interviewed even verbalized these fears by facetiously asking at the end of the interview, "How did I do? Did I pass? Did I cut the mustard?"

Through such experiences, we learned to save our questions about sexual problems until late in the interview, after a good rapport had been established. As with Brian, once the men realized they were not going to be judged or criticized, it was easier for them to open up about their sexual difficulties and the ways they handled them. This was the first time many of the men had ever discussed these sensitive issues. And, in general, they welcomed the opportunity for some constructive feedback. For a few men, the interview became almost a therapy session in which we offered information and expertise in response to the men's questions and concerns. But the fact is, most of the men we interviewed had, at one time or another, experienced some sexual difficulty and had found creative, sensitive ways of solving these problems that may be of value to others.

PERFORMANCE ANXIETY

As we analyzed the voluminous amount of material we had gathered for this chapter, certain patterns began to emerge. We often found that beneath the initial "cool" façade the men presented, were a variety of sexual fears.

Brian was typical in that the most pervasive and consuming of the men's concerns centered on the penis and its performance. Since sexual performance is the macho test of virility, many men had experienced some anxiety about the adequacy of their penis. They worried about its length, width, shape, and the angle of erection. In fact, some men confided that they couldn't imagine any man who had not mentally compared his penis, at least in its flaccid state, with his peers. Adolescent group masturbatory experiences, school locker rooms and showers as well as public bathrooms gave men ample opportunity to see the genitals of other men. Charles, age forty-five, was a former athlete who says it was reassuring to see what many other penises looked like:

> I spent so much time in the goddamn locker room that I learned there was a huge variety among men's penises. Some of them were a lot bigger than others. But most people had penises that looked like mine, so that was reassuring.

Erik, age forty-four, said, "For years and years, I was sure my penis was too small and too short." He felt better when he measured it. "I read books that said the average penis is so many inches long, and then got out a ruler and found, sure enough, I was average. Still, knowing it intellectually and accepting it emotionally was another matter. As he explained:

> Resolving this issue took time and some understanding partners. At one point I made comments like, "Gee, I've always thought my penis was too small." Getting the opposite reac-

tions, and then, recently, a spontaneous compliment—"You have a beautiful penis!"—really took care of an awful lot of anxiety.

The major reason most men worried about penis size was their fear of being too small to satisfy their partner. The impression given by pornographic movie stars is that only a penis sufficiently large to carry around in a wheelbarrow can please a woman. Men often conclude that the bigger the penis, the better the lover. And therefore men who believe this often think of the average penis as being too small.

Wayne, age twenty-three, came away with more confidence from a college class in sexuality which taught him, "It's not the size of the wand, it's the magic of the performance." Prior to the class, he says, he believed that "the bigger you were, the more manly you were—the more able you were to satisfy women." However, he started hearing women in his class say, "I don't like them big ones —you know, they choke ya up!" "The sexuality class," Wayne says, "has definitely been a plus to my sex life. It's cleared up a lot of myths." Through courses in school, reading, or discussions with their partners, most men recognized how unwarranted their concern was. They began to understand the importance of the clitoris in most women's sexual satisfaction and how little the size of their penis has to do with satisfying a partner. According to Barry McCarthy, author of *What You (Still) Don't Know About Male Sexuality*:

> The vagina is an extremely elastic organ that adjusts to the penis almost immediately, whether it is large or small. The idea of sexual incompatibility based on the size of a couple's sexual organs is, perhaps with extremely rare exceptions, a myth. Because of the distensible nature of the vagina, virtually any man and woman should be well suited, at least physically, to give each other pleasure.[1]

And although some women do prefer larger-than-average penises, other women express a preference for a smaller penis. In fact, the one hundred and twenty women we interviewed for *Shared Intimacies* cited love, comfort, familiarity, trust, variety, playfulness, and a partner's physical and emotional attraction as the qualities they considered important to a good sexual experience. Not one woman mentioned penis size.

Along with penis-size preoccupations, men had other concerns about their physical attributes. They worried about being physically attractive enough, about their waistlines bulging or their hair thinning. But mostly, men worried about their performance and not measuring up to macho male expectations. The worst fear of all was that they wouldn't be able to "get it up." As long as they could get an erection and have intercourse, at least the sexual event could be considered a success. Without one, they felt like failures as sexual partners and as men. Consequently, many men looked at the inability to achieve an erection as a major catastrophe.

Verner, a forty-year-old screenwriter who is separated, describes it as a "kind of sickening feeling":

> There is a sort of mini-second of silence—no erection—and you think, "Aw shit." You say to yourself, "Uh-oh," and you know it's going to happen. Then you usually think yourself into it. At that point, you can either relax and initiate masturbation, or try another kind of sexual business in hope of getting it back.

But the most common reaction Verner has is to "really panic":

> It's like being back in grade school. Your pants are over the chair, and you feel like you forgot your book, and you want to be back home with your mother. But all that's there is you and your limp dick.

Having erection problems or ejaculating prematurely tended to be more common during the first few sexual encounters with a new partner than with later experiences. It is during this stage of a relationship, before a sense of trust and comfort have been built, that performance anxiety runs high. Without the trust, men feared being ridiculed or rejected when their performance was not up to par.

"The fear lurking in every dark alley of male consciousness in respect to a failed performance," Verner says,

> is being with an angry woman who says something like, "Why did you fool around if you didn't want to fuck me?" Great men like Zeus himself had to limp across continents as a result of that sort of remark from some bimbo.

According to sex therapist Barry McCarthy, "the worst fear I've seen in men has been the fear of humiliation by the woman. This fear of being humiliated is more prevalent than the fear of a non-functioning penis." He told us of one client who had a horrible experience with a woman:

He was having trouble, and her response was, "Damn it, lay back. I'm going to make sure you get an erection." She really focused on the guy's penis and pushed him to get an erection. After she stimulated him as hard as she could and he still didn't get an erection, she threw his penis down and said, "You're absolutely hopeless. I don't know why you get up in the morning. I don't know why you live."

McCarthy said, "I think this story represents the ultimate humiliation for men. Even though I don't think it happens much in reality, it's a real fear."

However, the men we interviewed said that by and large women didn't have this reaction when erection problems occurred. Alan, for example, says most of the women he's been with don't consider lack of erection a failure:

They think it's great if you get hard, but it's not a disaster if you don't. These women care more about being close and don't believe fooling around always has to end in screwing. But I have a hard time accepting that, since I wasn't programmed that way.

Even if most women don't feel that way, men still worry that they do. And while one would have thought that the sexual revolution would have lifted some of the pressure off men to obtain an erection and to perform, this seems not to be the case. According to sex therapist Bernie Zilbergeld, men still feel pressure to perform, and:

The pressure's gotten greater. Even though men are more liberated and understand the importance of clitoral stimulation, they still feel they have to satisfy women in the old way— through intercourse. Sure, men are smarter than they used to be. For instance, it's rare to run into a man now who doesn't know what a clitoris is, or where to find one or what it's for.

But it's still not enough for a Real Man. He still assumes that even if she has orgasms that way, and even if she looks pleased, they still have to go on and have intercourse. Somehow the news about the clitoral stuff does not liberate the man to feel free not to have an erection.

In addition, many men assume it's their responsibility to bring their partner to orgasm. Again, Verner says it well:

"Can I make her come?" is right up there in importance with "Can I get it up?" Even though I've learned as I've gotten older that a woman's orgasm depends on a number of things that don't necessarily have to do with my performance or her enjoyment, I'm still preoccupied with the same old bullshit, which is: If you can't make her come, you're no good. Or else she's no good. I think in most men's minds there's always the question "Did I get her off or not?" It always feels better knowing that she did come—not necessarily because you're so interested in giving her pleasure, but because being able to make her come belongs on the checklist of being a good lover. Men have been indoctrinated to believe they're not so hot in bed if they can't get a woman off.

Wondering whether they're "hot in bed" comes up for men more often today than ever before. Since many women are as sexually active as men, or at least have had more than one lover, men sometimes encounter women who are even more experienced than they are. This disparity can be a source of anxiety. Many men fear they won't measure up to the performance set by a partner's former lover. This was true for twenty-year-old Peter, who is married to an older, more experienced partner. Peter told us he worries about his adequacy as a lover:

I feel a certain need to measure up to all of the people she's had past relationships with. There's a certain sense of competition with some nameless, faceless people. I feel in some ways like a novice, being married to somebody with experience. This is a society where men—not women—are supposed to be the experts. In my case, the roles are reversed.

With all these concerns, fears, and anxieties to perform well and please their partners, men found they could lose sight of their own enjoyment of the sexual act. In the words of Lee, a sixty-two-year-old consultant: "If I'm concerned about whether I'm doing all right or whether she is enjoying it, then somehow what is happening with me sexually seems to get submerged." As a man loses touch with his own involvement, the fears that preoccupy him often end up causing the very sexual problem he dreads. The anxieties themselves are powerful enough to keep him from attaining an erection, to cause him to lose it immediately, to ejaculate more rapidly than he would like, or to prevent his ability to ejaculate at all. This preys on his mind and generates anxiety over past "failures," which can spill over into the next sexual experience and cause the problem to recur. With a few such experiences in succession, the man may soon find himself with a full-blown sexual problem.

ERECTION PROBLEMS

The overwhelming majority of the men we interviewed had experienced problems with erection at some point in their sexual career. Most, however, had found the difficulty to be temporary. And, in fact, research shows that 90 percent of all males by age forty have experienced at least one episode of temporary erectile problems.[2] Although procreation is a survival need for the species, it is not necessary for the survival of the individual. Consequently, many things can interfere with the sexual arousal process in which sexual excitement causes the spongy tissues in the penis to become engorged with blood, resulting in erection.

This process slows down with age, resulting in erections that may be less firm (one fifty-nine-year-old man called it the "bend-in-the-middle" syndrome), and many men, both young and old, find that their erections wax and wane during sex.

However, the brain and not the penis is the most powerful actor in the sexual arousal process. Concern about appearance, performance, or a partner's response or approval, as mentioned earlier, can all cause the loss of erection. And, as thirty-eight-year-old Alan describes it, the result can be devastating to one's self-esteem:

I used to do an absolute number on myself when I couldn't get it up. It was as if my whole self-image, my sense of myself as a man, was completely tied up with getting an erection. So when my machine didn't work, my reaction was, "Oh, my God, I'm just not fit to function anymore."

In addition to the common fears and anxieties that affect most men, other, less pervasive, but equally devastating factors can inhibit erection. Stress and fatigue, lack of sleep, job obligations, and family pressures can all take their toll on the erection process. Even seemingly harmless medications can get in the way. Don, age sixty-eight, says that on the infrequent occasions he's taken a sleeping pill, "I notice for a couple of days afterwards that I'm relatively impotent. Obviously it stays in my system."

Alcohol also takes its toll. Men familiar with the dampening effect of alcohol on their sexual performance are careful to monitor their intake. Refraining from drinking is how Greg, age fifty-three and divorced, says he readies himself for a "performance." And if he doesn't feel up to par, "sometimes simply because of the fear of not making it," he says he'll withdraw from the sexual scene altogether so as not to be "mentally trapped into a psychological state of impotence."

Not feeling good about yourself often interferes with sexual expression as well. Says one man:

If I'm feeling lousy about myself, whether due to career, flu, or whatever, then nothing is going to help. Once I even went to a doctor and had a couple of shots of testosterone. He laughed at me and said, "You know goddamned well this isn't the problem," and I said, "Yeah, I do, but let's give it a try." All along I knew it was not a physical thing, so I just had to wait for the stress to lift and the difficulty to pass.

A number of men mentioned periods in their lives during which anxiety and guilt, particularly when caused by extramarital affairs, resulted in problems. Some men lost their erections after learning their wives were having affairs. A sense of emasculation and anger —as well as other powerful emotions—also inhibited erections. For example, one man reported: "There was a period in my marriage when I was confronted with some old affairs my wife had had and my reaction was to have difficulty in getting it up. This was a real devastating experience for me."

Other men often lost their erections when they tried to seduce a woman who didn't really turn them on. One man said:

Some guys think of themselves as always being ready for sex. They think all they have to do is snap their fingers and their penises will stand at attention. It took me awhile to learn that there are times when I am not in the mood for sex, and, more importantly, there are some women for whom I do not feel anything sexually—there is just no sexual mix. When a woman doesn't turn me on or I am not really in the mood for sex, the result is a flaccid penis and a very disinterested guy.

On the other hand, some men said getting an erection was difficult if they were *too* turned on. For instance, one man said, "Sometimes I just want it so bad that I can't get it up." Roger, a thirty-eight-year-old lawyer, had this happen to him when he first met the woman who eventually became his wife:

It was mystical when we met; we were so close. And yet I experienced an episode of impotence for about six weeks. I just couldn't make love with her. I couldn't get it up for anything. It was terribly embarrassing. But she proved herself to me through that experience since she didn't let it bother her at all. I shouldn't say "at all." It bothered her, but it wasn't as if she threw up her hands and said, "This isn't going to work; let's cut this relationship off." Throughout the six weeks of no sex, we went through the agony of trying with nothing happening. And we kept on trying and had faith that someday this was going to get better. And it did.

Some men had no trouble achieving an erection but had difficulty maintaining it—especially in situations where they felt particularly vulnerable. This was a fairly pervasive problem for men whose relationships had recently broken up and who once again found themselves back in the singles circuit, especially when former sexual relationships had been fraught with difficulties.

These men handled their erection problems in various ways. Only a minority sought therapy. Some men who experienced difficulty getting an erection with a new partner after a recent separation waited to have sex until they were in a relationship that was emotionally comfortable. This happened to Wyatt, who was six months divorced from his second wife at the time of our interview. Following the breakup of his first marriage of twenty-three years, he couldn't get an erection when he resumed dating again. Even though he was divorced, he says, "Mentally I was still with my wife. That piece of paper said, 'divorce,' and gave me the permission to be sexual with another woman, but looking back on it, I realize I felt guilty and thought it was taboo." His cure came when he met a woman he felt really comfortable with. "Bang! I was back," he remembers; "we made love and it was just like it had always been." George was in a similar predicament, but he dealt with the problem differently. His solution was to have sex with people who weren't important to him:

> After we split, I was sort of numb. When I finally got into a relationship after being freed of the encumbrance of the previous one, I found that I was not only out of practice, but incapable as well. That was horrifying. So to regain my fallen stature, I went through relationships with people who were not important to me. After a while and a number of successes, I got more selective and began to choose the kind of people that might be potential mates, because I was interested in a long-term relationship again.

The men we interviewed were almost unanimous in their feeling that the worst response to a flaccid penis was to "clutch" or "freak out." The best thing they could do was to try to relax, remembering that if it was erect before, it would be erect again—perhaps even later that same day. Roy, a sixty-one-year-old retired lawyer married for the third time, advises:

> If I start feeling a little bit uncertain of myself, and not very good because I'd lost my hard-on, then we talk about it. The way I try to handle those situations is to just have some faith that tomorrow morning or the next day or two hours later, my erection will come back. I don't freak. If it doesn't work, I just let it go. It works afterwards, maybe even right afterwards. Maybe we'll be listening to music and I'll touch her hand, and we'll start hanging on to each other, and suddenly I'll find myself ready to roll. Maybe it will be half an hour later—after whatever was in the way is out of the way. Other times it

might take longer. I might be tired. It helps, of course, to have a good relationship with somebody who's honest. That way, if I'm not really into it at the time, I don't have to perform. I can just let it go for a while.

If an erection isn't forthcoming, most men suggested carrying on with "lovemaking as usual," rather than dwelling on what was not happening "down there." For example, following surgery that seriously impaired his erections, one man was delighted to discover the pleasures of non-intercourse sex. He enthused over "the marvels of touching, hugging, and sensuality which can be so exhilarating because it can continue for so much longer than simply sexual intercourse."

Some men found that when they distracted themselves from their inability to get an erection by getting involved in non-intercourse sex, their erection would suddenly return. Young, a twenty-four-year-old medical student, says he realized that anxiety causes him to lose his erection. His "defense mechanism" when he becomes anxious, he says, is to:

Try to satisfy the woman orally or manually. I can rationalize by saying, "It's nice having erections, but actually the woman can have just as much pleasure without my having an erection!" And what would quite often happen is just when she was about to come, I would start getting an erection. So to solve the problem of no erections, I concentrate on the woman.

Whether they felt anxious or uncomfortable, had too much to drink, or for some other reason weren't getting an erection, the men we interviewed felt it was helpful, if not essential, to discuss it with their partner. Jack, a thirty-eight-year-old engineer married fifteen years, said:

If I'm not there sexually, I tell her, "Look, I'm just not with it." Either I'm not feeling well, not getting into it, or I can't concentrate or something. But I tell the lady straight out that I just can't perform. This is quite a change from five or ten years ago when, if things weren't going right, I blamed myself. Since then, I've realized that lots of things can go wrong in sex and you just have to accept it and deal with it. So now I try to communicate about it right on the spot. She takes it pretty well, too. I think the woman appreciates knowing what's going on when things aren't working rather than have you roll over and mope and groan about it without saying anything. I think that's probably the worst thing you can do. It's better to have it all out on the table.

These men recognized that they weren't the only ones with feelings, and that if they felt inadequate or humiliated because they couldn't get an erection it was also possible their partners were feeling undesirable and in some way to blame. One man described how he reassured his partner in such a case:

It was the first time I'd ever slept with this woman. Earlier in the evening, we had gone out to dinner with another couple and had a lot to drink, so later on I couldn't get an erection. She asked me why and I told her it was because of the alcohol. She said, "No, that's not true, it must be me." And I said, "Believe me, it's very normal, and it's nothing to worry about. I like you and I find you very appealing. It has nothing to do with you—it has to do with me." I tried to explain that it was not a fault of hers and not really a fault of mine either, it was just normal. And that's the important information that needs to be transmitted—that it's normal, that it's not anybody's fault, and that it's certainly not an irreparable situation or one that will continue.

Assuring your partner when difficulties arise goes a long way toward resolving them. Letting her know that your lack of erection doesn't mean you're not interested or that you don't want to continue being physical helps tremendously. But this kind of rapport and good communication take time to develop. When there hasn't been much time together and problems arise, Jerry, a scientist, suggests:

Maintain a sense of warmth and closeness. Hold your partner close and just touch each other. Try to make her feel relaxed, and then try to relax yourself. Let her know you're concerned, but not too concerned. If the problem is a flaccid penis, convey the idea that it doesn't usually happen, but occasionally it does. Remind her that it takes awhile to build a good sexual relationship. The solution is to try to stay together and work on it.

"But don't deliver this little talk in a deadly serious tone," warned Erik, age forty-four,

If there's trust to begin with, throw in some humor and—who knows?—maybe the erection will return. If I can trust that my partner will not ridicule me, but rather laugh and play with me, my trust level and self-confidence goes up. Then everything works out better.

Developing a rapport meant that if a sexual problem came up, these men would not have to assume the exclusive responsibility for figuring out a solution. They wanted to be able to count on their lovers or spouses for help. For instance, Verner says:

I would rather not have to come right out and ask a woman, "Could you blow me for a while?" To be so direct is embarrassing. And I think if she's tuned in to me at all, she will know that and help me out. I really appreciate a woman who takes some initiative. When a woman says to me, "Let me fix you up, let me do something for you," that is the sweetest nectar possible. My initial reaction is to think, "Naw, it won't do any good," but the fact is, I always seem to get right back into it.

Spike, on the other hand, cautioned us about the opposite response—women who, in their anxiety, try too hard to revive a flagging erection and, in the process, create even more pressure to perform. "I think if women would downplay the importance of erection problems," Spike says, "I'd be more comfortable and the erection would come naturally. Rather than stroking or sucking me harder, a woman who can just help me relax makes things much easier."

And some men felt that in situations where they weren't interested in sex, either because they were overly tired or just not in the mood, it was important to say no. Even though they found it difficult to tell an available, ready, and willing partner that they weren't in the mood for sex at the moment, when they listened to themselves and responded to what their body was telling them, the sexual experience generally turned out well. In sexuality workshops participants are asked to recount experiences that turned out poorly. Then they are instructed to replay the experience in fantasy so that it turns out positively. Almost everyone who carries out the exercise agrees that at the point when the situation started going sour, rather than having sex, they would either have talked about the difficulty with their partner or suggested that they not make love. Sometimes saying no is not turning down an opportunity but, instead, is avoiding the potential disaster of a dead-end experience.

RAPID EJACULATION

When men we interviewed talked about the types of sexual problems they had experienced in their lives, the most common of all was ejaculating more rapidly than they would have liked. And if this wasn't a current problem, it was one that had occurred at some point in almost every man's sexual history. However, the definition of rapid or premature ejaculation differed from man to man. Some men felt they had a problem if they lost control and ejaculated before they wanted to—regardless of how long they had lasted. Others considered their response premature if they could not prevent themselves from ejaculating before a certain fixed number of minutes had passed. Still others defined the problem according to whether their partner reached orgasm before they did. If she had not climaxed, they felt they had not lasted long enough.

Men cited a number of reasons for their difficulty in controlling ejaculation. The most common reason, particularly for men who experienced this problem when they first started having sex, was that they had become conditioned through their masturbatory patterns to ejaculate quickly.

Vince, a thirty-seven-year-old therapist, says that as a younger man, he had problems with premature ejaculation:

I think most people did. That's what the statistics say that I've read. I also think the fact that men masturbate really reinforces the probability that they're going to be premature ejaculators with their partners because, when they masturbate, the focus is usually totally on their penis and getting off quickly so they don't get caught. And, typically, if you're not masturbating in the bathroom, you're doing it in bed, or in another room; and if you live with someone, you're afraid they'll catch you masturbating. So you want to do it fairly rapidly. Most of the time you masturbate, it takes less than a minute—so you go from an erection to orgasm real, real quickly.

Men also learned to ejaculate quickly to avoid being caught making love with a girl in the back seat of a car or at home before parents returned or woke up. Men who visited prostitutes often experienced pressure to "make it quick" so the women could move on to their next trick. While these youthful experiences caused a number of men to ejaculate too quickly, other factors also triggered the problem. Men who developed the problem later in life named performance anxiety as the real culprit. This anxiety often cropped up particularly with a new partner. Jerry, a thirty-two-year-old single scientist, describes why it is difficult for him to control his ejaculation when he first has sex with a new woman:

You're trying to prove you're a good lover so you tend to think too much about trying to satisfy the woman and often, because of that, ejaculate prematurely. But as the relationship matures, the problem seems to go away. The anxiety goes away. You're not out to prove anything anymore. It's obvious that you're going to be together. Once again, the burden is off you to make the woman happy.

Some men said the strangeness of a new experience was likely to generate some intense emotions and therefore could lead them to ejaculate prematurely. Others said it might happen if they didn't feel anything for the woman. For instance, fifty-year-old Nicholas recalls, "I was a premature ejaculator only with women for whom I didn't feel any love. But it wasn't a problem when I went with women I really felt good about, for whom I felt very tender and deep feelings. So my rule became 'Don't mess with women you don't feel love for.'"

Those men involved in ongoing relationships said rapid ejaculation was a signal to them that something was amiss. Some said they ejaculated rapidly because their partner was not interested and wanted sex to be over quickly. Erik, age forty-four, says, "I ejaculated prematurely because my wife would indicate either verbally or physically to hurry up and get this over with. So I did hurry up for many years and that caused me a lot of anguish." Other men, dissatisfied with their relationships, came quickly because they were expressing their sense of frustration and anger through sex. Spike, a thirty-one-year-old investment counselor, says:

> If I have problems with an ejaculation there is usually some difficulty in the relationship and I am mentally blocked. Sometimes I'll have a hard time getting an erection, and then when I finally have it, I'll have an ejaculation right away. When that happens, it's really frustrating because I know something is fucked up with the relationship.

An extended period without sex also caused some men to ejaculate too rapidly. Spike adds that if he hasn't had sex for a couple of weeks, "I'm less able to control my ejaculation. But if I have it every day for a month, there's no problem at all." Paxton, age thirty-three and married eleven years, has the same problem if he and his wife haven't had sex for a while. However, for him, this sexual abstinence indicates that something else is going wrong. Says Paxton:

> It's been during our bad times that I have had problems with premature ejaculation. Three weeks would go by without sex and then, oh my God, I'd be premature to the point where I would come just at the time of penetration. This problem occurred when there would be withholding on her part, or teasing in the initiating of sex, or when I was expressing anger through our sexual relationship. However, our bodies work well for us when our heads are at least halfway together.

It was rare for the men we interviewed to seek professional help in solving their problem of rapid ejaculation. One who did see a psychotherapist felt the therapy was useful in reversing the problem. But most of the men who solved the problem did so alone. Some men, like Gary, age thirty-one, just gave up trying to change things and waited until the problem resolved itself: "I really tried to make it work, to get it to change. Then I just kind of gave up and said, 'Well, it'll change someday.' And it did—when I stopped worrying about it so much."

Similarly, twenty-four-year-old Young decided not to worry about his own responses and instead concentrated on pleasing his partner. Once she was satisfied, he figured it didn't make any difference if he came quickly. In addition, he was often able to regain his erection and have intercourse again. And the second time he was able to last longer.

Men who were unable to regain their erection after ejaculation suggested other alternatives. They tried to hold back their orgasm by concentrating on stimulating their partner manually or orally. They also avoided or minimized forms of sexual stimulation that entailed direct contact with their penis. And when they did have intercourse, they preferred a position other than the man on top, since this position was generally agreed to be the most difficult one for controlling ejaculation.

Others recommended keeping up an active sex life as a way to maintain better control of ejaculation. Spike suggested: "The more often I have sex with a woman, the easier it gets to know my own abilities and know when I'm going to come and how to stop it. Practice makes perfect."

Yet all men can't practice as often as they wish. Consequently, many men developed techniques—some psychological, others physical—to delay their ejaculation during lovemaking.

John, who is thirty-seven and divorced, says he prefers to concentrate on something other than the immediate sexual experience. While some people have advocated counting backward from one hundred or counting sheep or thinking about other things, John says:

What works for me is to get my thoughts off the physical feeling of penetration. I concentrate on something other than my partner and the sexual experience, like the pillow or something.

When Paul feels he's on the brink of coming, he stops and relaxes:

I relax from the hips down, physically, simply by willing myself to do it. I relax all my nerves. I just simply let go of the physical feeling. So it's a mental decision and then it's a physical letting go that slows down the orgasm.

Although quite a number of men used mental gymnastics to control ejaculation, many found this method less than adequate. Not only was it unreliable, but it also interfered with their pleasure.

Jason, a thirty-six-year-old married communications consultant, says:

> I know the old joke is that you're supposed to think about baseball or something. Well, that's what I did. I would think about something that would be totally irrelevant, something about business, but nothing having to do with the sexual act. And it worked to a certain extent. But I began to realize that was sort of cheating myself because I was really not enjoying sex as much. I was thinking about controlling the ejaculation, and thinking about something else—baseball or whatever—as well as what I was doing sexually, so I had three things to think about and that was really a waste of energy. Why bother stopping something if it becomes such an effort that it takes your mind off the ultimate pleasure you're trying to achieve?

Vince, age thirty-seven, says one problem in trying to develop ejaculatory control by shutting your mind off is that you might develop erection problems in the process. The reason, he explains, is:

> If you're thinking about your mother-in-law, you're not thinking about sexual feelings and sensations, and I think what's likely to happen is that your erection is going to start rebelling, it's going to go down. And that isn't the reason for ejaculatory control anyway. For me, ejaculatory control means being aroused *and* having control, *not* failing to be aroused but having control.

Vince's solution is to change the physical stimulation, and "use different intercourse positions and different intercourse thrustings," rather than turn off the sexual feelings. And the majority of men we interviewed agreed with this. For example, Ron, who is twenty-four, describes his method of postponing orgasm:

> As I'm coming close to an orgasm, I can sense that if we continue this rhythm for three or five more strokes I'm going to come if I don't change my position. What I usually do is slow down or change rhythm or change position. I sort of hold it, and then once I've lost the urgent feeling, I start again.

Other men would contract their pelvic muscles—the same muscles they used to stop the flow of urine—as they got close to orgasm. Besides contracting these muscles, changing positions or rhythms during intercourse were also suggested as well as practicing the stop/start technique during masturbation—as described in Chapter Four—to learn ejaculatory control.

Whether they were stopping or changing positions, most men agreed it helped to communicate what was going on to their partner. That way, she would know when to reduce the stimulation. Charles, age forty-five, describes how he communicates this message to his partner during lovemaking:

> I might put my hand on her stomach or something to get her to stop if she is writhing underneath me. Because, even if I stop, if she continues her motion quite independently, it will end it anyway. That's why it is good to know a woman very well. Then you can touch her in a certain way and she knows that means, "I'm slowing down, you've got to slow down too."

To reach that level of communication, however, the subject had to be approached at some point in the relationship. And talking about something even hinting of sexual inadequacy was difficult for most men. The problem was circular: men didn't want to have to deal with rapid ejaculation in the first place, and they figured if they didn't worry about it or bring attention to it, it would just go away. And while this worked in a few cases, most men found that their sexual problem didn't disappear unless they felt comfortable and secure enough with a partner to discuss it. Erik, a forty-four-year-old administrator, says he brought the subject up with a number of partners before he found one he was really comfortable with:

> I would tell them, "I'm probably going to come pretty quickly, and that doesn't mean it's over. Don't you worry about it; it's my problem!" And one time I happened to find a woman who was willing to talk with me about it. And then it was no longer of concern. For the first time, I could really play around and be relaxed about sex. It was a matter of relaxing and withdrawing and talking for a while. That's really what resolved it.

DIFFICULTY EJACULATING

Not being able to ejaculate was another sexual problem mentioned by the men we interviewed. It was much less common, however, than difficulties with attaining an erection or controlling ejaculation. Unlike the women we interviewed for *Shared Intimacies* who frequently spoke of periods in their lives when they had problems attaining orgasm, most men we talked to said orgasm came easily for them. Most who said they had difficulty were actually referring to lovemaking where they had already ejaculated and were having a problem reaching orgasm yet another time.

Those men who really did have problems reaching orgasm often found it difficult to ejaculate because they were so caught up in the mechanics of pleasing their partner that they couldn't really concentrate on enjoying themselves. Nathaniel, a twenty-nine-year-old poet, says he didn't have sex until he went to college, and then he experienced problems. The reason he couldn't ejaculate even when he had an erection for a long time was that he was "always thinking, always studying the other's reactions, seeing how they would respond." The result, Nathaniel continues, was that "a woman would come and I would still have an erection, because my mind was still going. I was still thinking."

With older men, those over their sixties, it is fairly common not to have an orgasm each time they have sex. The refractory period—the time it takes following one orgasm before another is possible—lengthens as a man gets older. Sometimes it takes a full day or even two or three before he can ejaculate again. And sometimes different types of stimulation must be applied simultaneously for him to reach orgasm. For example, if he is having intercourse, he might also need to have his partner kiss his ears and fondle his testicles. Sex therapists call this technique "flooding"—the man is flooded with different kinds of stimulation at the same time, the cumulation of which is sufficient to bring about orgasm.

Men who need this kind of intense stimulation often find it difficult to ask their partners for it, especially in the early stages of a relationship. With communication being so difficult, men who had a problem reaching orgasm sometimes dealt with it by faking.

Men faked orgasm for various reasons. Some were just tired and

wanted to go to sleep. Others, certain they wouldn't have an orgasm, wanted to get it over with. But for the most part, a man
faked orgasm to protect his partner from feeling she hadn't satisfied
him or to protect himself from feeling sexually inadequate. And if
the sexual experience had been fun, some men said that faking was
the easiest way to have it end on a positive note. Edmund, a forty-
seven-year-old minister, explains why he has faked orgasm:

> I knew that I could pump away for the next four hours and I
> wasn't going to come again. I was just going to get all sore.
> And also, I wasn't sure whether we were doing this for my
> benefit or hers. I think the times that I've faked, it would come
> under the heading of being a good sport.

Although twenty-four-year-old Rob didn't resort to faking orgasm, he did experience a recurring problem with retarded ejaculation after two unwanted pregnancies—one where the woman had
the child and gave it up for adoption and the second where she decided to have an abortion without consulting him, and then broke
up with him:

> So my associations have been: first, pregnancy, child, breakup,
> never seeing the child, never knowing who adopted the child;
> and second, being very much in love with a woman and her
> having an abortion and me being thrown out. These two expe-
> riences led to an incredible amount of fear. Then I got in-
> volved with a woman who used an IUD, and at first I was hesi-
> tant. It was hard for me to ejaculate at all because of this fear
> that maybe she wasn't using birth control. And when I finally
> realized that the next month she didn't get pregnant, and the
> following month she didn't get pregnant—that it really worked
> —it just melted this whole part of me that had been frozen. To
> realize that letting it out wasn't going to cause any bad reper-
> cussions was so freeing. And having orgasms with her was just
> incredibly satisfying.

CONTRACEPTION

Feeling secure that sex wouldn't result in unwanted pregnancy
was important for most men we interviewed. When we asked about

contraception, however, the men were split between those who continued to feel that the responsibility for contraception rightfully belonged to the woman and those who took an active role in preventing pregnancy—by either asking if their partner used some form of contraception or taking responsibility for it themselves by using a condom, inserting a diaphragm, or even going all the way and obtaining a vasectomy. Alan, who is thirty-eight and separated, says:

> Birth control for me has always been a female problem. This is one of the few subjects on which I'm a chauvinist.

And some men, like Bruce, age fifty-two and divorced, preferred to avoid the issue: "Sometimes you throw caution to the wind and gamble."

Some men said they didn't like to ask because they did not want to invade their partner's privacy. Twenty-eight-year-old Joshua says he used to ask women whether birth control was a problem and received mixed reactions:

> I would usually ask after it became clear that we were going to have sex. If there was no birth control available, then we would have oral sex or eventually masturbate or something like that. I got a number of—I can't quite call them negative—but very surprised reactions to my asking about it. I didn't know what to do with that. I know that I am less comfortable asking now than I used to be. In the past, my rule for myself was always to ask, and now my rule for myself is that I probably should ask but sometimes I don't.

"The reason for my hesitancy," Joshua explains, "has to do with an invasion of privacy. I know that that sounds very paradoxical, but if I ask, it is almost like I'm implying that she is naïve, and that I have to be responsible for her."

Other men who asked, however, said women were appreciative. Nathaniel, for instance, told us:

> I wasn't using anything, so I began to bring it up. That was good, because women said, "At least you're concerned about what will happen." It wasn't like I was taking advantage of them and didn't care.

And while contraception remains primarily the woman's responsibility, some of the men we interviewed, like twenty-four-year-old Ron, were more conscientious than their female partners:

One of my biggest fears is getting a woman pregnant, because I don't want to have a child. If I did father a child, even if the child was taken away from me, I would still feel responsible. So I'm very conscientious. First of all, I ask if she is using anything—if not, I'll use a condom. If she says yes, I'll still try to verify it. Of course, with the diaphragm or the IUD, you can usually feel it. I don't go so far as to do a pelvic exam, but I'll find some other more subtle way of checking it out.

Men agreed that the best time to ask was before beginning intercourse, but after it was perfectly clear that lovemaking would be a part of the experience. They felt that asking too early was awkward and might be assuming more than they should. Since thirty-one-year-old Billy didn't like condoms, he offered his partners a creative choice when they had no protection:

If I'm not sure, I wait until the woman gets undressed to ask, so that there's a good chance activities will continue. I might wait until the moment when I'm ready for insertion because I want the level of arousal to stay high. I will only use a rubber under very extraordinary circumstances, because it takes away sensation. So if a woman doesn't have any contraception, I'll give her a choice by saying something like "Would you rather have me come in your mouth or in your anus."

Whether or not they asked, men unanimously felt that every form of contraception was a hassle. Without a doubt, birth control pills and sterilization were considered the most trouble-free. But many men in committed relationships were concerned about the negative side effects of the pill on their partner's health. Others were unwilling to terminate their ability to father children. Some who had vasectomies experienced temporary erectile problems following the operation more because of their anxiety about how it might affect their sexuality than because of the operation itself. Men who had trained themselves to hold back their orgasm for coitus interruptus said that prolonged use of this birth control method at times made ejaculation difficult.

The potential problems caused by IUDs were considered to be worse than the pill by some physicians, and some men experienced pain during intercourse when the IUD string poked them. Condoms reduced the pleasurable sensations. One man compared the experience to "washing your feet with your socks on," while another described it as "fucking someone wearing a glove." Diaphragms, foams, and condoms all required a break in the lovemaking which was often long enough to diminish the man's level of arousal. "I've never been able to handle a rubber," complains forty-six-year-old Tim. "By the time I find it and get it on, I've lost my erection."

Bill, whose wife used a diaphragm for sixteen years, says "it was nice to get out from under it" once he had his vasectomy:

> To me, the diaphragm was a turn-off. It destroyed the spontaneity of just wanting to be together. If I said, "Let's just have sex," she'd say, "Okay, I'll get the diaphragm," and right then and there, I lost fifty percent of the interest I had, even though I knew she had to put it in. So after I got a vasectomy, it was a relief not to have to go through the same hassle. Sex itself didn't change. But psychologically it became more real, since we could spontaneously act on our feelings and didn't have to interrupt anything.

To help reduce the inconvenience, some men saw to it that the diaphragm was already next to the bed. Others preferred that their partner insert it before beginning any lovemaking. But this option raised some difficulties as well. Some women felt pressured to have sex if they were asked to wear the diaphragm beforehand. They wanted to respond to the sexual feelings that would spontaneously arise. Men who preferred women to wait to insert the diaphragm and cream until midway through the sex act, wanted to be able to have oral sex without smelling or tasting the spermicidal cream or jelly. Some even felt that putting it in midstream was part of the erotic experience of lovemaking. Edward, who has been divorced for six years, recalls a woman who made the inserting of her diaphragm part of the overall sexual experience:

> Rather than taking a break and losing the flow when she had to put in her diaphragm, she gave it to me and suggested I put

it in. I was a little intimidated at first. I'd never done it and I'd never seen it inserted before. But I realized pretty quickly that men don't come into the world knowing how diaphragms fit. She was so unhung up about it though that I quickly lost those feelings and she just showed me what to do. She got it all prepared, with the jelly and everything on it. She was an extremely sexy person and made the entire preparation of the diaphragm erotic. She told me what to do, she spread her legs and sort of guided me with her hand as I put it in. I think she positioned it herself more securely after it was in. But the sensuality was just in the air. Maybe it was the way she was sitting there with her legs spread or the general seductiveness of her movements as she was showing me how to put it in. She was talking about it as though she were talking about putting my cock in her. And I really enjoyed watching the diaphragm go in. I'd never seen that before, so it was a real turn-on for me.

For thirty-four-year-old Jeff, who had been married six years, inserting a diaphragm is no interruption in lovemaking:

I love it. I enjoy that little ritual. I'm not very good at it, but I try. I like to see her finger go in like that, and I really enjoy seeing that thing get taken inside. I don't feel put off in the least, and neither does she. I guess some people turn away to do it, but there's no reason to do it alone. It's really fun to watch.

Some men even managed to make using a condom a good experience. The men who used condoms recommended the lubricated kind, which they said didn't interfere as much with sensation. Thirty-four-year-old Jeff, for instance, says, "Condoms are pretty sexy, especially when you first put them on. They're so fucking greasy that they're great. I love to put one in my wallet and walk around knowing it's in there."

LACK OF SEXUAL DESIRE

The hassles of birth control, fear of pregnancy, as well as numerous other factors could result in a man losing his interest in sex.

However, what was considered a lack of sexual desire varied widely from man to man. It could mean anything from less desire than a partner's to less than the national average, or less than a person's expectations of a truly masculine man. However, whatever "low" meant, it could make a man feel inadequate. Even an average level of interest wasn't good enough for some men. After all, a real man isn't just average. As thirty-one-year-old Billy, an unmarried graduate student, describes it:

My normal rate seems to be about three or four times a week. But when I'm involved in a relationship, and I've been with women at times who wanted it more than that, I'd wish I could be a little bit sexier, and I'd think I would be a little bit more of a man if I could fuck every day. Although I've had streaks where it's gone twice a day for four or five days, usually the average is three or four times a week. And that's so average. Unfortunately, I have this inflated opinion of myself, so the dissonance between my desires and my expectations is painful.

Even if a man feels thoroughly satisfied with the amount of sexual contact he has, if he feels his sexual frequency is lower than an acceptable level, he may feel inadequate. Such was the case of Dean, who has been married for nine years:

We feel, as I guess probably just about every other couple in America does, that we should be doing it more often. And if two weeks go by and we haven't done it, we wonder, "What's going on?" We start to feel the tension and there's a need for discussion. At one level, that's good. But at another level, I wonder, if we had no societal performance demands on us, whether we might start having sex about once or twice a month. Left on our own, we might do other things, like masturbating, hugging, touching, kissing—other physically intimate things but not necessarily intercourse. But we might do the whole sexual number only once or twice a month because that might be our optimal number.

In fact, Dean believes that having sex less frequently could have a positive effect on his sexual relationship:

Anything you do really often becomes dull. Sometimes I feel

that maybe if we did it even less frequently, it would be that much more interesting and spontaneous and creative. There'd be more energy and more passion in it.

There can be many reasons why either or both partners have a diminished interest in sex. As with erection or ejaculation problems, a lagging sex drive is likely to stem from diverse causes, of which the most common are life stresses and time constraints. Feeling pressured by outside demands such as family obligations, financial concerns, or work-related tensions can devastate a sexual appetite. Stress must be alleviated before sexual activity can be revived. Men who recognized this gave priority to personal needs and even allowed some outside obligations to go unmet. Ned, a thirty-four-year-old graduate student, describes a time when he was under a lot of stress, and he and his partner had differing levels of libido:

I didn't want to be sexual, but my partner wanted to have sex a lot. I was under a lot of pressure from school and my internship, and she wasn't very understanding at the time. She said, "Well, whatever's causing it, I want you to change it. If that means giving up your internship and having to make it up somewhere else down the road, then do that. If that means taking fewer classes and being in school longer, then do that." And I told her it wasn't that easy, and we hassled back and forth and started doing this seesaw thing, where I'd get in a space where I didn't feel so pressured and then I'd start feeling sexual. But by then she'd have shut down, and she'd say, "Well, I'm tired of being disappointed, so I've shut down." And I'd say, "Okay," and I'd go back and shut down too. Then she'd come back and I'd say, "Well, I'm sorry, I'm shut down." This went on for months. What got me out of it was getting rid of the pressure. I stopped getting into my perfectionist stuff, my obsession that I had to read not only the books assigned, but all the ones on the recommended list as well.

For busy and involved people, handling stress is an ongoing challenge. Barry, a sixty-seven-year-old professor, shared how he dealt with this problem in his life:

When you have been a university professor for thirty years, you learn that when you go home you have to turn the switch off and forget it because the work is never finished. I always have unfinished work, so the only way I have been able to get any time to myself has been to ignore it occasionally. I just decide that I'm going to take off X number of hours or the whole day and enjoy myself. I just make the decision and do it.

If one holds to the myth that sex should be spontaneous, "spontaneous" for busy people often ends up meaning "infrequent" or "perfunctory." Men with this problem agreed that, to be satisfying, the sexual relationship often had to be scheduled just like other important aspects of their lives. Edmund, a forty-seven-year-old married minister, handled it this way:

We were talking last night about scheduling because my wife is going to go to school this fall. We realized that we schedule everything but sex. And the big objection to planning time to make love is that it's supposed to be spontaneous. You know, you're both supposed to be sitting there staring at the wall, and all of a sudden—zowie. That happens sometimes and it's really exciting. But if that's the only time you ever do it . . . Actually, even inspiration usually comes in the middle of some sort of discipline. So you're sitting there trying to write the poem, and sometimes in the process you get inspired. I don't know why spontaneity in sexuality should be any different. So we were talking last night about setting up schedules for having sex. For instance, Tuesdays would be just a God-awful day for us to attempt anything sexual, because we're going from eight in the morning until ten-thirty at night. On the other hand, Fridays are neat, because the week is over and I'm not yet under pressure for Sunday. Now when we were courting, I'd drive all the way to Kansas City and there was a lot of scheduling. Everything was arranged ahead of time, so we'd be free to make love if we wanted to. And that's all we had to do. When we got tired, we'd go to sleep. When we got hungry we'd go out and eat, and then come back and do it again. I don't think we expected married life would be like that, but observing the myth that sex should be spontaneous means less sexual intercourse, and, for that matter, other kinds of intimacy.

Not only did time have to be set aside for sex, but it had to be a priority for both people. This meant that when sexual activity began to ebb, both partners, especially the man who was expected to initiate it, had to be willing to put extra effort into regenerating it. Larry, who is thirty-eight, considers his sexual relationship with his wife of fifteen years to be a high priority. Says he:

One of us will say something to the other when we've gone through maybe a period of a week or two when we might have been fucking but haven't had the experience of really getting off in the way that we like. We'll ask whether we should cancel everything we're going to do Wednesday so that we can just be in the sun, listen to music, go rent a dirty movie, or go down and look at another vibrator. God, we wore out the old vibrator a year ago. When things are not all that turned on for the two of us, we use toys. To revive things, Sheila will dress up in black hose and a garter belt. I'll double my frequency of jerking off because I've assumed for a long time that that's a way to prime one's pump to bring that kind of sexual awareness back up.

In my relationship with Sheila, sex is usually number nine on the list of the ten most important things. But when sex is not part of our relationship, for whatever reason, it becomes damned important. It becomes number one or two. And I'll make it that important until I feel like I'm back into it and then it takes care of itself. But it takes consciously paying attention to get it there.

When outside stress or time constraints were unavoidable, men generally found that focusing on nonsexual contact was one way to get through the difficult period without hurting the relationship. "After my wife had our baby, she was sore and not interested in sex," recalls thirty-four-year-old Art. "During that time I made sure there was more touching, more hugging, more back-rubs. We maintained the intimacy more along the lines of nonsexual contact."

Diminished interest in sex frequently occurred following a fight and lasted until enough time had passed for wounds to heal. Then sexual interest regenerated itself. More commonly, however, a lack of sexual interest signaled problems in other areas of a relationship. According to sixty-two-year-old Lee, married for thirty-eight years:

Sex for us is a way of expressing and maintaining intimacy. So we just don't have sex when we're not feeling good about each other. We have to feel close with each other to have it, and we have to deal with whatever stands in the way first before we can have sex. We don't have sex to bring us together. We have sex when we're feeling together.

Like Lee, couples who experienced an undercurrent of unspoken anger, disappointment, or hurt had to resolve their nonsexual problems before they could increase their sexual activity. Some married men looked elsewhere for sex to feel better about themselves, to strike out at their partners, or to end the marriage. One man called his extramarital affair "the instrument of my deliverance" because it enabled him to get out of an unsatisfactory marriage.

Others who sought to escape problems at home by having an affair decided, when their wives found out, to use the crisis as a way of strengthening their relationship. Gene, age sixty-six, for instance, says his affair was a turning point in his marriage:

My wife found out about it, so I was caught. But maybe I really wanted to get caught. Anyway, I came home, and I sat on the side of the bed at two in the morning and said, "We can do one of two things: we can either fight about this for the rest of our lives, or we can find out why I did what I did and resolve the problem." So I took the bull right by the horns and we each went into therapy and from that time on we never had serious problems in our marriage.

After the kind of normal fights or relatively brief periods of anger or disconnection that take place in even the best of relationships, men were able to bridge the gap and resume sex relatively quickly. Gary tells how he and his wife renew closeness after an argument:

After a fight, things are very difficult because when I feel hurt I feel distant. I have to feel unguarded to enjoy sex, so sometimes we just sit down and talk or cuddle. Or sometimes we play solitaire together. That helps create a bridge between us. We feel like we're doing that together, not against each other.

Sounds weird but it works. Usually a day has to pass after a fight before that can happen. It just takes time.

Others felt that sex was a good way to resolve a fight. This was the approach used by Jeff and his girl friend, Janet:

One afternoon we had a terrible fight. Janet had had dinner with her parents, and she came over afterwards. She looked lovely, very dressed up—you know, New York chic. When she sat on the bed with me, she lifted her knee up so I could see right up her skirt, and I looked and I thought, "Oh, God, this is really a good idea." So that's what I told her. And she said, "You bet it is. We both need it. Wait till you see how good it is!" That was so nice. Especially since I was very, very worried. I thought I had really hurt her. And then she comes in looking really sexy and says, "We're going to fuck it away."

Most men reported that lagging sexual interest in a relationship usually came from their partners rather than themselves. The men complained that though their partners were responsive during sex, they did not initiate enough. The men considered this a problem because it made them feel sexually undesirable. And though they realized that often their partner's response was the result of her female role scripting, which taught her it was not ladylike to initiate sex, they still wished she would be more assertive.

Sometimes what seems like a lack of interest on one partner's part is really a different level of interest between the partners. One partner may simply have a consistently higher sex drive than the other, or, during a specific period of time, one person's interest may be greater. Given that any two people are physiologically different, under varying levels of stress, and are subject to different erotic stimulation or erotic thoughts during the day, it seems only reasonable that their levels of sexual desire would not always be in sync.[3]

There are a number of things that can be done when levels of sexual interest don't mesh. Some men accepted these differences as a part of life and did not let their partner's disinterest bother them. Stanley, who had been married forty-three years, shares his perspective:

I have found that at different times in our marriage either myself or my wife was not interested in sex. And I guess when I was younger that made me angry, and my anger would last a long time. Whereas now I say, "Well, the heck with it. If that's the way it is, that's the way it is." I just forget about it. I don't carry a grudge. I learned that in the long run carrying a grudge was self-defeating.

Jim found that talking to his partner and letting her know how important sex was for him was the key:

She probably had more sexual experience than I had, but the desire wasn't there as much for her. In other words, I'd want to have it once a day, and she wanted it much less. At first when I would say that we weren't having enough, she would say, "Well, don't get on my case. I'm just not that interested. You can't make yourself be interested." So, it was a problem, but now we're moving toward a balance. I told her that sex is very important to me and suggested we try to work out some way that I don't become frustrated and she doesn't feel put upon or guilty. Now that she knows sex is a priority for me, we have begun to slowly increase our frequency. And the more we have it, the more she enjoys it. So it's become her priority too.

A number of men found that it was possible to compromise by having the more interested partner be the one who was more active sexually when sex drives were unequal. Lee, who is sixty-two and married, for instance, says if he wants to make love and his wife doesn't feel like it, they might go ahead with it anyway, with her taking a much more passive role:

I can appreciate that sometimes she's not there when I am so we have a couple of alternatives: either I masturbate myself or she stimulates me, but there's enough caring and concern for each other so that it isn't a problem if I feel horny and she doesn't.

WOMEN'S SEXUAL PROBLEMS

A lowered sexual desire on the part of women was just one of several partner-related problems that impeded men's own sexual satisfaction. Others included: lack of orgasm, inability to be penetrated, and sexual inhibition, which often included negative feelings toward oral sex.

Lack of Orgasm

While there are men whose concern over their partner's orgasm stems from the belief that her response is in some way a validation of their lovemaking skills, most of the men we interviewed were primarily interested in their partner's happiness. Gene says: "It was as important to me that she had an orgasm as it was that I had one. Keeping that in mind relieves a lot of tensions and anxieties in the relationship."

The consensus was that women took more time and more attention to reach orgasm than men did. Silas, age fifty-four, suggests:

Foreplay is crucial for having the woman enjoy sex. I think the man is excitable from the start because his organs are on the outside of his body, but the way a woman is made, she has to be brought to that point.

Also, women often required very specific, individual stimulation for reaching orgasm. For example, John, who is thirty-seven and divorced, describes some of the differences he has observed among his various partners:

One woman I was with was only able to achieve orgasm in the female superior position. The reason, as it turns out, was that she had always masturbated on the corner of her bed, and being on top was the closest position to the corner of the bed that we could get into. Eventually, once or twice, she was able to achieve orgasm in other positions, but it was so much work that it didn't seem worth it.

Another woman I dated was only able to achieve an orgasm when I was on top and deeply penetrated her, but didn't move in and out. She liked me to stimulate her clitoris by moving up and down. I was in her vagina, but what brought her to orgasm was my pubic bone rubbing against hers. Other women had other ways of reaching orgasm. One preferred the side position because I was able to achieve deeper penetration and could stimulate her manually this way.

But most women, men agreed, required a certain amount of clitoral stimulation to reach orgasm. It was clear that the sexual revolution and the women's liberation movement had made an impact: virtually all of the men we interviewed were fully aware of how important clitoral stimulation was to most women's experience of orgasm. And when men had difficulty finding a partner's clitoris, an increasing number were willing to ask rather than stick to the macho script and act omniscient.

Edgar, a twenty-seven-year-old bachelor, says it's really hard to find the clitoris on some women:

> When this happens, I just say, "I cannot find your clitoris, where is it?" I have my hand on her genitals and I say, "Which way?" And I keep going until I find it. I haven't run across a woman yet who didn't know.

Clitoral stimulation could be applied in many different ways and at different times within the sexual experience. Raymond, who is twenty-seven, says his wife needs a lot of stimulation to come to orgasm:

> Usually more than I can provide with intercourse alone. So sometimes I'll stimulate her manually while I'm inside of her. Other times I'll stimulate her until she climaxes, and then I'll come inside of her afterward. Other times I'll just arouse her, and then come inside of her before she climaxes and then continue to touch her. It's just however it works out.

Some men thought the time-consuming task of bringing their partner to orgasm was a hassle, particularly if they themselves had already come. That was Farnsworth's opinion:

> I would try to bring her to orgasm, but by that time I was finished, so I would have to masturbate her. And that got to be a drag, because, when the man's done, he's ready to go to sleep, and having to satisfy her can get to be a hassle.

Those men saw to it that their partner reached orgasm before they allowed themselves to climax. However, most of the men we interviewed agreed with Raymond that the extra effort required was "no big deal."

I know in the past, if I was with a woman who took a lot of stimulation, I felt like it was my problem—that I couldn't keep an erection long enough, or that I couldn't satisfy her. But with my wife, it's no big deal to me. I enjoy watching her climax so much. Watching her come really turns me on. So I don't mind that it takes a little extra time.

When a woman had difficulty reaching orgasm, men felt differently about whether she should fake it. Among those who say no was fifty-four-year-old Silas:

Sometimes she says, "I'm tempted to fake it because I know how important it is to you for me to climax." But I say, "No, I don't ever want us to come to that point. If you don't feel up to it, just say that." So, for instance, last night we went to the mall, and later on, as I was playing around, she said, "If you're into what I think you're into, I can't even meet you halfway tonight. I walked too much." I said, "I know that. I just came over to tell you that I love you and I just want to be tender." Had she felt good enough to go through with it, I was ready to go, but the fact that we didn't, didn't lessen my affection or feeling for her, so we just kissed and hugged and stayed in each other's arms for a while and then I rolled over on my side and went to sleep.

Spike, age thirty-one, felt differently. On occasion, he appreciates being fooled:

You never really know if a woman is faking it. Sometimes it depends on how they react after it's over. If it's, "Oh, that was great," and she seems like she's drained and really been through something, then you can tell. But it's often very difficult. I think many times women fake it more for me than for themselves, which I appreciate. I don't mind being fooled. I appreciate their trying to fool me to make me feel good.

PAINFUL SEX

Although pain during intercourse was far less prevalent a female sexual problem than lack of orgasm, it had a much more devastating impact on a man's sexual enjoyment. In some cases, the woman felt so much pain that penetration was impossible. Such situations required men to display extreme tenderness and patience. The men handled this problem in a number of ways. For example, fifteen years ago, and after a year of marriage without being able to have intercourse, Larry finally mustered up the courage to talk with his professor at the seminary school he attended about his wife's inability to be penetrated. The professor referred them to a physician who practiced his own brand of sex therapy since sex therapy, per se, was not yet popular. The therapy helped them solve their problem.

After months without intercourse, Jim says he and his girl friend worked out the problem one night by getting drunk. The intoxicating effect of the alcohol helped her relax, and with plenty of additional lubrication, he managed to slip his penis in.

Paxton, who is thirty-three and has been married for eleven years, stumbled upon a procedure to stretch the vaginal opening, which made intercourse possible. The process he used is similar to the one recommended by most sex therapists today:

> Early in our marriage—I hate to sound clinical about this—but I think she bordered at times on vaginismus. Not having any notion about sex therapy or how one should proceed, we sort of stumbled around together and worked our way through it. Sort of half-assedly we found that it worked to insert my finger in her vagina to stretch the opening. Then later inserting two fingers seemed to work. Eventually, just some holding with the penis inserted without much movement or thrusting seemed to work out okay. We discovered that the woman-on-top position worked best—so that she would feel some control over penetration. Finally it got to where she could move in ways that pleasured her and she sort of overcame that problem. But we struggled with that some in the first couple of years. I think one of the things we've always appreciated about each other is our mutual patience as we stumbled through those times where there was pain. Neither of us went nuts, or called the other one names. We just found something that worked.

It was evident that the men whose partners experienced pain with intercourse cared for their partners and their relationships far more than the sex itself. In fact, some, like sixty-seven-year-old

Barry, said that, in the greater scheme of things, intercourse was relatively unimportant. Barry wasn't completely satisfied with mutual masturbation but says it is an acceptable alternative to sex in a relationship where love and closeness are higher priorities. He describes his wife's particular problem:

> She has some kind of a cyst or a pulled muscle or something in or near her vagina that makes it extremely painful for her when I insert my penis. Doctors don't seem to be able to do anything about it, so I stopped trying and we haven't had penetrative sex for a couple of years. The way we make love is to masturbate each other. It's not unpleasant, in fact, it's very pleasant. This is going to sound like a cliché, but things become clichés because they're true. There's a difference between lust and love, and though my wife and I fight sometimes, there is love between us. We have a good relationship even though we're not having standard sex right now. We're close and tender and loving anyway. Even if we go for long periods of time with no sex, it doesn't matter a great deal. We communicate in many other ways.

Sexual Inhibition

In this culture, many women have not been taught that sex can be positive and fulfilling and, as a result, feel inhibited sexually. Men who married women from very strict backgrounds filled with negative attitudes about sex have had to be patient. Frequently it took a long period of time before they could build a truly rewarding sexual relationship with their wives.

Jonathan, a thirty-seven-year-old history professor, says his wife was brought up believing "nice girls don't," and this attitude followed her into marriage:

> I would imagine our biggest problem was the guilt associated with sexual feelings and sexual relationships. In my wife's family, having sexual intercourse before marriage was positively forbidden. Men were considered evil, dirty, awful. Sex was considered evil, dirty, nasty, and oral sex—that was the ultimate sin. You would die immediately and go to hell if you had oral sex. So our initial dating was very platonic. She did let me caress her breasts once or twice, but there was always a surge

of guilt. Afterwards she wondered whether or not she was a bad person and whether I was an evil creature because I was doing it to her. That went on for years before we got married.

To correct the problem, Jonathan says he was willing to be patient:

You can't pressure someone into overcoming or unlearning a lot of learned behaviors, thoughts, and ideas overnight. It can't be done. The only thing you'll do is just jam them or block them. They'll be unable to function. Telling them they have a problem doesn't help; they realize that. What helps is being patient and spending a lot of time with them, letting them know there isn't anything wrong with them and talking it through.

A complaint quite a number of men had was that their partner did not enjoy oral sex, especially fellatio. Says Nicholas, who is fifty and separated:

My partner has a problem about oral sex. I enjoy it and she tolerates it. She doesn't want to disappoint me, but I believe she finds fellatio and cunnilingus distasteful. But she accommodates me so I try not to press her.

Other women, however, were unwilling to accommodate their partner, and some men who wanted oral sex sought it outside their relationship. Others managed to successfully alter their partner's initial negative attitude toward oral sex. Again, patience and consideration were required. John realized it was important not to push his partner too far too fast:

The way any problem is solved is by talking about it. However, just because you communicate your feelings doesn't mean that the problem is going to go away. It took time with this particular partner who did not enjoy oral sex. Talking about it, reading about it, and letting her work at her own pace helped solve the problem. I suggested that she work her way up to feeling comfortable by caressing my body a little bit nearer to my penis each night. By the time she got comfortable caressing my chest with her mouth and had worked her way down, she was in close contact with my genitals but still not performing oral sex. That way, she felt she was in control of the situation, and when she felt comfortable doing it, she went ahead and did it. Obviously licking my chest and legs didn't bother her very much at all, and it got her closer to my penis. I think it took a week before she actually performed oral sex. I made sure I had showered and put on some cologne so there would be no objection on her part. It worked out very nicely. I found that even after she started sucking me, if I allowed her to be in control without pressing her to do it every single time we were in bed together, she became more comfortable doing it and eventually the problem went away.

Bob, fifty-two and married for twenty-six years, said what his wife needed to enjoy oral sex was encouragement and reassurance:

When I got married we were young. In the first years of marriage, I had a desire for oral sex and my wife didn't. And over the years, she gradually got to the point where she enjoyed it too, but it took a great deal of gentleness, consideration, and reassurance on my part for her to achieve that. Specifically, the way I did it was to first get her sexually aroused by fondling her breasts and manipulating her genital area with my fingers. Then I verbally encouraged her to try it. Of course I had to reassure her that nothing was wrong with oral sex. Also, she wonders whether she's doing it right. Throughout it all, I try to be encouraging and show her how much pleasure she's giving me. I think my happiness breeds a certain degree of happiness in return. There's also a sense of satisfaction and reward when I say, "That was wonderful. I feel great. You're fabulous."

Beyond the enjoyment of oral sex, some men felt it was very important for their partner to willingly allow them to ejaculate in their mouth. This, we found while interviewing for *Shared Intimacies*, was probably one of the most difficult things for many women to do. Yet men such as thirty-eight-year-old Alan said it was necessary in order to feel completely accepted:

I wish women realized how important it is to allow a guy to come in their mouth. As far as I'm concerned, being able to come in someone's mouth is a perfect ending to a beautiful experience. I just wish women were comfortable with it. If they could just swallow it, it would be great. I had to learn to like tasting a woman. I knew that oral sex was a very natural part of sex, but I had some inhibitions about it. When I was younger, I had some experiences with women where it smelled like dead fish. I didn't want to put my face down there. I thought, "You got to be nuts!" And for a long time, I didn't. When I finally got around to it, though, I found it was an enjoyable experience. I got to a point where I decided I wanted to get comfortable with it, and I did.

While a number of men we interviewed like Alan had some difficulty becoming accustomed to women's genitals, most found them to be sensual, attractive, and the source of sexual satisfaction from the beginning. Those who had to get beyond initial feelings of distaste, discomfort, or disgust had to overcome negative messages learned as children.

Wayne, a twenty-three-year-old college student, said that the first obstacle he had to get over was the message he received while growing up that blacks don't have oral sex:

I noticed that other people just come on out and say, "I have oral sex," "Yea, I eat, I eat," but blacks never say they do. So still today, I'll play that game: "No way, you'd never catch me down there." And I wouldn't do it, because I was afraid that the woman might tell and then I'd get a reputation that I eat. When I get with a lady, neither one of us wants to reveal that we do that. And I'd be kind of afraid that if I say it, she won't kiss me anymore. There's a chance that she probably would do it too, and that we both can indulge in it, but it's just like a competition—which one of us is going to let it out first. I'll say, "What do you think of oral sex?" and they'll usually say, "Euh, nah, not me." But then if they say, "What the fuck, hey? It's a way of expressing yourself," or whatever, then we usually do it. That's why, when I first meet someone, oral sex is usually out of the question.

The primary obstacles to oral sex for most men seemed to be getting used to the taste and smell. Wayne continues:

One thing that helped me with oral sex was meeting a woman

younger than me who hipped me to this: the vagina is the cleanest part of a woman's body because it was getting ready for that baby to come out. And I said, "Hey, maybe that's right." But at first I thought, "That's where they urinate, have their periods, no way I'm going down there." But when I got sexually aroused, I got just like an animal. The first time wasn't hard. I was scared of what it might taste like. I didn't know whether I was going to spit on her or if I was going to keep on with it. But it looked good and I didn't want to come up. It was all right. I liked it and I was a master at it the first time. It was just like tongue-kissing to me. But then I learned even more by being with older ladies who liked me going down on them.

Some men said they felt pressure to be proficient at oral sex right from the start, even while they were unsure of themselves. Others said they felt guilty or perverted about the act—not because of the woman's genitals, but because they felt there was something inherently unnatural about it. Edward, age thirty-five, says, "What I had to overcome was just the fear of the unfamiliar and some vague and cloudy feeling that what I was doing was not okay."

After getting used to oral sex, some said the appeal was its animalistic aspect. At least that's how Joseph, a thirty-four-year-old divorced social worker, sees it:

There was a breakthrough when I first kissed a woman's genitals. I had had an aversion to that. I thought there was something wrong with it, and felt, "Oh, I can't do that." So that first experience was another breakthrough. One of the things I like is the whole primitive part about it. I mean, God, that part of a woman is so special and so fleshy, it's great. And I like the smells, too, although I have done it a couple of times when I haven't enjoyed it as much. It's the chemistry, I guess. The good part about it is feeling like an animal in a way, the sniffing, the smelling, the slurping. You get totally into the experience. It totally encompasses your face, all your senses. That's what I like about it.

Many men considered oral sex distasteful during menstruation and some even considered intercourse unpleasant when a woman was bleeding. Recognizing how little blood there actually is—four to six tablespoons or one to three ounces throughout an entire menstrual cycle—helped some of them change their attitude. Others had their partner insert a diaphragm on days when the flow was heaviest.

Ron, a twenty-four-year-old medical student, recalls that when he was about nineteen he was confused about menstruation and therefore abstained from having sex with a woman during her period:

> When I was first starting to have sex regularly, I didn't know what was going on when women have their period. I thought they gush blood, and so during their period I didn't have sex with them. I figured if I went in there maybe I'd come out with my whole penis red and there would be blood all over the bed and stuff. I didn't know. But at some point, I noticed that there was not much blood on a tampon and I could go in there perfectly safely and just have a few spots of red. I thought, hell, there's no reason to abstain.

HEALTH PROBLEMS

The great majority of sexual problems are the result of cultural messages, which create unrealistic expectations and pressures to perform. In addition, however, sexuality can be affected by physical factors such as illnesses, infections, and accidents. Anything that alters the state of our health and our bodies naturally affects our sexuality.

With the exception of heart disease, diabetes, surgery, disabilities, and other major illnesses, men had far fewer sex-related ailments than the women interviewed for *Shared Intimacies*. Men seemed to be healthier than women in this regard, probably because their sexual "plumbing" is less complex. As opposed to menstrual and vaginal problems, pregnancy difficulties, and menopausal discomforts, men were primarily concerned with venereal disease and prostate problems.

Venereal Disease

Venereal disease—gonorrhea, syphilis, herpes, and others—was mentioned far more frequently by the men we interviewed than by the women. One reason for this may be that the women were more ashamed of having had a venereal disease and therefore omitted mentioning it. It is also possible that men are more comfortable with casual sex and so are in a position to contract a venereal disease more frequently. Most men who had had a venereal disease found the experience to be humiliating. Erik, age forty-four, once picked up molluscum, or small warts, and unknowingly transmitted them to another partner. As he said, "It was an incredible embarrassment for me to have picked up warts and then to have transferred them from one woman to another. I wanted to die because I consider myself extremely clean, so it had to do with my self-image." Alex had had similar feelings when he had a simple urinary inflammation which had the same symptoms as VD:

I was feeling terrible about myself, feeling dirty, not wanting to contaminate anybody, and I was feeling very, very asexual, which is unusual for me. I just wasn't interested in sex for a good month or two. Even when the diagnosis showed it wasn't VD, it took me awhile before I got comfortable with the notion of being sexual again. And even then I wasn't exactly opening my black book to get back on the circuit.

Men with herpes talked about feeling like untouchables and how they often went to great lengths to fabricate reasons not to be sexual rather than divulge the fact that they had herpes. One man said: "I just don't even like to mention it to a woman anymore. When I do, I feel like a leper and some women treat me like one and I just can't deal with it." Other men, while not generally comfortable telling just anybody, were conscientious about not infecting a partner when their herpes was active. This is how recently married thirty-six-year-old Jason handled the problem in the past:

Unfortunately I contracted a case of herpes several years ago and initially I went through a period of about a year and a half when it was quite active. I used to have outbreaks maybe every month and that definitely interfered with my sex life because I was very careful not to have any intercourse when it flared up. If I had an episode of herpes, I was always upfront with the woman about it. I would tell her exactly what I was going through and what she had to be concerned about and what she didn't have to be concerned about. But that didn't stop me from doing oral sex on her. And I don't think I ever found a woman who objected to it.

Many men who did not have herpes had become careful about whom they chose to sleep with. There was a growing tendency to wait until they knew a partner well enough to inquire about venereal disease before having sex with them. Erik says:

Lately I have become much more direct with a new partner and will ask, "Do you have anything?" or "Have you ever had anything?" before I have intercourse, especially with herpes being so common. I want nothing to do with that. I'd rather go home and read a good book. So now I'm more selective with partners and I wait until the second or third date before having sex.

Prostatitis

Prostatitis is another common problem which causes discomfort. The discomfort can range from a mild burning sensation upon urination to pain that makes sex virtually impossible. Prostatitis is an inflammation of the prostate gland. The prostate gland manufactures the prostatic fluid that forms the bulk of the male ejaculate. Although men of all ages can experience infections of the prostate gland, the problem is more common among younger, sexually active men where it is often acquired through sexual contact. In older men, the bacterial infection is frequently due to prostatic changes resulting from the aging process. And while all of the causes of prostatitis are not entirely clear, it can also result from an acute increase or decrease in sexual frequency. Because of the symptom of pain with urination, some men think they have VD when they have a prostate infection. For obvious reasons, the pain involved in prostatitis can lead to a lack of interest in sex or an inability to attain an erection.

Treatment for a prostate infection generally includes antibiotics and a moderate amount of ejaculating. Although initially painful, these ejaculations cleanse and filter the prostate. In addition, curtailing or eliminating the intake of alcohol, caffeine, and spicy foods is considered valuable supportive therapy. In severe cases or frequently repeated episodes, a prostate operation may be required.

The removal of the prostate cuts down severely on the amount of the ejaculate a man produces. While some men feel that this makes no difference in their enjoyment of ejaculation, others find the sensation at the moment of orgasm less pleasurable.

Medical Conditions

In general, the more serious the medical problem, the greater effect it had on the man's sexual activity. The major problems experienced by the men we interviewed included arthritis, spinal fusion, diabetes, heart attacks, and permanent disabilities, including spinal cord injuries.

Pain from medical conditions such as arthritis, and various surgeries, required men who had had these conditions to move slowly and adjust their position during lovemaking to compensate for the physical problem. As sixty-five-year-old Stanley said, "I have arthritis and it is almost impossible for me to perform the sex act if I'm lying on my right side. So I have to make sure I am lying on my left side or that I readjust my position if I feel any pain."

Chuck found that sex was possible following an operation if he was particularly careful:

I had a spinal fusion and I couldn't have sex for quite a while. I was in the hospital ten days. It was probably close to two months before I had sex. I wasn't really functioning well for a year. And then it was really difficult. I was in a metal corset, and it was really painful, and I remember lying on my back and having my wife masturbate me, and then sit on me, and it was real delicate and really painful to put any pressure on it. But we got pretty good at it. She learned how to do it on top and not jar me too much. And it worked.

Heart attacks were the most common health problem that impaired sexual activity. Even after the pain had passed, vigorous sex was impossible until sufficient healing had taken place. However, contrary to common belief, men found that they could resume a full and active sex life after healing from a coronary. What was required was building up physically to the point where they could handle the amount of physical exertion that was required for intercourse. This was done through various forms of exercise until gradually the necessary stamina was developed. Until this was achieved, most heart attack patients assumed the passive role with the woman on top. Consequently, most men with serious cardiac problems modified their lovemaking by slowing the process down and having more touching and foreplay, and less vigorous thrusting during intercourse.

But on the whole, men felt that a heart attack was no reason to put an end to sex. Says Forrest, sixty-eight, and now retired:

> The heart attack affected my sex life to the extent that at first I didn't want to have sex. I didn't want anything else except to get well because the pain was so terrible. But once I got over the pain, I got back into the natural day-to-day of living. Then I started fantasizing and wanting sex again. However, I still had this fear that something would happen to me if I had sex because my heart had been so taxed. I talked to the doctor about it and he said it was up to me to judge my own capabilities. If I thought I could do it, I was to go ahead and try it. But if I noticed anything unusual happening, I was to stop and not continue. Even now I still have some angina pain when I overdo some activity, or if I have too much stress. But I don't feel stress when I'm having sex, and I think the positions we use help—like lying on my side or having my wife sit on top of me.

Even men who were disabled and confined to a wheelchair were capable of maintaining a satisfying sex life. According to thirty-five-year-old Ben, who was injured as a young child and is paralyzed from the waist down:

> I think it's important if you have to live with a disability not to let it limit you any more than it has to. And your sexuality is something you shouldn't give up. As a kid, I got in trouble in hospitals a lot for being sexual. But nobody told me what to do with my sexual feelings and luckily I never really felt so guilty about it that I stopped being sexual. You can't stop living because you're institutionalized.

Ben says he has choices:

> Just because I'm disabled doesn't mean I don't have the same choices as other people. It's just that there might be a wheel-

chair involved, or a crutch, or somebody may have to push me up to the bed, but I can still do it. Just because I'm disabled doesn't mean I have to have less of a sex life.

However, the disabled men did mention differences between their sex lives and those of able-bodied men. Much of their sexual joy came from turning their partner on and experiencing the pleasure of satisfying her. Once they could overcome the idea that the only way to satisfy a woman was through intercourse, they realized that they could be more than adequate lovers. And even though their genitals may not have sensations, being stimulated in that area was arousing.

Ben describes his situation:

I still find myself at times fantasizing about being genital or wanting to use my genitals in some way. Even though I don't have sensations there and I don't ever remember having them, I still sometimes like to rub them or have them touched or have them kissed. I live with all of me and I like all of me and I want the person I'm with to like all of me too. It's maybe the same kind of experience as watching porno—it can be exciting for some people even though they're not directly participating. It's a turn-on all the same.

Almost all of the disabled men we interviewed were orgasmic. They had learned to eroticize different areas of their bodies and, even without an erection or an ejaculation, were capable of experiencing orgasms. One man even said his orgasms were much longer and far more intense than they had been before his injury.

Disabled men found it important to talk about their particular situation with their partners before making love. They felt it necessary to communicate their needs to assure their satisfaction and to prepare their partners for what they could expect to encounter in making love to someone with a disability. Says Blake, a thirty-eight-year-old TV producer:

I have had more sex since I was disabled than I ever had when I was not disabled. I have to start telling women what I like, because when they don't see the classic response of my cock getting hard when they stroke my chest, they start to feel insecure. Sometimes when they realize that this guy can't just climb on top of them and get off, that he needs more attention than that, they have to look at their own sexuality. So I talk to them about me. I didn't used to talk about any of it. But now, when I feel comfortable with the person, I talk about the realities of not having bowel control or bladder control and what it means to me. Making love with me is a little bit different and there are things that may need to be explained. Sometimes people are apprehensive about whether they are going to hurt me, or put me in a position that's not comfortable. I have a ureter that comes out of the skin directly from the kidneys and that has to be explained. Some people are blown away by it, which sometimes makes me a little self-conscious.

Approaching the sexual experience is a risky venture if you're disabled, according to Gilbert, a thirty-four-year-old clinical counselor. But communication helps:

I always want to be honest and tell them what lovemaking would be like with my disability and find out if they're interested in taking that risk. And if they are, I go into some of my personal cares and needs. I also ask them about their needs. For example, what do they think about oral sex? What about trying some other things? There's many ways to make a woman feel good. A lot of women don't like their breasts handled; maybe they'd rather be kissed on the neck or around the ears. So you need to check these things out before you actually get involved. Then, after we talk about these things, I enjoy myself and I think they do too. Psychologically, even if I might not have sensual feelings in a lot of places, knowing that she is happy will make me a lot happier. Also, I fantasize at the same time and that makes it even more exciting for me.

Although many men with serious medical problems that interfered with attaining an erection said an erection was not necessary for enjoyable sex, a few had a prosthesis, or artificial penile implant, and felt satisfied with it. There are many different kinds of prostheses. Some are normally flaccid but can inflate with the push of a button located in the scrotum. These are obviously complex and therefore more subject to malfunctioning. Malleable and semi-rigid prostheses are less complex as far as surgery and functioning are concerned. The malleable device can be easily positioned to the resting state so there is no noticeable permanent erection. The semirigid device leaves more of a noticeable bulge when the man is clothed. Fifty-eight-year-old Emmitt, who had a series of medical problems ranging from diabetes to heart failure, had a semirigid prosthesis. Emmitt described what the penile prosthesis has meant to him:

I couldn't find anybody to help me. I even went through self-hypnosis and biofeedback to see if the problem was mind over matter and whether relaxation would help. But it turned out that the diabetes had worked on the nerves and, of course, I had circulatory problems because of the heart disease, and gradually I lost my ability to have erections. I had been married for over twenty-five years and I was heartbroken that I couldn't do it anymore. I even told my wife to go out and find somebody else. She wouldn't hear of it. Then I found out about the penile prosthesis. It improved my sex life and my marriage. My wife started saying, "Hey, at your age, what do you think you're doing?" Actually, I think it increased our harmony at home. It's a great ego feeling, and I can go when I want to, any time, morning, noon, or night, to please my woman or please myself.

I have a rigid prosthesis, which causes some problems, because when I stand up, there's a bulge. My wife's embarrassed but it doesn't bother me a goddamn bit. I think no more of it than I do of wearing these orthopedic shoes, a hearing aid, or glasses. They're all a form of prosthesis. And I don't give it a second thought. The implant can't be too long or too thick because it can cause problems, so you lose in length and diameter —which I wasn't keen about—but I figure half a loaf is better than no loaf at all.

Men such as Emmitt, who openly talked about his prosthesis, and Brian, who discussed his performance anxiety, were initially hesitant to talk to us, but they did so because they wanted their contribution on record so other men could benefit from their experience. "I want to save some other guy the unnecessary grief I've gone through," said one man. Brian added, "Maybe if I had known earlier how other men have handled ejaculation problems, I could have recovered more quickly."

Even if the men we interviewed had problems that interfered with their sex lives—whether psychologically or physically based— they still found ways to cope. However, some disruptions to sexual activity are a normal part of the life cycle. Pregnancy, for example, can have a profound impact on a couple's sex life. And while more attention has been focused in recent years on how pregnancy can affect a woman's sex drive, little has been paid to its impact on the male libido. Even less attention has been paid to the ultimate impact pregnancy and delivery have on a couple's intimate life, which is the subject of our next chapter.

CHAPTER NINE

SEX, PREGNANCY, AND THE NEW BABY

The macho men of the past, always rational and in control, seemed to crumble, predictably, as their woman brought new life into the world. In *The Flame and the Flower*, by Kathleen Woodiwiss, the hero, Brandon, is tall, dark, handsome, worldly, arrogant, and in complete control. Yet in the following passage, which describes the birth of his son, Brandon feels helpless and overwhelmed by the mysterious world belonging exclusively to women. This man's experience of being an alien intruder during childbirth rings true for many men even today:

> [He] felt a strong need of brandy, but declined, wanting to stay and comfort his wife in any way he could. She clung to his hand tightly, seeming to want him there by her side, and he could not leave her when she was so tortured with giving his child birth.[1]

As with many men who today still feel like an intruder during childbirth, Brandon is a stranger by his wife's side and is instructed by the midwife to leave: "Master Brandon, you best let Master Jeff fix you something strong. You don't look so good." Gently but firmly guiding him to the door, she tells him: "You go and get drunk, Master Brandon. Go get drunk and don't come back until I call you. I don't want you fainting while I tend to the missus."

Until very recently, the man's role in the birth process hadn't changed much. Although the setting of childbirth moved from home to hospital, the man was still banished to a hallway, the waiting room, or a nearby pub. And as he waited, he plied himself with steady rounds of coffee or whiskey. Like our fictional hero, men today have often felt excluded from the birth of their children.

In the past, rarely did a man question his status as an outsider in childbirth. His job was to plant a hearty seed; hers was to have a receptive, nurturing womb which eventually would produce a healthy offspring. The roles of men and women were clearly delineated. Both husband and wife knew with unshakable conviction what was expected of them in the reproductive process. And each paid a price for these rigidly defined roles. The woman had to face the pain of labor and the unknown perils of childbirth alone. And the man, who had no biological function in bearing children, was assumed to have no corresponding instinctual urge to participate in the delivery. So he wore his manly mask and denied his very genuine male instinct to play a part in the birth process.

In *The Birth of a Family*, which explores new roles for fathers during childbirth, Nathan Cabot Hale recounts how left out he felt when he was prohibited from witnessing the delivery of his children:

> I felt that I was being denied something that was my right as a man and a father. I really felt a sense of loss of a very important life experience. Later, when I was finally able to witness and assist with labor and birth, I knew for sure that the feelings that I had had before were both true and natural and, what is more, necessary to my mature development. I say with full assurance that childbirth is not only the greatest human experience, but one of the finest experiences that a man and woman can share. The instinct that makes a man yearn for direct involvement with the birth of his children brings him close to the creative principles of the universe.[2]

Within the last twenty years, alternative childbirth practices in this country have emerged. Now men are not only allowed to stay with their wives during labor, but some have become an integral part of the birthing process. An entirely new philosophy and method of preparing for childbirth has increased in popularity over the last ten years, which considers pregnancy and birth as a decidedly two-person endeavor.

In the Lamaze method, the Bradley method, and others, the husband is involved as a full-fledged partner of a team, attending classes with his wife to learn breathing, relaxation, and concentration techniques to prepare for the delivery. The husband becomes his wife's coach, helping ease her through the labor and delivery. Jack, a thirty-eight-year-old engineer who has been married fifteen years, had the experience of working together with his wife when she gave birth to their second son, now ten years old:

The Lamaze training requires you to participate with your wife, so you go to the classes together and you practice the exercises together. You even go to the doctor together. You're with her in the pre-delivery room, you're with her in the delivery room, and you're with her when she's wheeled back to her bedroom afterwards. You're there with her for the whole thing. You basically share the delivery. You hold her hand. You help her push. You help her when she's hyperventilating. You wipe her face when she's sweating. You just help her all the way through. It makes you feel like you're part of the overall thing and that goes a long way to making it a lot easier for both of you.

Underlying the Lamaze philosophy is the belief that the husband is the person best able to recognize the signs when his wife isn't relaxing or concentrating. He knows her better than any health professional could. It is important for him to be nearby during labor, say supporters of the Lamaze method, because a woman often reaches a point at which she feels emotionally and physically drained; she gets discouraged and feels she can't continue. The husband steps in at this time to provide her with the emotional support she needs.

A couple who decides to adopt one of the natural childbirth methods during the birthing process adopts as well a new attitude: that the entire pregnancy is a joint venture, with both people fully and actively participating. Although the woman is still the only one who physically bears the baby, in a psychological sense, the man carries it to full term as well. Even though the natural childbearing classes don't start until the last trimester, this partnership in pregnancy is likely to begin with the decision to have a child. The husband then accompanies his wife on doctor's visits, on shopping trips for the newborn, to films and parenting seminars, and eventually to classes where he will be trained to assist her in the birth.

Based upon the interviews we've conducted, we've come to believe that this joint participation in the pregnancy not only leads to greater cooperation and investment throughout the childbearing process, but also enhances the intimacy between husband and wife. Jack continues:

My wife and I became much closer during her second pregnancy because we communicated about our feelings and concerns with each other and the doctor and other people who were going through the same experience. We'd already been through it once the old way, so we knew the negative side. The first time around, she was totally knocked out and did not experience any of the delivery at all. She was very disappointed. So when we had our second child we took a whole different tack right from the beginning. We decided we were going to enjoy this one, and it turned out we enjoyed it beyond imagination.

What made the second birth so much more satisfying, says Jack, was the sharing of responsibilities—and rewards—of both the pregnancy and delivery.

Of course, not every father we interviewed had participated in the pregnancy and delivery. Many of the younger men had, and others, like Jack, chose it the second or third time around. But some hadn't considered it at all. Therefore, in the course of our interviews, we wanted to learn if participating in the pregnancy had any effect on the sexual intimacy of these couples.

The picture of the traditional couple, according to rigid role models, portrays the man a bit overwhelmed—and turned off—by the wife's swollen condition. And who could blame him, his buddies might say, if his eye roamed and he looked for someone on the side. With nausea and physical discomfort, the nine months of pregnancy between some of these prospective parents was to be nine months of reduced sexual interaction, if not complete abstinence. And sometimes, sex remained nonexistent or at a very reduced level for months post-delivery.

However, many of the men we interviewed told us a far different story. They wanted to continue making love with their wives as long as it was physically possible and emotionally desirable for both partners. And even when the time came when they wanted or had to stop, they preferred to work within their relationships to strengthen their intimate marital bonds rather than seek fulfillment elsewhere.

GETTING PREGNANT

Although most couples conceive within six months after they stop using contraceptives, there are a substantial number of women who, a year or two later, still haven't become pregnant. With their desire for a child constantly thwarted, these couples find that their sex lives often suffer. And in order to determine which partner isn't "functioning properly," many submit to a battery of tests. The man must masturbate and send his sperm to a laboratory for immediate analysis. The woman must record her monthly ovulation cycle on a temperature chart. The clinical scrutiny of these tests not only invades the couple's privacy, but also can transform their spontaneous lovemaking into routine sex. Recreational sex and lovemaking become procreational sex—planned, programmed, and charted at every turn. Some men we interviewed recalled that this period prior to conception greatly stressed their sexual relationships. The pressure to perform was on. How deep and effectively could the virile seed be planted? And sometimes this urgency to perform produced the opposite effect: a man's penis would soften and the all-important ejaculation wouldn't even happen.

Although the performance pressure was certainly great, several of the men we interviewed were able to lessen the stress by viewing things in a more positive light. For instance, one man pointed out that because sex becomes a number one priority when trying to get pregnant, more time is often allotted for it:

It's easy to get into the habit of infrequent sex in a marriage, given conflicting or taxing work schedules and the normal aggravations of day-to-day living. But if you have a problem conceiving, at least you can turn the difficulty into an opportunity for fairly frequent sex.

"Trying to conceive becomes a mandate for having sex," says Douglas, a thirty-two-year-old lobbyist, who recently fathered a son after a long period of trying. "There was no guilt, shame, or secrecy attached to it. Everyone was encouraging us to make love." So make love they did:

> We had almost forced sex for a year and a half to two years. One time I was traveling and met Helena at the airport in Los Angeles. I commuted there from Chicago and she came from Houston. We got into a hotel room at one o'clock in the morning and had intercourse, and the next day I left to go back to Chicago. It was crazy but exciting. Furthermore, there were no headaches, no issues that were strong enough to prevent our having sex. You know that sex is going to take place and so you just try to flow with it. You feel like the whole world is patting you on the back because you're making love. Even your parents, who want grandchildren, are giving you permission to have sex.

BODY CHANGES

Shortly after a woman becomes pregnant, sex is likely to improve. Suddenly there's no more guilt, performance pressure, need for birth control, or concern about failure to conceive. Sexual relations are often freer and more spontaneous.

Douglas says:

> We had so much difficulty getting pregnant that we went through a three- to four-year ordeal of exploring the possibility of adoption. So having that business over with when she finally got pregnant was a great relief. Also, it was liberating not to have to worry about fertility or the birth control issue. Sex was just worry-free.

But the pregnancy itself brings on hormonal changes which can cause bouts of nausea, increased fatigue, and, of course, the enlargement of breasts and belly. Not only can these changes create physical discomfort and dampen sexual appetite, but they can also trigger a series of emotional and psychological doubts that can disrupt a sexual relationship. The woman may begin to worry, "Am I still sexually attractive?" "Will I have a healthy child?" And the man in turn may question, "Will I hurt the baby if we have sex?" "Can I earn enough money to support all of us?" "Am I ready to be a father?" The weight of these accumulated questions—questions which have no immediate answers—can negatively affect the couple's sexuality.

All of these stresses and anxieties, coupled with the tremendous physiological changes a woman undergoes throughout her pregnancy, can result in sweeping mood fluctuations. A basic understanding of the chemical changes a woman goes through during pregnancy is really helpful for the husband, according to Dan, a thirty-one-year-old doctor, who has two daughters under a year old. "Mood changes become more prevalent as the pregnancy advances," Dan says,

> and many times men will take these mood changes personally and feel that they're doing something wrong or that their wife doesn't love them anymore. Usually it's their wife's own insecurity or lack of self-esteem, or the common feeling that pregnant women are ugly, that are behind her feelings of depression.

He goes on to describe how these mood swings can be handled:

> With this understanding of what many women go through in a pregnancy, I found myself allowing my wife to cry or even yell at me without taking it personally. We'd talk about it and sometimes lie in bed and be close to each other. I'd let her cry, or she'd allow me to cry if I needed to. And we'd try to investigate the underlying fears, like feeling ugly or inadequate because of the pregnancy. These are feelings which many women seem to deny. Some are afraid that their husband is going to go out and cheat on them because they're not sexual enough or attractive enough. And it can become a vicious cycle where, without effective communication, the husband does get pushed away. So we talked about it and didn't make light of the very real emotional changes she was going through.

Other men felt it was also important not to deny or hide any negative feelings that they might have about their wife's ever-expanding belly. One man said that midway through his wife's pregnancy, it suddenly occurred to him that:

> This isn't exactly appealing to me. It's no longer aesthetically pleasing anymore. Sure, I would have liked to have a mental

picture of the woman who is bearing my child as the object of my sexual desires, but sometimes it doesn't happen that way.

Some men watch their wife's body swell and see it as big, fat, misshapen, and unattractive. This situation can be sensitive and emotionally charged, and unless a couple talks about it, the problem can escalate. Howard, a thirty-five-year-old land use planner, says that during his wife's first pregnancy he was reluctant to tell her that her increasing girth did not turn him on, and she couldn't tell him that she wanted more sex than usual. Their failure to communicate made a touchy problem worse, and, "in retrospect," Howard says:

> We've both realized it would've been much easier if we'd talked about it. But it seems that at the time I was afraid I would hurt her feelings. I didn't want to say, "I don't want to make love with you when you stick out this far." And because she was feeling neglected and insecure she wanted more sex, but she didn't say anything because she was afraid she would be putting too many demands on me when we were both under a lot of pressure. Finally, when we read a book after the baby was born that said husbands think everybody else's wife but their own is really attractive when she's pregnant, Liz said, "I just wish I'd known that last summer." And that got us talking about it and we were able to understand and accept what had happened.

Art, a thirty-four-year-old physician, managed to cope with his wife's expanding size by accentuating the positive:

> There are other ways to perceive the physical changes of pregnancy as opposed to being just negative or threatening. Pregnancy, like anything new, has its good and bad points and you just have to focus on the good points. The physiological changes can also be sexy if you let them. Often you can see a glow coming from a pregnant woman. You just have to be more sensitive to that part, that glow.

Mark, age sixty-one, recalls his wife's childbearing period as a "trade off" in terms of her sexual appeal. He was excited by her pregnant state, but because her size had a tendency to interfere with lovemaking, and she was not as limber, she was also not as exciting. He describes the effect of her pregnancy as being both inhibiting and enhancing:

On the one hand, the idea that my child was growing in her body gave me a sense of tremendous intimacy and a greater desire than ever. And on the other hand, the fear that I might in some way harm the child had an inhibiting effect. So I struggled with both things at the same time.

Douglas also had mixed feelings about his wife's changing shape during her pregnancy. He liked her swelling breasts but felt odd when the baby kicked while they had sex:

Helena is not big-breasted, so that was brand-new. And I found it arousing. It was a different feeling, like I was with another woman, without having to go through the dangers of that. But when the baby moved, it was not, in my opinion, sexy at all. It's an intrusion to know someone else is there in bed with you. It wasn't always sheer pleasure to put my hand on Helena's stomach and feel the life within. It was kind of freaky.

Then there were the men who had no ambivalent feelings at all about the physical changes their pregnant wives underwent. They loved seeing their wives pregnant and enjoyed watching their bodies change. Burt, a thirty-four-year-old attorney, felt this way:

I was extraordinarily attracted to her when she was pregnant and I really enjoyed making love to her. Her breasts were very large, and I liked that. Her nipples enlarged and turned dark, and her skin was beautiful, really beautiful, when she was pregnant. I loved to touch her stomach and her skin. She was kind of round and cuddly and I found her very, very attractive. I enjoyed holding her. I found the physical changes that she went through enormously attractive and sexually exciting.

Albert, a forty-two-year-old schoolteacher, felt that his wife was not only beautiful while pregnant, but also absolutely erotic:

We were sexual right up until the time the baby was born. I

thought my wife was beautiful when she was pregnant. She was like an overripe fruit. There was something succulent about her, like juice running down the corners of your mouth.

Many men like Scott, a twenty-seven-year-old teacher, made love with their wives up until the day they gave birth:

I found her very sexy, and it became a challenge, as the nine months went on, to see how long we could do it. It became a kind of contest. We were trying to set a record by doing it right up until the baby was born.

Unlike Scott and his wife, a number of couples discontinued intercourse before the delivery date, mostly out of fear of hurting the baby. This fear, a Lamaze instructor told us, is the most prevalent one voiced by both men and women during pregnancy. But unless a pregnant woman has a history of miscarriages, or shows unusual bleeding or other physical signs of a problem, there should be no cause for concern.

But some were concerned nonetheless, and for Paul, a forty-two-year-old stockbroker, the concern itself caused problems:

I was quite careful about my weight, and as her pregnancy developed, we used the position where she would be on top or I would be behind her, entering from the rear. But that took the spontaneity out of sex. It was no longer a mad scramble to excite each other. It became more formalized and less spontaneous, which, I think, contributed to the loss of sexual desire on my part. I was more concerned about my wife's feelings, her attitude and mental receptiveness to having sex, and the physiological safety of the baby, which made sex more of a calculated kind of thing, where in the past it wasn't.

Douglas, thirty-two, says during his wife's pregnancy she was "spooky about deep penetration," and he, being conscious of the life growing inside her, kept that in mind during sex. "Our lovemaking," he says, "wasn't as vigorous as usual, it was more subdued, more laid back. And I guess we ultimately found intercourse positions that weren't so conducive to deep penetration."

Men experimented with different intercourse positions because of their fear of physically hurting the fetus and also because certain positions became too difficult for the women to manage as the pregnancy progressed. The three most common positions that men told us they finally settled on during the later months of their wives' pregnancies were female-superior, rear entry with the woman kneeling, and the side-to-side position, where both partners lie on their sides with the man behind the woman. None of these positions placed extra weight or pressure on the woman's stomach.

Dan, age thirty-one, describes how he and his wife managed to make love face to face on their sides during her pregnancy:

> We particularly liked the position where we would lie perpendicular to each other with her legs over my hips so the penis would be inserted into the vagina sort of sideways, which was quite pleasurable. This way we had flexibility and movement, and the position seemed to stimulate many of her vaginal muscles that were not stimulated in the usual sexual positions. It also gave me the opportunity to manipulate her clitoris at the same time.

MEN'S ANXIETIES

While a woman can be quite preoccupied with the physical and emotional changes that accompany her pregnancy, the man often struggles with his own concerns. Many men we interviewed worried, at various points in their wives' pregnancies, about how they would handle the role of father and all the responsibilities it entailed. Many confusing and uncomfortable feelings often emerged for men during this emotionally laden time. And in some cases the emotional turmoil dampened their sexual desire.

Worries about being able to handle fatherhood plagued Howard during his wife's first pregnancy. He said:

> I became more protective rather than sexual toward my wife, and I was always thinking, "Oh, my God, I'm about to become a father. But I don't know how to be a father. I haven't the vaguest idea. And I'm much too young." So it's hard to say how much of my sexual interest diminishing was actually a result of anxiety.

Larry, thirty-eight, a minister, experienced a different kind of anxiety. Accustomed to the exclusivity that their close relationship brought him, Larry felt a profound sense of loss as he noticed his wife's attention shifting to the as-yet-unborn baby, and he worried that after the birth he would be shut out completely:

> For twenty years, Sheila and I had been pretty much constantly together. She was always really present, and now she really wasn't. I understood her preoccupation with being pregnant, but I wasn't prepared for the sense of loss I felt, the sense of absence in my life, the abandonment, and the anxiety—even fear—about the future. I wondered whether I was ever going to get this back. And that frightened me. I was also disappointed in myself that I would be so hurt by her appropriate preoccupation. And I think I was jealous, too, which I didn't like. There was a lot I didn't like about myself then.
>
> But the last week of Sheila's pregnancy, we took off some time together. We were practicing our Lamaze together, and just talking about the excitement of what was coming up, getting the tape recorder ready and all that. Finally I was able to talk to her about some of these feelings, probably because I had gained some understanding and some perspective and I was not feeling so lost or so bad about myself. Her response was real caring and that was very helpful to me. And within four or five months after the birth I was feeling okay again.

Another fairly common problem men experienced during their wives' pregnancies was their tendency to see prospective mothers as holy and asexual. The inner glow then took on an almost religious quality. And some men found that if they put their partners up on the pedestal of motherhood, they had difficulty switching back to seeing them as their sexual playmates. Adam, age forty-nine, remarked: "Sometimes it struck me that in this state my wife was becoming a little bit more like a mother than a wife, and maybe this is what caused my sex drive to diminish."

And forty-three-year-old David, who felt similarly, interpreted it this way: "It somehow just didn't seem right to me that sexuality should be interesting to her while she was pregnant."

Neither Adam nor David was aware, while it was happening, that he had been reacting to an unstated assumption or attitude that mothers are not sexual. Only in retrospect could they figure out why their sexual activity with their wives had diminished during pregnancy.

More often, it was the woman who lost her sexual desire. Fatigue, nausea, stress, and carrying around all the excess bulk often curbed her appetite for sex. As a result, some couples led sexless lives during this period. While some men were understanding, others suffered. Terry, a thirty-six-year-old college professor, recalls that during the early years of his marriage sex was the major vehicle for expressing intimacy. And during her pregnancy, when his wife's interest in sex waned, he felt totally cut off from her:

> The frequency of our lovemaking dropped off pretty dramatically as she got bigger and bigger. I think the doctor advised us not to have sex for the last six weeks and the first four weeks after the birth, so we were celibate for quite a while. I remember that that was really hard because Glenna and I didn't know how to be intimate apart from being sexual, and I felt very alienated. Now I wouldn't feel so alienated. I know how to take care of my needs in other ways. I can ask her to hold me if I need that, and she'll do it. If I need to lay my head in her lap, I can do that. Even though I would guess that our sexual frequency has probably decreased rather than increased over the years, our relationship is much stronger. And the sex, while less frequent, is better.

Some men found other ways to have their intimate needs met during this period. Roger, a thirty-eight-year-old lawyer, used the late pregnancy period as an opportunity to express affection that didn't have to lead to sex, which brought him and his wife closer together:

> I think being pregnant makes a lot of women sick, and late in the pregnancy they're big and they don't feel very comfortable or attractive, and all of that causes them to feel less sexually happy. My wife just wasn't as interested in sex during that time. So I tried to be a good boy and to be real understanding, even though it wasn't always possible. Generally I just tried to accept it and realize that it was only a transitory situation that would be over soon, and that it was really harder on

her than it was on me. It wasn't pleasant, and neither of us really liked her being pregnant, but there we were, we had to get through it, and that's what I kept telling myself. Instead of sex, we did some things that were sort of semisexual. A book I read said that it makes delivery easier if the perineum is loose, and that a good husband will massage his wife's perineum, so I used to do that. And I really wanted to help her avoid having varicose veins, so I used to massage her legs to help the circulation. It made her feel good, it relaxed her, and it made me feel good because I was being helpful to her on a physical level without being sexual about it. We both enjoyed being physically affectionate, hugging, kissing, massaging, having back-rubs, without feeling that it had to lead to sex. It made me feel good to be able to give her pleasure with no strings attached. And while I think, on a certain level, that there's no substitute for sex, on another level it's nice to know that we could be close and affectionate without its having to lead to sex.

Those who wanted to maintain sex as well as intimacy found ways of working around the problems. And while sex was infrequent, at least it occurred at times. George was instrumental in helping his wife adapt and adjust to her new pregnancy. Before conceiving, she had been an active career woman, operating at a high energy level. During her pregnancy, she often wasn't aware that she was feeling fatigued. George was the one who would suggest a nap so she could replenish herself and could possibly have enough energy for sex later on. He says:

It's very important for a husband to recognize that his wife is tired and to say, "Let's go to bed and get some rest." So you go to bed, only with the idea of sleeping and being together. Suzan sleeps much better when I'm with her. After a half hour to an hour's nap, we wake up feeling better and then when we do want to make love, she has enough energy for it.

Morning sickness is another common symptom of pregnancy that interferes with sexual desire. Women with morning sickness describe it as a constant feeling of seasickness or an ongoing bout of the flu. Raymond's wife had a continual case of nausea during the first three months of her pregnancy, yet she was still sensitive to his sexual and emotional needs during this time. Whenever she was free from the nausea, she would tell him, "I'm not feeling bad. Let's go. Let's make love."

Other couples, who used to have sex during the morning, switched to the evenings if the woman had morning sickness. As always, sexual solutions hinged on open communication and a consideration of each partner's needs.

DELIVERY

Finally, after a very long nine months, it's time for the baby to arrive. The men interviewed had gone through many significant emotional changes as their wives' pregnancies progressed. But regardless of how different their experiences of the pregnancy had been, all the men shared one common thought as the ninth month approached: let the baby come already!

Many, especially those with another child, had decided to be directly involved in the labor and delivery if possible. Those who were, felt they would not have missed being there for anything and planned to be in the delivery room again if their wife had another child.

Marvin's reaction to the birth was that it was among the most exciting and memorable experiences he had ever had:

I couldn't be there for the birth of my daughter. That was when we were in Cleveland and they didn't let you do that. But I was able to be there for the birth of my son. It was just one of the most incredible experiences of my life.

Caulder, age thirty-five, agreed:

I felt feelings of exhilaration just rushing through me when I saw the baby come out of the womb. I had no idea I would feel that way. It was totally different from the feelings I've had in nature, or sexually, or in my fantasies, or with music. Nothing has ever made me feel that way. And I finally realized what people meant about having children.

In describing how he felt when witnessing the birth of his children, Roger, thirty-eight, compared his feelings to those he had during an all-encompassing orgasm:

> Our first child was born in a hospital and I was there, coaching. The second child was born at home, and there were just my wife, the midwife, and me. I rubbed my wife's back and tried to be encouraging and it made us very close. So both times I assisted. The experience is unbelievable. It's a very high moment. I can't really describe what it's like. It's like a great orgasm in a way. It's just unbelievable. When I experience a great orgasm it's like I go up to another plane of existence and I'm not even aware I've been there until it's over and I'm back and then I realize I've been somewhere else. And it was the same when the children were born. I realized I had been someplace where I totally—emotionally, intellectually, psychically, physically—felt wonderful. At the moment when the child comes out, you almost cry with joy, but you're not really here on earth, you're off somewhere in some other sphere. It's fantastic!

The fathers who experienced the joy of watching their children being born, or those who held and cared for the baby immediately afterward, said they would cherish the memory forever. And what grew out of the experience for them was a sense of closeness with the child which translated into a more close-knit relationship later on. Therefore, these men were not fully prepared for the conflicting feelings they experienced after the child was born. Suddenly there was a newcomer whose insistent emotional and physical needs invariably upset the intimacy that had been building between husband and wife during those nine months of pregnancy. This disruption inevitably affected their sex lives. For some couples, it took months to restore their sexual relationship to its previous level of activity and intimacy.

THE IMPACT OF NEWBORNS

Five months after his son's birth, Douglas, a thirty-two-year-old Washington lobbyist, said:

> The interruption in our sexual life is unreal, absolutely unreal.

It is a total drain on our time and energy, and our sex life has deteriorated without our batting an eye, without any malice, even though we had had a fairly good intimate relationship up to this point.

Douglas seemed typical of the men we interviewed who felt very strongly about their roles as parent and supportive mate, so his response intrigued us. We wondered whether the sudden drop in sexual activity he experienced was unique. But as we interviewed more men, we found that Douglas' experience was the norm. No matter how prepared a couple was for the birth of their baby, almost without exception, fathers reported that they were not at all prepared for the chilling impact the new child would have on their sex life. According to Roger, a thirty-eight-year-old lawyer:

Children are wonderful to have, but they can be dangerous from the standpoint of sustaining a good marital relationship. Kids are innocent and you can't blame them for it, but if you don't watch out, they can ruin your sex life.

Couples formerly accustomed to the freedom of making love whenever the mood struck often felt themselves prisoners of a squealing, dependent, and demanding seven-pound infant. A complaint we heard frequently from the men we interviewed was that the infant's needs often overruled their own sexual desires. In the midst of trying to be more understanding, many men harbored resentments. Roger recalls the difficult period following the birth of his first child:

There were so many times when we would just get something started, and the baby would cry; it was hungry, and my wife would have to get up and go get the baby and feed it. That usually took about half an hour. By the time she'd put it back to sleep and come back to bed, the momentum was gone.

Often, when couples enter sex therapy, we find that the beginning of the sexual problem can be pinpointed to the period following a child's birth. For most couples, sexual activity slows markedly after the delivery and, for some, comes to an abrupt halt. The stress, fatigue, distraction, and anxiety a new child causes can siphon sexual energy and threaten the couple's intimacy. While this can be expected initially, if prolonged, it can cause tremendous concern and can make reversing the process more difficult. If, during this time, a couple does not concentrate on keeping the intimacy in their relationship high—even though intercourse may be infrequent—resentment and negative patterns can develop which may have long-lasting effects.

POSTPARTUM

Even if the stress and fatigue caused by the new child could be overcome, the physical trauma of the delivery makes the immediate resumption of sex impossible for most couples. Most women who have a vaginal delivery undergo an episiotomy—an incision in the vaginal wall at the perineum to prevent the baby's head from tearing the tissue at the vaginal opening. Time is needed for the cut to completely heal. Time is also required to heal the weakened stomach muscles and stitches in the abdominal wall that occur with a Caesarean birth. Some men are turned off sexually in the first weeks after delivery because of the physical trauma and the feeling that their wife has been injured. This happened with Edmund, a forty-seven-year-old minister:

> The afterbirth was a bit of a turn-off, especially the first week or so when she came home. She had stitches and I had to help spray those with Dermaplast to keep them from getting infected, and that was a turn-off because I felt like this part of her body was an infected area.

Other men, who were not turned off by the physical trauma, held themselves back sexually out of concern for their partner's physical well-being. Roger says:

> I was really sexually frustrated, but we really tried to wait because even though she didn't have an episiotomy she had some tearing of the walls of the vagina. It was minor, but still I was conscious of the fact that she had been physically injured, and so I really didn't want to rush it, even though I was ready.

Some of the changes that prevented reinstating active sex were more emotional than physical. Depression sometimes characterized the postpartum period. Many women experience a postpartum depression or "baby blues," which is thought to be, at least in part, the result of an abrupt hormonal change that occurs following childbirth. Although this period generally lasts less than a few weeks for most women, some struggle with depression for several months, during which time they have little or no interest in sex.

Another contributing factor to diminished sexual interest is the extra weight that has accumulated during the woman's pregnancy. Some women gain twenty-five pounds or more, and losing this weight, especially while breast-feeding, takes time—sometimes as long as a year or more. In the meantime, women often don't feel good about their bodies. A lowered self-image can result in a loss of libido. And this extra weight gain can sometimes make them less sexually attractive to their spouse as well.

Interestingly, some spouses also gain weight during their wife's pregnancy. Two men who were reluctant to resume sex told us they had put on weight simultaneously with their partner. One gained thirteen pounds, and the other, a physician, said each time his wife became pregnant he gained as much weight as she did. Both men said this extra poundage made them feel less sexually attractive and contributed to their diminished sexual desire after the delivery.

Both men and women often lose sleep and suffer from fatigue as they attempt to adjust to the newborn baby's sleep cycle. Since it sometimes takes several months before the child sleeps through the night, new parents may feel continually disoriented and lethargic as sleep deprivation leaves little energy left over for sexual diversion.

Anxiety about being a good parent as well as preoccupation with this new little person can also interfere with the desire for sex, particularly for the mother. While some fathers felt left out and sometimes jealous of their wife's preoccupation with the baby and looked forward to sex as a way to reestablish closeness, some men were more interested in forming a bond with their infant than in making love.

Nathan, a first-time father at thirty-seven, felt that both he and his wife were less interested in sex because they were so preoccupied with their new role as parents:

A great deal of time was consumed by the baby waking up at all hours of the night. Both my wife and I were tired a great deal of the time with the first child. But we also felt a lot of responsibility toward the child, and our worries about how we were doing as parents so consumed us that sexuality dropped considerably on the scale of things that were important to us. This probably lasted for a year until we mastered our role as parents and felt more comfortable with those responsibilities.

During this period of sexual abstinence, men felt it was important to be close and intimate with their wives in other ways. Paxton, a thirty-three-year-old therapist, says:

It took a couple of months to begin actual intercourse again. That was really okay, that wasn't a problem at all because there was a lot of really nice holding, touching, and affection during that time.

Dean, a thirty-four-year-old professor with an infant son, says that his sexual needs throughout his wife's difficult postpartum period were met largely by the emotional intimacy he and his wife shared:

Although we had no sex, I think of that time as one of the most intimate in my marriage—and my life—in terms of the touching, the holding, the kissing, the shared experience. To give you a concrete example of what I mean, the hospital where Hal was born had a candlelight dinner for the new parents. It sounds kind of corny, but we went into this little room for the candlelight dinner, and Hal was wheeled in. He was sleeping. I just took Beth's hand and looked at her, and we both started to cry. The moment was so moving, so intimate, that we were overwhelmed. I can't ever remember feeling closer to her. And that feeling carried over for quite some time. For me, that meant I didn't feel that much of a sexual need. I guess the intimacy needs were being met to a large extent by sharing the childbirth experience. So every now and then when I felt blue balls coming on, I'd jerk off in the shower. I could take care of genital sensations without any problem because my needs in the intimacy department were being met.

When intimacy was not enough and the sexual need prevailed, men talked about using masturbation or oral sex as a substitute for intercourse. They would masturbate either alone or with their partners. Caulder, a thirty-three-year-old urban planner with two young children, says:

> Jeanne was generally very tired, but when she wasn't she was pretty good about non-intercourse sex. She was really willing to make a lot of effort. I think Jeanne was very conscious of the fact that we weren't having intercourse, and so she tried to make up for it this way.

Several men appreciated that their wives were sensitive to their sexual needs and initiated oral sex more often. One man recalls that, in the couple of months following childbirth, "we resumed our high school practices and became oral dreamers again."

RESUMING SEX

The standard advice an obstetrician/gynecologist gives a new mother about resuming sex after a vaginal delivery is: "Wait six weeks." This is to ensure that the cervix, which dilates during delivery, has closed up again. While it is open, it is easy for an infection to occur when a foreign object, like a penis, is inserted. Though six weeks' abstention from intercourse is advised, the cervix may close up more quickly. The cessation of bleeding is a good indication that it is probably safe to have sex again. However, even if there is little chance of infection, many women, particularly those who have had an episiotomy and whose scar still feels tender, need to wait longer to begin intercourse.

Douglas, for instance, says that although his wife was sexually interested and even initiated sex two months following their child's birth, she felt severe discomfort when he tried to penetrate her:

> It was frustrating. It took four months until she was really comfortable. We had reduced sexual contact and self-touching and oral sex, but Helena was physically drained by the baby. The demands on her body were enormous. She was nursing, we were up two or three times a night—and with everything else, I began to look at myself as another demand. She wasn't able to handle that one until after four or five months.

THE FIRST TIME

Even if a couple waits long enough, they are often unaware of how to proceed to make the first sexual experience after delivery comfortable. Most doctors don't provide the details. They leave the "how to's" up to the presumed sex experts in our culture—the men. However, the new father is often as ill-prepared as his wife for dealing with the very real pain she might experience. Of course, some women are able to resume sex with ease. But those men who found their wife's first intercourse attempt after childbirth to be genuinely painful, remember it as a difficult time. Feeling responsible for making it a successful experience, yet not knowing what to do, often stressed the relationship.

The men who found solutions shared the methods they used to gradually ease into intercourse and handle the common problems of lack of lubrication, vaginal tenderness, and vaginal tightness.

Among the solutions offered for dryness were: substantial foreplay, particularly cunnilingus; water-soluble lubricants, such as K-Y jelly; and prelubricated condoms.*

In attempting intercourse with a woman whose vagina is tender, men we interviewed generally suggested using soft caresses and proceeding slowly. If the vaginal entrance was too tight, some men slowly stretched the opening by inserting a finger and pressing it outward toward the walls in a circular motion. Gradually two, three, then four fingers can be inserted until the opening has been stretched sufficiently to be able to accommodate a penis. One couple used a dildoe to prepare the vagina for intercourse. Relaxation exercises can also be helpful. John's wife was particularly uncomfortable with penetration after her delivery because her doctor had made very tight stitches after the episiotomy. The way she eased into intercourse, John says, was to do Lamaze breathing exercises which relaxed the vaginal opening when he entered her.

* Conception is possible even if menstruation has not yet resumed or the woman is lactating, so using a condom is advisable if another pregnancy is not immediately desirable. Pills should not be used by nursing mothers, an IUD is considered by many to be potentially harmful, and a diaphragm cannot be fitted until the woman's body has totally recovered from the changes which occurred during the pregnancy.

Another helpful hint men suggested was using positions where there was little pressure on the incision or where the woman could control the amount and angle of penetration. Rear entry and female superior positions were generally preferred. Art, a thirty-four-year-old physician, says:

> It seemed that it was less painful if Melanie was on her stomach and I was behind her. That didn't put as much pressure on her perineum. It put more pressure anteriorly than posteriorly.

While Art's wife had had a vaginal delivery, women who underwent Caesarean births also preferred this position, since it kept the man's weight off the abdominal incision.

Sometimes it wasn't the pain that created the initial problem. For some men the long period of abstinence put a damper on their libidinal drive. Larry, a thirty-eight-year-old minister and father of a two-year-old, says that his wife's libido waned during pregnancy and completely died during the postpartum period. Because they'd been married so long and felt so connected, "when the bottom dropped out of her libido, it dropped out of mine too." The way they resurrected their sexual activity was to follow the advice they read in books:

> We changed the time and place of sex, bathed the senses, made sure we began with goofy, grab-ass games in the shower or in the hot tub. We started off with either a playful kind of tickling or massage. We paid attention to changing the lighting in the room, changing the room we made love in, changing the music, changing the smells. We even started watching pornography on our home video. We made a conscious decision to get *Behind the Green Door* and some John Holmes flicks. Sheila picked up several copies of *Playgirl*. We just tried to restimulate the whole thing. And now our sex life is pretty much back to the way it was.

BREAST-FEEDING

From our interviews we found that breast-feeding could enhance or detract from the sexual intimacy a couple shared. There is no doubt that breast-feeding is good for the baby. Breast-feeding promotes an important sense of bonding between mother and child. Most doctors will also tell you that nursing a baby is the most safe and natural way to feed an infant. Antibodies in breast milk will protect a baby against some infections for the first three months. Breast-feeding is also good for the mother. Studies show that there's less breast cancer in women who have nursed their children than in women who have not breast-fed at all.[3] These and other health considerations were a major reason many men supported their wife's decision to breast-feed.

Some men had a sense, as did thirty-six-year-old Terry, that their wife's breasts were "certainly off-limits" while she was breast-feeding. They were often a source of sexual discomfort rather than arousal for the woman since they were swollen with milk and, because of the suckling baby, her nipples were often tender. Terry says that "although Glenna didn't have any particular problems with breast-feeding, there was some soreness associated with it—a kind of hyperawareness of her breasts, and I couldn't really touch them during that time."

And some men really didn't want to fondle their wife's breasts during the nursing period because, as Art put it:

There was all this milk coming out and dripping and the idea of sucking milk from her breasts didn't turn me on; it did the opposite. She would get engorged or full, and if I manipulated her breasts they would start to hurt. So breast-feeding really robbed me of her breasts—which had been important to my sexual pleasure. But there wasn't much we could do about it until she stopped nursing.

Some men felt they not only lost their wife's breasts during this period, but their wife's attention as well. They felt shut out from the close biological link between mother and child. One man admitted that it was his profound jealousy during his wife's nursing period that led him to develop an obsession with gardening. He couldn't feed the baby when she cried for milk, and he felt like a bystander watching his wife in the starring role. In retrospect, he realized some of those feelings were redirected into nurturing his lawn and growing flowers.

The sense of standing on the sidelines as the intimacy grows between mother and child stirred up powerful emotions in many new fathers. And although logically the men knew it was ridiculous, some said they felt they were competing with their newborn baby for their wife's attention and for her breasts. Says Terry:

> I began to feel more estranged, more alienated when Glenna was nursing, because nursing every three to four hours required a lot of attention. We had been married three and a half years before the baby was born and I felt left out. I really did. I didn't feel like she loved me any less, but I felt like I got less attention.

Burt says that he felt the little affection he had gotten from his wife before the baby's birth dwindled down to nothing afterward:

> After the baby was born I felt my wife took away affection from me and gave it to the baby. Problems developed right away. We didn't really get to go out that much because she was nursing and the baby had odd sleeping hours. And I kind of felt, "Hey, what about me?" As a consequence, everything suffered. The sex suffered—she was tired all the time, I was tired all the time. The once every three or four weeks when we'd be really up for sex was not enough, and I felt left out. I began to feel like the hired helper rather than the husband participant.

As a result of interviewing these men, we realized that those who successfully navigated this period handled the newborn baby's insistent demands and the reduced attention from their wife in a number of ways. First, they would give themselves permission to experience the anger and negative responses, and to accept the fact that it was all right to have ambivalent feelings. As a result, they didn't have to repress these feelings or feel guilty about them. Sometimes they could dissipate the intensity of their feelings by expressing them directly to their wife in a nonthreatening way. They also spent more time developing a relationship with the baby and therefore felt less jealous of the bonding between mother and child. Finally, and if all else failed, recognizing that nursing was time-limited and that the end was in sight helped to keep the issues in perspective. As one man explained, "I know breast-feeding won't last forever. I can live through it."

Then there were men who had a completely different response to the nursing period. They weren't just tolerating the fact that their wife had a baby suckling her breasts, they enjoyed it and some even found it to be sexually provocative. Scott, a twenty-seven-year-old father of a four-month-old son, really enjoyed his wife's enlarged breasts:

> I was never a breast person before and at first, when my wife developed these great breasts, it was a joke, and we would laugh. But suddenly it became very sexually arousing to be able to be smothered, to be secure, to be enfolded with these beautiful breasts.

Dean, a thirty-four-year-old professor, says he didn't expect to be so turned on by watching his wife breast-feed their infant son. Her breasts were sensitive at the time, so he couldn't play with them during lovemaking. "But this totally unexpected sexual turn-on more than compensated for that," he said. "At first I felt a little perverted about my feelings, but as time went on, I felt okay about it and just enjoyed them."

And Dan, a thirty-one-year-old father of two girls aged one year and one month, says that breast-feeding is so stimulating that once he and his wife even had intercourse while she was nursing the baby:

> There was one time in particular that we felt like doing something really wild and my wife was breast-feeding the baby, so we engaged in intercourse while she was breast-feeding. It didn't cause the baby to get a stomachache, or the milk to sour, or anything. It was quite a pleasant experience for all three of us. The baby didn't seem to notice anything and it didn't create any discomfort for my wife.

Scott took nursing a little further. He and his wife are co-workers who often travel together for business. Sometimes when they are out on the road Scott's wife needs to be relieved of her milk since she cannot nurse, so he gladly helps by sucking her breasts. "I don't drink the milk," Scott says, "it's too gooey and I never liked milk, period, so I just spit it out. But it's a very sexy thing to do and she enjoys it so much that she wishes I would do it more often."

FATHERHOOD

The arrival of a new baby produced some powerful emotional reactions many men hadn't anticipated. These reactions—sometimes overwhelmingly positive, at other times negative—were not in response to the emotional or physical changes their wives were undergoing, nor were they associated with the intense mother-child bond; they were in response to their own role as father.

For men like Roger, fatherhood meant they were fulfilling one important aspect of their masculinity. They saw it as an accomplishment and, says Roger:

It almost made me feel more manly to be a father. Once the child was here, I finally felt all grown-up. "I'm a father, I'm a parent; I'm a part of the lineage in my family. I'm finally producing children and I can stand on the same level with my father and my grandfather." I don't want to overemphasize it, but it was there and in a very subtle way it added some extra dimension to my sense of male sexual power.

With fatherhood also comes a sense of responsibility, which made many men anxious about their ability to be an adequate provider. Those who faced uncertainty in their jobs understandably were concerned about their role as breadwinner. They wanted to give their babies a secure home and promise for the future. Some told us they were thinking about life insurance for the first time. One man had been out of a job for a year, and although his wife had returned to work, he worried about the future and felt a loss of esteem, as if he were less of a man. He also admitted that these feelings had interfered with his sex drive and his ability to maintain an erection. However, keeping these issues in proper perspective can help prevent them from causing serious sexual problems.

MOTHER VS. LOVER

Another potential threat to a man's sex drive during this infancy period was the role of mother detracting from his wife's sexual attractiveness. If this problem did not arise during pregnancy, it sometimes occurred after the child was born. Paul, a forty-two-year-old stockbroker felt this way, but he wasn't sure why:

> After the birth of our son, I was less attracted to my wife as a sexual partner. I saw her as a mother, although I don't understand why that should diminish my sexual desire for her. But I feel that also goes on with other men who are fathers.

Within our culture, what is erotic is often connected to a sense of the illicit, and some images or fantasies found to be exciting are tinged with a sense of the forbidden. These acts, of course, are carried out with lovers, mistresses, or erotic sex partners—not a woman who has delivered a baby. Once the woman becomes a mother, unconscious associations with saints, virgins, purity, and so on arise and can create sexual disinterest or erection problems. For example, although John and his wife had been through couples therapy prior to our interview, he had not been able to understand the actual reason for his dramatic drop in sexual interest following the birth of his child. He had been too embarrassed to bring up the specifics about his illicit sexual fantasies which conflicted with his new image of his wife as mother. However, once he could verbalize those feelings in our interview, their intensity dissipated.

With good communication, caring, concern, and compromise, many issues and anxieties new parents face in the aftermath of the pregnancy and postpartum period that affect their sexuality can be resolved in the months that follow. Women begin to shed some of the weight they have gained. The crisis of confidence many men feel in their role as father has abated. Both parents are more at ease caring for the infant and have adjusted to having another family member around. And as the sexual interest returns, the practical problems of how to find the time to be sexual while infants, youngsters, or teenagers are around is an issue faced by every couple with children.

CHAPTER TEN

FATHERS ARE STILL LOVERS

When Barry McCarthy asks students in his sexuality courses at Washington, D.C.'s American University whether they could imagine their parents having sex, only one out of four raise their hands. McCarthy, a sex therapist and author, usually laughs and reassures them: There *is* sex after marriage—there is sex *even* after the children arrive.

But some fathers we interviewed said they weren't sure whether their sex life would ever have the same vitality it had before their wives became pregnant. In the aftermath of the difficult postpartum period, many fear that the former level of frequency and enthusiasm for sex will never be recaptured. Most couples are reassured as the demands of family life settle into a comfortable pattern and sexual interest returns. Yet, with reawakened libidinal drives comes a new dilemma: How will they find uninterrupted time for an active, satisfying sex life and still be responsible and responsive parents? Most parents say this is an ongoing problem that gets more difficult as the baby grows older, particularly if other siblings follow. Time, not lack of interest, is the major culprit. Leisure time for parents is a precious commodity and one that can easily be interrupted by family responsibilities, such as supporting, feeding, chauffeuring, and entertaining youngsters. A husband-lover turned father wears many hats, and unless he and his wife can schedule time for lovemaking, according to one new father, "your sex life can deteriorate to nothing in the blink of an eye." Most couples see the lag in their sex life as a temporary phase. They often decide that family needs and outside obligations will, for a while, take precedence over lovemaking. They agree that if an opportunity for sex arises and they both have the time to enjoy it, they will; but if other things get in the way, they won't worry about it. With time, they believe, their sexual relationship will regain momentum by itself.

And this works for some couples. But most who leave the responsibility for picking up a waning sex life to nature are disappointed. They are bewildered when their sex lives don't pick up momentum on their own. Four or five years down the road, many of these couples end up in sex therapy, their sex lives virtually nonexistent.

Men who were still struggling with this problem in their marriage, or who had dealt with it successfully in the past, suggested ways in which a couple can maintain an active sex life. During the early years of raising a family, they need to consciously make sex a priority by planning for it, yet be flexible enough to take advantage of unexpected opportunities to make love.

PRIORITIZING SEX

Prioritizing sex means scheduling daily activities so there is enough energy and time left for sex. If sex is to be a priority, it must be kept at the top of the agenda. The usual times, late at night or early in the morning, may have to be replaced by periods in the day when fatigue and early-rising children won't interfere. According to Ben, age thirty-five:

It's easy to get caught up in doing housework and taking care of the kids, and pretty soon, even if you want to have sex, you're really too beat. Who wants to have sex then, anyway? So to prevent that situation from arising I'll say, "Well, how would you like to have a date tomorrow?" What that means is, we'll go to bed early and close the door and block out the house and the kids and maybe we'll even take in some champagne with us. It's a way of creating a situation where we can relax and be intimate.

Making sex a priority often means eliminating some other activity: the Sunday football game, that class you've been wanting to take, your favorite TV show. It may mean "reserving" Wednesday nights for the two of you, arranging things so that you're home alone on Saturday mornings, or setting aside time once or twice a week on a regular basis. It also means talking over your plans so that you can create time to be together in a way that is comfortable for both people. Let your partner know that you miss the intimacy that occurs with more frequent lovemaking. In all likelihood, your partner feels the same way. Once the issue has been aired, you can work together to resolve it.

Roger, thirty-eight, gave us a rundown of the factors he and his wife consider important for ensuring that the few precious hours they set aside for each other will be quality time:

If I call her from work and say, "I want an appointment tonight," and she agrees to that, we try not to deal with all the petty stuff of our lives. When I come home we don't talk about her problems with the kids or my problems with the office. We try to keep everything on a really romantic, loving level. In a way, it's a pretense. We try to ignore any hardships; it's as if they don't exist. We'll get the children to bed, have dinner at a leisurely pace, and just talk about pleasant things, bathe or shower, have a glass of wine or whatever, and then go to bed. If we ignore the hassles and get to bed early enough, we're in a much better frame of mind the next day to deal with problems like finances, kids, or whatever.

Prioritizing sex becomes particularly important when both partners have full-time jobs. Juggling work, home, and family responsibilities can be an enormous task and it is often imperative for a working couple to make prior arrangements in order to have sex together. Art said he and his wife, both doctors, would never find time for making love in their busy schedules if they didn't make appointments with each other:

My wife is on call every third night and spends those nights at the hospital. In addition, she works almost every day. I also work a pretty tight schedule, including some nights. Sometimes a week goes by and we don't see each other. We try not to arrange it that way but often it can't be helped. And sometimes when we're home alone and we're thinking of having sex, we're too tired. So we have to literally plan—"Next Thursday let's try to get laid." And when Thursday comes along we make an attempt and see how it goes.

But what if Thursday comes along and you're so strung out from a tough week of work that you can't shrug off the pressure and relax? With all the responsibilities of a two-career couple, merely setting aside time is not sufficient to nurture the intimacy. Some couples find it helpful to include what we call "transitional activities"—activities which ease the daily pressures and tensions and even encourage sexual feelings. For some, this means taking a nap, sharing a drink or a relaxing bath, or listening to music for a period of time before initiating sexual contact.

Art says:

Before Melanie started her residency and the baby was born, we had a lot more free time for spontaneous afternoon sex. But now we have to do a lot more scene setting. Now when we get together, if there is any fatigue, any frustration about something that happened at work, worry about some patient, or anger about having to go back again the next day or the nagging thousand errands that have to be done, it can be really tough. We have to concentrate on trying to make the time together nice. Sometimes we even get a little drunk, just to forget the rest of the world.

Many couples are reluctant to plan for sex. They believe that good sex should be natural and spontaneous, that scheduling takes away the magic. Sex early in the relationship, they recall, was totally unplanned and spontaneous. To a large extent, however, this memory is sheer myth. Sex was almost always planned. The expectation when a date was made, was that there would probably be sex. In preparation for that possibility, showers were taken, cologne splashed on, and the proper outer- and under-garments carefully chosen.

Another reason couples often find it difficult to prioritize sex is that there have been few role models for this behavior. Television sitcoms or movies don't usually show couples talking about how to arrange their schedules to accommodate their sex lives, and few of us can recall hearing our parents even mention their sexual relationship.

But if you think about it, you may be aware of some situations where your parents were trying to occupy you or send you off somewhere so they could have time for themselves. During our interviews for *Shared Intimacies*, a forty-year-old divorced mother suddenly recalled:

> My mother made such a big thing about our going to Sunday school on Sunday morning. She would get up bleary-eyed and, no matter what, take us to Sunday school. And now that I look back on it, I realize that that was their time to fuck.[1]

Years after he was grown, one fifty-two-year-old man says he realized that the money his father slipped him every Saturday to take his brother to the double feature was designed to keep them gone for the afternoon. In fact, he says, there were times they'd go all day Saturday and Sunday too.

Sometimes the men we interviewed carried out the role of the planner, but, most often, setting aside intimate time was the woman's role. Forty-eight-year-old Justin's wife took on this responsibility:

> My wife comes from a broken home and she has one goal—to keep our family together, to keep our marriage together, and not let anybody come between us. So she always made sure I was as busy with the children as she was. She also made sure they went to bed early enough so that we had the rest of the night to ourselves. In the afternoon she saw to it that the children took naps, and since my work has always permitted me to be home at different hours of the day, we took advantage of that time alone and that helped keep us together.

The men who did assume responsibility for promoting sex in their relationships enjoyed the role. Silas, a fifty-four-year-old minister, has been married happily for thirty years and he believes the longevity of his marriage is no accident. Since sex is important to him, he takes over some of his wife's household chores so she'll have energy for making love. He doesn't feel he is making a sacrifice for her; he does it in the best interests of their relationship:

> I seem to have much more energy than my wife. I have always done quite a bit of the work around the house, aside from my regular work in the office. I washed the diapers and did a lot of the cooking, even when she was home with the children, because she had a limited amount of energy. So I tried to con-

serve and preserve it so she could be a better lover and still enjoy being a mother. Also, I thoroughly enjoyed doing it.

BE FLEXIBLE: SEIZE THE MOMENT

First, men suggested setting aside time for their sex lives— scheduling it in, so to speak. Then they seemed to suggest the opposite: Be flexible. The truth is that both are essential in maintaining an active, ongoing sexual relationship while raising a family.

Being flexible often entails changing the time and/or place that have become customary for making love. Dean, a thirty-four-year-old professor, considers flexibility to be of number one importance in keeping his sexual relationship alive. For him, flexibility means adapting the time for lovemaking to the baby's sleep cycle:

> The baby goes through phases of getting up every morning at 5 A.M., and then he'll sleep till 8 A.M., and we've got to adapt everything, including our sex life, to his schedule. If he's taking a long afternoon nap, we do it in the afternoon. If he's falling asleep early at night, we do it early in the evening. If he is sleeping later in the morning, we do it then. With us, it's not too difficult because we're fairly flexible in terms of time of day and things like that, but I think for couples who are not, it can be a major problem.

Dean shared with us his most recent experience of spontaneous lovemaking that entailed being flexible enough to work around the baby's nap time:

> Yesterday we had a good experience that was very spontaneous. I bought her a sexy negligee for Christmas. Well, the baby went to sleep soon after I gave it to her. While I was in the kitchen, doing some stuff, Beth went upstairs to try it on and then came back into the kitchen to show me how it looked. It looked fantastic. It fit her perfectly. So she was kind of walking around modeling it, and I started to get very turned on. Neither of us knew it was going to happen. It was a sudden turn-on and I guess this was why there was more passion than at other times. The whole sequence of events was so unexpected and spontaneous. Neither one of us would have pre-

dicted it would happen, and I think it felt a lot more intimate and special for both of us for that reason.

Being flexible usually means being willing to suddenly change your plans when the children are occupied or off somewhere and you unexpectedly find yourselves alone. But some men found that they could even seize the moment when the baby was around. Justin, a forty-eight-year-old minister, recalls: "We had no misgivings about having sexual relations right there with the baby on the bed beside us. She was just a young thing, and we felt very comfortable about it."

Scott, a first-time father at twenty-seven, was not only comfortable with the notion of making love in front of a baby, he was positively enthusiastic about it:

The primary suggestion I can make to all parents is, forget about all those taboos about babies watching sex or being in the same room. Put the baby on the bed with you and have a blast, because the vibration, the bouncing of the bed, makes the baby relax and feel warm and secure. And that's about the only way that we can have sex now, with our son in his infant stage and going through so many different changes. If the baby is old enough to roll off, surround him with pillows. Unless you're involved in a lot of screaming and wild, hysterical sex, which could frighten the baby, he will be thrilled to be surrounded by all that love, affection, and good feelings.

Other men, however, were totally opposed to the idea and considered it a perversion. According to Roger, age thirty-eight:

Even when they were little tiny babies sleeping in bassinets, we were never that comfortable making love when they were in the same room. And we certainly wouldn't do it with a two-and-a-half-year-old in the bed. The thought has crossed my mind, but I have to admit I think it's perverted. I assume my daughter's not totally conscious of what it's all about, but then, on the other hand, you'd be surprised at what they know.

PRIVACY

Even the men who willingly disregarded the taboo about having sex in front of an infant felt differently once the baby became a toddler. This next stage of a child's development forces parents to consider the question of privacy: how to secure it without giving a child the sense that he or she is being neglected or shut out. For the men we interviewed, the issue of privacy became an ongoing concern they would have to confront time and again.

Most men handled the problem by waiting until the child was safely tucked away in bed before they made love. Some men reported that this restriction on their sex life was a source of frustration, a constant reminder that spontaneous sex was a luxury of the past. However, Clint, a forty-five-year-old consultant, said he and his wife found a way to turn that frustration into a sense of anticipation that actually enhanced their lovemaking:

> There have been times when we've had to stop ourselves because we couldn't make love in the middle of the living room floor with the kid around. So what we do is turn that frustration into a positive thing. We'll say, "Let's wait until tonight, when he's asleep in bed." That's something to look forward to. That way I don't feel cut off, and the excitement can build. So it works out okay.

Other men found ways of getting their children into bed early, thereby having more time to be alone with their wives. Valiant, for example, a father of six, tired his kids out through vigorous play so they would go to bed early:

> I guess I just wore them out early. Then my wife and I had our time alone after they were tired and had gone to sleep. A fringe benefit was that playing with them kept me in good shape.

Roger pays special attention to his children, and he finds that when they have all shared an especially fun evening, they don't resist bedtime:

> I just try to get them out of the way without giving them a

sense that I'm trying to get rid of them. I've noticed they will pick up on exactly what is happening. If we're behaving in a loving, friendly manner towards each other and we're really working at keeping things calm and peaceful, it's much easier to encourage them to play by themselves or eat their dinner quietly and go to sleep. If I feel I really want to have sex that night, then I'll interact with the kids much more than I usually do to try to keep things calmer, and keep them in a more placid state of mind so we don't have any problems getting them to go to bed.

Getting your children into bed might be a cinch, but keeping them there so they don't interrupt the lovemaking can often be more difficult. After all, a child might awaken at night and come looking for Mommy and Daddy or wander into the bedroom just wanting to join the folks in bed. For many parents, this raises an uncomfortable issue: Should there be a lock on the bedroom door? The men we interviewed had mixed reactions to this question.

In general, they appeared less concerned than their female counterparts about whether their children knew about their sexual activities. More women than men cared if the children overheard them making love or suddenly burst into the room while they were in the midst of it. Chuck's response was typical:

We would usually seclude ourselves from our three children to make love. We'd be in the bedroom and we would close the door and lock it. I know that was important for my wife, although less so for me.

A number of the men, however, felt uncomfortable having their children walk in on them during sex. Some men chose to lock the door and not discuss it with their children and some preferred a closed door with no lock to teach them the meaning of privacy. Closed, but not locked, is how Jack, a thirty-eight-year-old engineer, handles this issue when he and his wife have sex:

We just tell the children we're going to the bedroom and we'll be out in half an hour to an hour. I guess we never really say we're going to make love or something like that. We just say, "We're going to be together, so you boys amuse yourselves." Until now we haven't really had any particular questions or comments about it, but now that I have a son approaching adolescence I suspect we might get some questions along this line.

Justin, a forty-eight-year-old minister, whose three daughters are now grown, went a step further and always left the bedroom door open—even during lovemaking. There were times, Justin says, when he—and not his wife—was embarrassed by the girls' interrupting. But they wanted to create an open attitude in their family, and he believes no one has suffered as a result:

We practice a no-closed-bedroom-door situation in our home, so we always have an ear to the kids. And they have walked in at times and my wife has always broken out laughing because my reaction is to roll off real quick, to get out of her arms fast. They never let on that they knew, bless their hearts. But we never had a closed-in family. Our girls have a healthy attitude as a result. We can sit down now and talk with our daughters about their boy friends and husbands. We try to be to our children what our parents were not to us. I think it has been a very healthy situation.

Aside from locked, shut, or open bedroom doors, the men were often very creative about finding private time for lovemaking. For many, Saturday mornings were a favorite time to be together because of the continuous cartoons on television. Leaving food out or suggesting the child prepare something simple also bought some time. Says one man:

We tell our son when we're staying in bed, like on a weekend or something, that we just want to talk and be alone. And he can go ahead and watch TV and if he wants he can have some yogurt or toast or whatever he can get by himself. And that seems to work. It's the mutual respect the three of us have for each other that makes the difference. We trust each other and we communicate with each other.

The modern version of "sending the kids to the double feature on a Saturday afternoon" was to tape a string of shows on the videocassette player. Some fathers liked this idea because it also enabled them to select the best of the week's programs and control their children's viewing.

Other suggestions for securing private time for sex were:

- pick up the children a little late from the day-care center;

- walk the children around the block on a Saturday morning to tire them out so naptime is extended;

- send the children to the store with a dollar each and a promise to shop carefully so it will take some time;

- hire a babysitter to keep the children busy in the house and sneak off to the bedroom;

- take the children to a babysitter and spend the day home alone.

Men lucky enough to live near relatives or friends found that they provided a respite from parenting for a few hours on a regular basis. But there is nothing like getting away from it all. A vacation can provide the occasion to renew a love affair. Time away from the children and the stress and cares of everyday life can do wonders for renewing the romance. Recalls fifty-two-year-old Bob:

Once we had been apart traveling and we met in a hotel in Washington. She got there first. I got a big kick out of going to the hotel because they'd never ask for my name—in Washington it's very delicate. So they said, "Sir, you may go upstairs, here's the key to room 247." It was great.

It is a particular pleasure to have relations with your own wife and feel free of the emotional strain of having young children around, of "Shh, they'll hear us," or, with older children, at one in the morning when they haven't called or come home, worrying, "Do you think they had an accident?" Being away from all that stuff, you're down to two people who really care about each other and are lovers, and that's fun.

SINGLE FATHERS

Even with this trend toward greater intimacy and stronger family ties, many marriages fail. Half of all marriages today are likely to end in divorce,[2] and in cases of marital rift, men need to decide how actively they will pursue their roles as single fathers.

Many of the men we interviewed valued their close ties to their children and did not want to give up this special relationship after a separation or divorce. They wanted to continue to have a substantial impact on their children's lives and didn't want to become merely a "Santa Claus," or visitational father, showing up bearing gifts and promises of fun-filled outings. These men wanted to assume a more meaningful role as a parent.

The fact that ever-increasing numbers of fathers are choosing to bear more of the burden of parenting is a significant departure from conventional role scripting. Traditionally women are considered to be the nurturing, caring child-rearers, while men assume the primary responsibility for supporting the family. And even though the roles have dramatically changed, many men still consider child-rearing to be an inherently feminine activity. As one man, who is currently discovering the rewards of fatherhood, points out:

> In society, raising children is talked about as being extremely important, but if you ask a man what's important, he'll say, "Work, money, sports. Kids? No way." I think the most exciting trend today is that men are getting involved in parenting.

Yet, undertaking the role of a single parent is not easy. Many men are not familiar with the traditionally female skills of parenting and are struggling with their own stereotypic attitudes about fatherhood. Leif, a thirty-seven-year-old economist, had been married eight years and had two young sons when his marriage ended in divorce five years ago. He says, "It was mainly my wife's role to do the parenting. And I didn't have much background or training for the role as primary parent." Right after the divorce, he and his wife worked out the conventional arrangement: she took custody of the children, while he had visiting rights and provided child support. But now, since they live in the same neighborhood, he and his ex-wife have decided on a custody arrangement whereby they each care for the children on alternating weeks. This change made a tremendous impact on Leif:

> I've always been brought up to believe that women have a nat-

ural facility for the parental role, and my ex-wife had always reinforced this by telling me in a lot of not-so-subtle ways that she was by far the wonderful parent and I was just the secondary parent. She was always, for instance, checking up on me and sending instructions with the kids about how to do particular things. But when I went from being the visitation parent to becoming an alternative custody father, I made the choice of being much more of a real parent.

Men who want to become primary parents in their own right say that, no matter how many strides they make, they still are seen as the auxiliary parent. Albert, for instance, a forty-two-year-old schoolteacher separated for two and a half years from his wife, says:

I get so angry at being stereotyped. I was in the store the other day with my boys, buying a Mother's Day card. And the saleslady said, "It's so nice that you're helping your boys do this." And I said, "Do you say that to women customers who come in with their kids? Because, you know, I raise my children as much as their mother does, and I don't think there's anything wonderful about me doing this at all. It's just one of the things I do with my children." I was mad, and my voice was shaking.

The assumption that women are the primary parents and men the helpers is apparently deeply entrenched. Albert gives another recent example:

A nurse-practitioner who isn't familiar with me or the boys turned to my woman friend and told *her* the whole routine for taking care of the kids when we got home. I thought, "Lady, she's not their mother, she's my friend. She's just sitting in the corner, for God's sake."

The supposition that women are inherently better parents continuously irks Alex. "I resent that implication," he says. "I can love, care for, clothe, and provide a home for my kids just as well as my former wife. And if I need to learn new skills to do it, I will. As far as I'm concerned, the only advantage a woman has over a man in the parenting department is that she can breast-feed and I can't."

Sexual stereotypes, however, are deeply ingrained. And those who challenge conventional expectations usually don't find the support they need from society at large. The men we interviewed who were taking on increased parental duties said the payoffs came from the closer emotional ties they developed with their children. Says Leif:

> Learning to be a parent was not easy. But slowly and surely I started getting feedback from the kids; they were talking to me more, telling me how they felt about me, and our relationship was growing. I think that closeness was there all the time, but I just wasn't aware of it, sensitive to it, or tuned-in to the fact that I would want to be a parent and could get something out of it.

Whether their deepening involvement with their children resulted after separating from their wives or whether it began much earlier, the men we interviewed derived a significant amount of self-esteem from their role as parents. Yet, as important as this father-child connection was, few wanted to pursue their fathering role at the expense of their sexuality.

For the most part, men wanted to feel fulfilled in their role of father as well as lover. The exceptions were men whose self-esteem and pride had suffered extensively after the breakup of their marriages, or men who were feeling inordinately sexually insecure themselves as a result of sexual problems with their ex-wives. Many were too scarred by the divorce to immediately involve themselves in a new relationship. Others, after years of marriage, found the dating scene so alien that initially they were overwhelmed and immobilized. The singles scene left them feeling like bumbling adolescents on a first date. Others, continuing to feel emotionally married to their wives, were uncomfortable about being sexual with another partner. They too preferred to give themselves time to adjust to the separation before plunging into new relationships.

Most men, however, were not only ready to date but needed to date. Men who had married early were often looking forward to a number of partners to broaden their sexual expertise and to make up for "lost time." Others sought a variety of relationships with women to help them get through the painful separation period or to help them rebuild their sexual self-esteem. And since most of these men were not ready for another permanent relationship, they purposely dated a number of women as a way of avoiding any serious emotional entanglements.

The problem faced by most of the men who were ready to date was how to meet their emotional and sexual needs without further upsetting a child who was already dealing with the painful reality of the divorce. This meant weighing their own needs for sexual intimacy with the impact dating would have on their children. And there were no easy answers about how best to carry out this balancing act.

Most of the single fathers we interviewed were in an emotional quandary after their marriage broke down. With no guidelines to follow, each reacted to his own situation differently, choosing to balance his sexual needs with his parental responsibilities in his own unique way. Some let their children know they were dating but didn't introduce them to the women they were seeing. Others occasionally brought their children along on their dates but drew the line at having their dates stay over on the nights their children were with them. And finally there were a few men who had very few qualms about introducing their children to their girl friends and having their dates spend the night right from the start.

The single mothers we interviewed for *Shared Intimacies* were almost universally concerned about a man staying overnight and perhaps encountering their children the next morning at breakfast. Those few men who were relaxed, even cavalier, about introducing their lovers to their children were in direct contrast to their female counterparts. Valiant, for instance, who has been divorced for eight years, says:

I never worried about having a woman stay over the same time the kids were visiting. I wouldn't have a different one every week, or something like that. But if it was someone I had seen for several months, or someone I planned on seeing for a while, I would expose her to my kids. And I felt comfortable with this right from the start.

Valiant's ease at exposing his six children to a series of women, in the years following his divorce, may in part reflect a culture that gives men permission to be openly sexual and to display a steady stream of new partners, while women are usually expected to adhere to a more strict behavioral code. "After all," points out one man, "it makes sense that women are more sexually discreet than men. The red-blooded American male likes to show off his conquests and is less concerned about how this appears to his children. After all, if a woman screws around she's a tramp; if a man does, he's a champ."

The majority of men, however, were very concerned about the impact of their dating on their children's lives and took a number of factors into consideration before deciding whether to introduce their children to a woman they were dating. One factor was the circumstances surrounding the separation. The more recent the separation, generally the more sensitive were the child's feelings, and the more they needed to be considered. Also, the nature of the breakup—whether it was an amicable settlement or a bitter fight to the finish—influenced a father's decision about whether to introduce new women to his children.

For instance, Claude, forty-four, recently went through an explosive separation from his wife of eleven years. The separation arrangement they worked out is one in which Claude keeps his seven-year-old son on alternate weekends. Because the breakup was so recent and the feelings so raw, Claude thinks more time is needed before introducing his son to the woman he is dating. Claude says, "I just feel that at this time he seems to be better off when I don't share our time together with anybody else."

Burt, thirty-four and separated from his wife for three years, thinks he made a mistake by going on a vacation with his six-year-old son and a woman he was dating so soon after his marriage broke up:

> It bombed. It was too soon. My son really reacted very adversely. He was sullen toward this woman and, even though he knew her before this, everybody kind of had a lousy time.

Some men decided to keep their private lives separate to allay any fears a child might have that the separation or divorce meant that they would lose their father. The best way to assure them that this bond would not be broken was to establish a regular schedule of time reserved solely for the child. Some men, like sixty-eight-year-old Don, who didn't handle the situation like that, wished, in retrospect, that they had.

Don says his two adolescent sons had a difficult time, following his divorce, eighteen years ago. He originally thought it was because he saw so many women during that time. But Don said his sons told him years later that it was not so much the number of women he saw, but the lack of time left over for them to spend together that bothered them. It was a difficult period, and he was drinking as well. He quoted one son as saying:

> I resented it when you would bark at me. I would know you had a hangover. And when I would try to talk to you about something you were either half in your cups or you were busy with a woman.

"That didn't mean busy in bed," Don explained. "That meant busy because whenever I took them somewhere I usually had a date with me."

The individual child's reaction to the separation was another factor that influenced a man's decision about introducing a new sexual partner. In general, a child's reaction will vary depending on his or her personality and the family situation. However, according to Larry Brain, a Washington, D.C., child psychiatrist, children tend to have a number of general reactions regardless of how well they have been prepared for the divorce. They tend to feel shocked, abandoned, sad, anxious, angry, and more dependent once their parents split up. In reaction to the crumbling of their family unit and the fear that they are losing one or both parents, many children also temporarily regress to an earlier, more dependent, stage of development.

One man we interviewed had a four-year-old boy who regressed to the infant stage after the divorce. The father, who was given joint custody, says: "My son was always sucking his thumb, whining and crying for me to hold him. And when he saw me with a woman, he'd start asking her, 'What are you doing sitting next to my daddy? I want to sit next to him.'" His son demanded a lot of his attention and the father handled it by trying to meet as many of his son's infantile demands as he could. "Until things stabilized, and I moved into a house near my ex-wife," he told us, "I would really cater to my son's wishes and coddle him as if he were an infant. It's taken some time, but now that he's more secure, he's functioning at his appropriate age level."

Along with the more general emotional reactions most children display at the breakup of their parents' marriage, recent studies show that some behaviors are more typical at different ages.[8] These reactions are mediated by the child's unique personality and degree of internal stability:

- The infant or toddler's world is an ego-oriented one, so if the parent the child is closest to and most dependent upon is upset or depressed, he assumes personal responsibility. "Did Daddy go because of me?" or "Did I make Mommy cry?" would be overriding concerns of a child this age. Internally, such a child may feel he or she has been bad and caused the divorce. However, if given consistent, warm, nurturing care by both parents, long-term negative effects of the separation can be minimized.

Paul, a forty-two-year-old stockbroker, assumed full custody of his two-year-old son. Although he and his wife were emotionally upset at the prospect of breaking up and spent many difficult sessions with a counselor, Paul was able to be fairly consistent in the manner in which he cared for his son. "I had other outlets for my emotional reactions: friends and, later on, my own therapy, so I was able to be there for my son," says Paul. "Edward is now five and, as far as I can see, he's adjusted well. He sees his mother fairly regularly and, in his mind, we've always been two single parents."

- By the time children reach school age, they are more able to understand the situation and are less inclined to feel responsible for their parents' breakup. Still, the loss of a parent and the shakeup of the family unit tend to make them feel lonely, helpless, and depressed. At this stage, some children develop psychosomatic illnesses or have problems in school.

- During adolescence when teenagers are striving for self-expression, trying to separate from the family and develop unique identities, a divorce can be experienced as devastating. Adolescents often feel overwhelmed, abandoned, as if their stability has been pulled out from under them. In desperate attempts to cope with a situation which is beyond their control, adolescents tend to react by distancing themselves emotionally from the powerful feelings they may be experiencing by acting aloof, by becoming excessively self-controlled, or by trying to control others around them. Some begin experimenting with drugs, alcohol, or sex in an attempt to cover over feelings of anxiety, shame, or depression. And, a teenager is likely to test repeatedly the limits of a new household following a separation.

In addition to concerns about their child's emotional well-being, men had a number of other reasons for keeping their children and lovers separate, reasons which revolved around their own needs and comfort levels. Some men didn't include the woman they were dating when their children were around because, in addition to their children's need to be alone with them, they needed to be alone with their children. These men felt the time they had to share with their children was too little and too precious to include others, and jealously guarded the moments of intimacy they had together. Says thirty-nine-year-old Alex:

I got tremendously close to the kids after the separation and learned to cherish the time that I had with them. I've become very possessive of that time. And I just don't want any of my friends messing around with the limited amount of time that I've got to spend with my kids.

Some men were uncomfortable about exposing their children to a number of partners because it conflicted with their own values. Charles, a forty-five-year-old man who was single for four years before he remarried, used to occasionally stay over at a girl friend's house when his children came to visit because he didn't want to confuse them or expose them to a series of relationships that might not go anywhere. "Besides," he says,

I was terribly embarrassed at the thought of having a woman spend the night while the kids were there. So I did not do that. Though I would have them over to eat and I might give them a hug, or something, I would feel guilty about it. I wasn't living a kind of life that I would call so loose that I was afraid of the kids' seeing something that I basically disapproved of. But some part of me still didn't want them to see me with women I wasn't married to—women I was just dating. I was seeing a number of different women and I didn't know how long a relationship would last. I guess I felt it would be a burden on them

—seeing me with too many people might be a little unnerving. When the kids spent the night at my house I solved it by staying at her place.

Leif, a thirty-seven-year-old father whose divorce five years ago gave him partial custody of two young sons, says that while he personally feels good about his single life-style, he is "not entirely comfortable about what it might be teaching the boys." They are nine and thirteen, and, according to Leif:

> One of the things I've been most concerned about is what values my kids will pick up. As a single parent, I want to be with a series of women. But, on the other hand, one of the great advantages of a long-term, committed relationship between two people is that children can see through example, not through some great lecture, that sex is the outgrowth of the caring two people have for each other. I worry about how they see me in relationships with other women and what they're learning about this. I personally feel that what I'm doing is right for me, but I'm not entirely comfortable about what it might be teaching the boys.

To handle their own discomfort, as well as to offset any unpredictable reactions their children might exhibit following their separation or divorce, most of the men we interviewed waited until they were in a stable relationship before they brought up the issue of dating. Lester, a thirty-four-year-old physician, divorced one year, has his children three nights a week. He handles his dilemma by keeping his dating life separate from his life with his children:

> Since I've been single, my kids have never been with me and a date. They've never seen me with another person other than their mom. I'm not comfortable with that yet, because I'm not comfortable with dating yet. And I feel like I need to get that straightened out first before I can get my kids involved. I don't know if that's right or not, but that's the way I feel.

Since most men are still not usually awarded custody of their children by the court,[4] unlike single mothers, they can have the luxury of maintaining two separate lives—one as a father tending to his children, and the other as a single man free to participate in the social scene. Such was the case for most of the single fathers we interviewed. Whether the children alternated one week with them and the next with their mother, or lived in the same neighborhood as their former spouses so they could go freely between the two homes, most of the nine men who were co-parents initially restricted their dating to those days and evenings when their children were away. Those three men we interviewed with full custody had to face the same limited set of options single mothers face. If they wanted to separate their social lives from their family lives, these men hired babysitters or live-in help and stayed over at their girl friend's house.

While the majority of men we interviewed decided to keep their social lives separate until they were involved in a serious relationship, many made a point of letting their children know that they were dating. They wanted them to realize they were social, sexual people without exposing them to these facts in a confrontive way.

Lester, for instance, says he's been involved in three relationships since his ten-year marriage broke up a year ago. He lets his children know he is dating by talking about the particular woman he's currently seeing. "I tell them that I enjoyed going out with so-and-so last night. They'll say, 'Well, who's so-and-so?' And I'll say, 'Well, that's somebody that I've been going out with, and sometime you'll get to meet her, maybe.'"

By talking about her for a period of time beforehand, a man made sure his child knew there was a woman who was important in his life and had heard enough about her to make any eventual meeting no surprise. As Burt, a thirty-four-year-old attorney, suggested:

For the most part, unless it's something serious, I tend not to talk about women and not to get the children involved. And I think, when I'm at the point where I'm seriously involved, then I'll say, "Well, look, this isn't an anonymous stranger, this is someone I care about and I would like you to get to know her so we can all spend time together." I would stress the fact that she isn't going to be a replacement "mom," but that she is going to be around and that I'd like us all to get along.

However, telling the kids that this new woman is also going to be sharing Daddy's bed can be awkward. And while some men never dealt with it directly and allowed the woman's appearance in the morning to speak for itself, others wanted to handle the issue more sensitively to help minimize the emotional stress the child would experience. Alan, who has joint custody of his ten-year-old daughter, was surprised at how difficult it was for him to bring up the subject compared to how easily his daughter accepted the situation:

> It was about four months or so after I separated when I had a date with this lady I had gone out with a number of times. I knew I was going to have my daughter Alison that night so I asked her out to dinner with Alison and me. I had never done this before, but they absolutely hit it off with each other. When we got home I remember how nervous I felt going into Alison's room to explain to her that I wanted this lady to spend the night with me. And I remember the conversation because I felt so awkward. I told her that it's lonely sleeping alone and it's nice sometimes to sleep with someone and that I liked this lady. I was surprised when Alison's response was only, "Oh, does that mean I get to play with her in the morning?"

Alan says another reason he feels his daughter so easily accepted the notion that Daddy wanted company for the night was her sense that she was still his first priority. As he said, "She sees that no one is living with me and that she gets to spend a lot of time with me but that sometimes she has to share."

Other children may not react so positively. According to Larry Brain, many children fantasize for years after the divorce that their parents will be reunited. Although their fathers might mention they are dating this or that woman, until he brings the woman home, children often do not accept the full reality of the marital rift. When children meet their father's new woman, this often puts the "final nail in the coffin of the fantasy about their parents' reconciliation," says Brain. However, this situation can be used as an opportunity to probe a child's feelings about the divorce. Brain recommends that a single parent allow feelings of anger or sadness to be expressed by the child. The fact that these feelings can surface and be discussed, he says, is another sign to the children that their relationship with their father is secure. When a child reacts negatively to meeting Father's new girl friend, many men we interviewed suggested handling it by reassuring the child that he can be involved with another woman and still be close to them.

Although the aftermath of divorce has its complications and no one felt they handled the variety of problems that arose as well as they could have, the men we interviewed agreed that eventually most children managed to cope with the new circumstances. The fact is that most school-age children expect that their divorced parents will date and are suspicious when they don't. Divorce no longer carries the same stigma it formerly did and most children have friends who have already gone through the same process.

One man remembers that after his separation his eight-year-old son was often seen with another classmate whose parents had split up six months earlier. His son's explanation was that she was his "adviser." And although his son felt sad, anxious, and initially stuttered and had trouble in school, he too did fine once his home life and his parents' once-volatile relationship stabilized. He even stopped stuttering once he developed a closer relationship with his father.

Jeff, a thirty-four-year-old lawyer who has full custody of his six-year-old son, feels that his son's awareness of his personal life hasn't had an adverse effect on him. Jeff has been seeing one woman regularly now, so he doesn't have to confront the complexities of exposing his son to several different women. Jeff says:

In the past, he wasn't always thrilled when a woman was over. But now, I love to hear him say, "Daddy, when Janet comes over, will she give me a hug when I'm sleeping?" You know, that's such a nice thing. Plus, we're very open about our relationship. Sometimes he opens the door while we're just lying in bed and he comes in. I never say, "Get out of here," or anything. He's not an interference. Obviously, we like our privacy, but we always have time for him when we spend time together as a couple and that's important to him.

Jeff says there have been times when he has wondered whether he is doing the right thing by being so open, but recently his son's teacher gave him a glowing report, saying he's the most socially advanced child in his class. "And I felt, 'Wow, I must be doing something right.'"

Whatever a man's marital status, it is important for his well-being to have his intimate and sexual needs met despite the presence of children. As the men in our study suggest, with a bit of planning, sexuality can continue to be a vital part of a parent's life even if he is parenting alone. And a man's desire for an active sex life is likely to continue even after the children are grown and have started families of their own. Yet, popular opinion suggests that men have a storehouse of sexual energy that at some point is depleted. In their autumn years, so this prevailing viewpoint goes, men lose their ability and interest in sex. Yet, a different picture emerged from our interviews. Even as sexual patterns change, sexual interest and vitality continue. Many of the men we interviewed reported that their intimate lives with their partners were a source of continuous enjoyment well in their sixties, seventies, and even eighties.

CHAPTER ELEVEN

THE GOLDEN YEARS CAN BE GOOD YEARS

Have you heard the one about:

The seventy-five-year-old man who was arrested for attempted rape with a dead weapon?

Or the eighty-one-year-old man who walked into the bedroom one night and found his seventy-year-old wife standing on her head? When he asked her why she was doing that she replied, "Well, I know we're going to have sex tonight and I thought if you couldn't get it up, maybe you could get it down!"

Or, finally, the sad story of Abie and Sadie who had been married for fifty years. Abie was eighty-five and Sadie was seventy. One day Sadie came home early and found her husband in bed with a twenty-five-year-old girl. She was so angry that she barged into the room, dragged Abie off the bed and threw him out the window. Abie died instantly. When the policeman came, he said, "Sadie, you and Abie were married for fifty years. Why did you throw him out the window?" Sadie said, "I came home and found him in bed with a twenty-five-year-old girl. I figured at eighty-five, if he could fuck, he could fly!"

If these lines don't leave you rolling in the aisles, it may be because this deprecating humor is used to cover up a deep anxiety many of us share. What will happen to our sexuality when we get old? For women, the looming fear is loss of sexual attractiveness. And for men, the fear is loss of sexual effectiveness. As comedian Tom Lehrer put it, "In all probability, I'll lose my virility and you your fertility and desirability."

When older men find it more difficult to obtain an erection, they interpret this as a sign of waning potency. Some men begin to view themselves as sexual eunuchs, believing this to be an inevitable consequence of the aging process.

Some of the older men we interviewed admitted they had given up on their sexuality. There was a sixty-nine-year-old man who had had a prostate operation five years previously and since then, because he couldn't talk to his wife and explain that he needed more direct penile stimulation, they had not had sex. Another man, a sixty-five-year-old lawyer who had been separated for three years, sublimated his sex drive by burying himself in his work. The reason? He claimed, "I wasn't as reliable sexually as I used to be in my youth."

But is a sexless life after youth necessarily inevitable? After interviewing nineteen men over age sixty, we found that the effects of the aging process vary from person to person. Each man's sexual response to aging is unique. And at the same time, some general patterns did emerge. Based on our study, it seems that as a man grows older, he may eventually experience one or more of the following:

• He may need more direct penile stimulation to obtain an erection

• His erections may not be as firm or as full as in earlier years

• He may need more time to reach orgasm

• He may not reach orgasm or ejaculate every time he has sex

• His ejaculations may be less forceful

• He may take longer to attain an erection after ejaculation

So it appears that getting old does not necessarily mean losing the ability to have an erection or to ejaculate. It just means a gradual slowing down of these responses. Rather than dwindling with age, a man's sexual performance can, like a fine wine, actually improve. And many of the older men we interviewed felt their sexual enjoyment had never been better. This response corroborates a recent sexuality study by Starr and Weiner. Of the eight hundred men and women over sixty who filled out questionnaires, two thirds said their sexuality was the same or better as compared to when they were younger.[1] With this as the reality, why do so many men pack up their sexuality and store it away, as if the pleasures of sexual intimacy ended with youth? One reason is a lifetime of conditioning that has ingrained in men the belief that this slowing-down process indicates a flaw in their masculinity. After all, we know a virile man:

- is always ready for sex
- can always get an erection
- needs only to think about sex to get turned on
- consistently has enormous and rock-hard erections
- always ejaculates

These responses are not the rule as men grow older. After decades of conditioning about what it means to be a man, many men who live to be a ripe old age find they don't match the image. Men raised under the macho credo are devastated when all they can do is "foreplay" and "afterplay," which, in effect, to them means no play at all.

The men we interviewed, however, were willing to reexamine their image of male potency and power. One man, who is now sixty-four, says:

A manly image for me, and I think for most men, was connected with how hard your dick gets and how fast and how often you score. This was a very powerful message, and one thing that happens when you get older is you begin getting internal warnings that say, "Oops, you're slipping." Then you begin to worry and the problem builds and gets more debilitating because you've always associated power with erections.

When they do not have an erection, many men say to themselves, "Well, I must not be ready for sex," or "Something must be seriously wrong with me," or "Maybe I'm not attracted to my partner anymore." This kind of concern can further interfere with sexual functioning until eventually they begin to avoid sexual situations altogether. This is the real killer of sex in later years: the belief that a man has a limited storehouse of sexuality that runs on full power in adolescence and early manhood, cruises through the middle years, and shuts down after that. Men who have this belief often make it come true. They interpret the signs of the aging process as forecasters of their future doom—the beginning of the end. So they abstain from sex and their responses decline more rapidly. The tragedy is that they cheat themselves out of a continued enjoyment of a fruitful, albeit more relaxed, sexual existence.

Many men make this decision to give up on sex because of life circumstances that demand and drain their energy and attention. Our society portrays the elderly as lonely, physically ailing, mentally deteriorating, and financially strapped—all of which would dampen sexual appetite regardless of age or gender. No wonder that as a man approaches his later years he braces himself for the eventual loss of his sexual prowess.

Although the common consensus is that "old" equals "sick," the statistics paint a different picture. The overwhelming majority of elderly people live independently and are in good health.[2] Currently in the United States, there are twenty-five million people over sixty-five, and the number increases each year. In fifty years, the figure is expected to double and reach the fifty million mark. Of the present figure, only 5 percent live in institutions or nursing homes. So the remaining 95 percent—nineteen million—live and function in the community. And contrary to the notion that the aged are enfeebled and dependent, 70 percent of these older people are home owners.[3]

The men we interviewed who were satisfied with their sexuality bore out these statistics. The majority continued to have active, vigorous sex into their later years. And since we are in dire need of positive role models, these are the men whose responses we have chosen to highlight. We wanted to find out what actual changes, both physical and psychological, they had to confront as they aged, and how these men who experienced rewarding sex lives had come to terms with these changes.

PHYSIOLOGICAL CHANGES

The more men we interviewed, the more we realized that each man had a unique sexual pattern. Some men felt that the aging process had slowed down their erection process but had not influenced their ability to ejaculate. For others, the time required between ejaculations grew longer, but their erections were as firm as ever. And some men, like Patrick, had experienced very little physical change in their sexual functioning. For Patrick, who is eighty-six, the most apparent change in his bedroom habits has been his need for more sleep. As far as sex is concerned, he and his seventy-six-year-old wife enjoy making love two or three times a week. Besides not noticing any significant change in the frequency of their sex together, Patrick said he still gets firm erections with no trouble and ejaculates each time—sometimes more rapidly than he would like. Patrick said: "I read in the paper that sex keeps elderly people young, and I believe that there are *young* old people and there are *old* old people. I think our sexual relationship is what keeps us young."

And Clarence, a sixty-seven-year-old college professor, reports that he and his second wife have about as active a sex life as he had during the early years of his first marriage:

We probably have sexual intercourse two or three times a week, sometimes one day apart, sometimes four days apart, except when one of us is sick. When that happens, my wife says we've gotta get a raincheck! On our honeymoon last June we did it every day. As far as sex goes, I think I've had a pretty good adjustment over the years.

Of the men we interviewed, however, those who reported no change or only slight changes in their sexual responsiveness and frequency as they aged were unusual. The majority of men were able to cite very specific changes in their sexual response patterns as they entered their later years. For some, these physiological changes actually began at thirty, for others, over the years that followed. But almost all of those who talked about changes contrasted their current sexuality to the sexual image they held of themselves around the age of eighteen—when hormones had surging lives of their own and erections appeared on the scene suddenly and unannounced.

Riley, age seventy, remembers:

I'd get on a bus sometimes and there'd be some smashing woman there, and I'd have a hell of a time getting off the bus. I'd have to hold my briefcase in front of me. Now, no way.

That just can't happen. I need to be physically touched to have an erection.

While sexual changes may have crept up on these men gradually through their twenties and thirties, it was often the fortieth birthday that caused men to reflect and take stock of their lives. For many men, this age marks a crucial milestone. It can be a time to look in the mirror and confront oneself on many levels—professional, personal, and sexual. At this point, many men come face to face with the reality of growing older. In his first-person account for *Esquire* magazine, Digby Diehl wrote: "Turning forty means you're changing from a sprinter to a long-distance runner."[4]

Some men were able to roll with the changes, while others fought back and some even lost control of their lives temporarily. In any event, the sexual changes that accompanied the aging process almost always required making readjustments in their self-image as well as their personal relationships.

Justin, a forty-eight-year-old minister who has been married twenty-three years, said:

Here I was almost forty and I noticed some of the problems I've continued to experience, like not being able to have an erection as quickly as in previous years—because I'm one guy who really enjoys his sex life. Sometimes I would have an erection and, just before penetration, bam—flab. Or I'd get involved in the act and all of a sudden it would disappear and I'd have to get a searchlight to look for it. And it bothered me.

Fourteen years ago when Leo was forty, he was also concerned about the longer refractory period he required between erections:

I noticed that, as I aged, I came more slowly, especially with oral sex. I also didn't get hard as quickly as I did when I was seventeen. But it is hard to tell which changes are physical and which are mental. I used to get mixed up about it and worry about it, but the worrying just slowed me down more. So I've just quit worrying about it.

If a man has crossed the threshold of his forties with no discernible signs of aging, he can probably expect to encounter these changes at some point in the future. Changes in erection and ejaculation patterns of the vast majority of the men we interviewed, supported the literature on aging. Many of the older men reported a need for direct stimulation of the penis in order to get hard. The sudden springing to attention—spontaneous erection—was largely past history. Their erections now took longer to achieve and were often not as firm as they had been in the past. They had what one man called the "bend-in-the-middle" syndrome, an erection firm enough for penetration but less firm than in younger days.

Once intercourse was in full progress, many men told us they didn't always feel a need to ejaculate. For instance, one man says that he reaches a peak during sex, but it isn't necessarily an orgasm. Another says, "I get so damn close, like I'm just about to go off the cliff, then I deflate, and that's the end of that." He adds, however, that this inability to reach orgasm doesn't leave him frustrated or irritable as in bygone days.

Riley, age seventy, elaborates on a similar experience:

There's no way now that I can have sex night after night and ejaculate night after night, but that doesn't mean I always have to wait three days or something, either. I can have sex two evenings in succession, or tonight and tomorrow morning, and ejaculate both times. But sometimes I'll have a roaring fine damned sexual experience and feel higher than a kite, be very much into it, and, at a certain point, I just physically and emotionally tire. I feel stretched out, at the outer edge, and I just suddenly come down from it. Then I have to assure my friend that I feel fine, that I've gotten everything I could get out of it for the night, and that's it. Once I got some information about the process and knew what was happening, I felt okay with it.

Sometimes even when a man did ejaculate, his experience of the ejaculation changed as well. Some men noticed less of a separation between the feeling of ejaculatory inevitability, just prior to the ejaculation, and the ejaculation itself. The two blended together. Others noticed that their ejaculation was less forceful. "I've noticed in the last ten years," said one seventy-year-old man, "that when I do come, my ejaculation is less powerful. I feel my semen seeping out rather than shooting out like it once did." Yet he doesn't let these changes trouble him. "It's like I play handball every day and know I'm not as good as I was ten years ago. But I still play well and I still enjoy the game."

Because of a variety of physiological changes—muscles growing weaker, strength diminishing, the body losing tone, and a general waning of stamina—sexual interest may also decline. Many of the men we interviewed in their sixties, seventies, and eighties said they felt less physically powerful. Stanley, age sixty-five, said he has less drive than he used to. "Sleep becomes more important, perhaps more important than when I was very young and all the hormones were working."

What this means to an older man's sex life, according to some of the men we interviewed, is that sexual encounters usually occur in the morning, after a good night's sleep, or on weekends, when there's more leisure time and fewer worldly demands. Fatigue becomes more of a concern than it may once have been. "I'm not as active as I once was," says Lee, age sixty-two, who calls himself a "weekend warrior." "I wonder if it would be different if I were more active, but I don't think so. I'm not sure if the variable is my age or my physical condition. Perhaps if I were in better shape I might not get tired so easily."

Rest was clearly important to these men. In fact, eighty-six-year-old Patrick felt that his restful retired life was critical to his active sex life:

The most important thing to being able to keep having sex is rest. I rest all the time. I tell the guys I won't stay up till ten o'clock playing cards. At eight o'clock I go upstairs, watch television, read the paper, then when my wife comes in from playing cards, I'm plenty rested and ready for sex.

BODY IMAGE

Many of the men we interviewed refused to accept the idea that as their body changed their sex life would necessarily decline as the years passed. They looked in the mirror and either made peace with themselves or, if they didn't like what they saw, made the necessary changes. They had to come to terms with the wrinkles, sagging stomachs, slouching posture, and thinning hair. Some men didn't let these changes affect the picture they had of themselves as sexually attractive. Rolfe, for instance, is sixty-six, and says:

I'd be happy to walk along a beach nude and not give a damn. My philosophy is to grow old graciously, and if I have a few wrinkles or sag here and there, I couldn't care less.

Greg has always been thin but lately has acquired a belly. "I feel all right when I'm dressed," he says, "but when I'm undressed, when I'm getting ready to go to bed with a woman, I'm very aware of it." The way he deals with it is to "just ignore it":

I've never had anybody complain. It's just something that sticks out there that makes me a little more huggable. It's more important to me than to the women I know. It's not very important to them, which always surprises me.

Then there are the men who couldn't ignore the changes they saw in the mirror. Rather than "grow old gracefully," several men we interviewed refused to let the aging process ruin their self-image. They fought back, committing themselves to a vigorous regime of exercise. The result, for some, was like turning the clock back. Mark, age sixty-one, told us:

I have a better sense about my body now than I used to have. I feel better about it although it is older. My body feels stronger and more flexible. I wasn't a great athlete as a kid. My mother inhibited my physical activity and discouraged me from using my body athletically. So I started from way behind. But now I've gotten more friendly with my body, and I've overcome a lot of the inhibitions, very gradually and slowly. I've strengthened my body. A year ago, I got seriously interested in jogging, and I started jogging more, and farther, and longer. I also began doing other exercises that I hadn't done before. As a result, my body has gotten stronger. And I feel like I'm getting younger. I have an advantage over men who in the old days, I would envy for being so athletic when I was unathletic. Now, I look at other men my age and I see them as being paunchy and stiff and aging in lots of ways, while I feel like my body is lithe and trim and stronger than ever.

Then we interviewed a man who, at seventy years old, says:

I'm in the best shape I've been in for ten or fifteen years. Three years ago, I took up Tai Chi. And now I'm using my body every day. Of course, my arms sag now and my skin feels like crepe, and, goddamn, I don't like it. It doesn't look like it used to, but I know that, underneath it, everything is terrific.

These men, who consciously maintained their physical activity, had good news to report about their sex lives. Their stamina improved. They found they had more energy for sex. Their bodies were strong and muscular and they felt more virile. People paid them compliments and they appreciated the acknowledgment. Although they would never recapture their youth, their good health and fine physical condition enabled them to feel more sexual as they grew older.

SEXUAL SOLUTIONS

Keeping the body taut and in prime condition through exercise, however, is not sufficient to stave off the physiological slowing-down that inevitably comes with age. You can tighten your stomach muscles by doing leg raises and sit-ups, but they won't help keep your penis fully erect. And while jogging may strengthen your heart, it won't guarantee an ejaculation each time you make love. How, then, did the men in our sample confront the physical changes that altered their sexual pattern?

One way men managed to cope with these problems was to expand the definition of what comprises a masculine sexual response. As they aged, some of these men reported that this aspect of their lives acquired a new definition. Said one:

I've come to recognize that my sexuality is both very powerful and very fragile. Sometimes, it's not so easy to get hard and many times I don't come. Yet there are compensations in growing older—like more staying power and, for me, more sensitivity.

If an older man can accept those aspects of his sexuality that are delicate, sensitive and, at times, fragile, he can then redefine his idea of what comprises adequate sexual performance. He no longer has to mourn the loss of the knee-jerk response to stimulation he experienced so powerfully as a younger man. The result, for those who have peeled off their he-man masks, is a deeper sense of their own sexuality.

But a man can't take off his mask with his eyes closed. With all the changes taking place during the aging process, each man must become familiar with his individual responses. More than ever before, he needs to understand his orgasmic pattern if he is going to be able to enjoy the changes—just as a surfer must be in tune with the sea if he is to ride out the wave.

The difficulty for most men is that they rarely assume responsibility for their erections or orgasmic responses. Instead, they often attribute them to their lover. "She was so sexy," they say, "it just happened." Is a result, men may not be familiar enough with their sexual arousal process to recognize what is happening. When their set of responses changes, they may sense a loss of control. Step one, then, is to understand the changes your body has gone through so that you can learn to adapt to them. Masturbation is a good way to understand your arousal pattern and the ways in which it has changed.

If your erections are less firm, but feel just as pleasurable, become familiar with the tactile sensations of a less-erect penis. Perhaps a variety of new strokes and caresses to your penis can make it harder. Experiment with yourself. Know where, when, and how you enjoy being stimulated. If your sense of ejaculatory inevitability is fainter, then listen more acutely for the signals leading up to it, and if your ejaculations no longer burst forth but slowly exude, recognize that this change in rhythm can be accompanied by a whole array of new feelings.

Step two in removing those macho masks is to share this new information about yourself with your partner or, together, experiment and explore in order to develop a new, more rewarding sexual pattern. What could be more reassuring to a wife, lover, or friend than to be included in the process by a man who has become comfortable with himself.

As Justin explained to his wife:

My mental acumen is not so powerful when it comes to sex as it was with our early years. I recall, earlier, all I had to do was just think about sex and I'd experience an erection. Now, I can

think all I want to and nothing happens. Now, I really need
you as an outside stimulus. I need your hands, I need your
voice, I need your body pressure, I need more action from you
to me.

Many of our interviewees didn't start out as such super com-
municators. It was not easy for them to communicate openly about
their most basic sexual needs, especially when they were doing this
for the first time in their lives. In many cases, it was the support and
active involvement of a caring woman that helped these men adjust
to their evolving sexuality. Some men had dropped out of the sexual mainstream, often following divorce or the death of a spouse,
thinking their potency was used up and that sex was a thing of the
past. Often, in these instances, the admiration and affection—and
active encouragement—of a supportive partner was what they
needed to once again experience their virility.

Seventy-two-year-old Alvin, for instance, thought his sexuality
was all but dead after a long-term sexually inactive marriage that
ended in divorce and was followed by a platonic relationship with
a woman whom he took care of for several years until she died.
Since at least ten years had elapsed since Alvin had had any sexual
contact, he assumed his sexual functioning had ceased:

I believe I was still sexually interested, but I shied away from
it. I hid behind the fact that I was so many years old. I suppose
I was secretly afraid that I wouldn't function "properly," and
often I wasn't able to because there wasn't any encouragement or whatever it takes from the other person to help with
the stimulation. Naturally, at an older age a man can't expect
to have an erection as quickly or as long. Men *should* know
that, but many don't and are ashamed when they can't perform
like they used to. Many older men still have an interest in sex
but they hide behind their age when what they're really afraid
of is exposing themselves. But if they felt that their partner
would be sympathetic and cooperative, they would still be interested in sex.

Alvin's confidence and participation in sexual activity were revived with the help of a woman who appreciated him. She told him
that his body was beautiful, that she found him attractive and liked

being with him. "If you hear this over and over again," Alvin recalls, "you begin to believe it, and you begin to respond."

Another reason this woman's approach was so successful was that she downplayed the importance of intercourse and therefore the emphasis on having an erection. She taught Alvin that sexuality was not synonymous with intercourse—that holding, caressing, and fondling were important aspects of lovemaking. Through her, he was reintroduced to the joys of oral sex—not as a substitute for intercourse, but as an alternate way of expressing their pleasure with each other.

Dan, a seventy-three-year-old, reinforced this view and says he would tell others who consider themselves too old to have sex that:

Solo sex or mutual masturbation can be just as exhilarating as intercourse. Sexuality is a life force, and a very powerful life force. If tapped, it can keep you alive and vigorous and full of dynamic interest. It's not something to abandon depending upon whether you got a certain erection or not.

Dan felt like a crusader of sorts. The message he wanted to share with those in his age group who, like himself, had been raised thinking of masturbation and oral sex as "dirty" and "unnatural," was that there were ways of continuing sexual activity regardless of erection.

Says Dan:

All men fail at one point or another. But rather than get depressed, the marvelous way to react is to celebrate life, to realize that although the penis has indeed deflated or failed, the man can still continue to caress his partner with his hand most tenderly, almost with a religious dedication, and with his tongue, if she can accept that. His tongue and his hands certainly aren't going to deflate. And instead of committing suicide, let's have a learning experience. Rather than feeling that it's totally lost and there is no reason to live, we can learn to accept all of our sexuality, so that ten years from now, when both the husband and wife have less vigor, this great life force of sexuality, warm and alive and surging right within their command, will help carry them through all kinds of difficulties.

More so than when they were young, a couple in their autumn

years who want satisfying sex together have to become a team. It's like dancing: when the music is rock, the energy is high, and two young people dance separately to the rhythm. An older couple often dances to the beat of the big band sound. The music is somewhat slower, and when they dance they do better when they move in unison.

For many men we interviewed, this meant that women sometimes had to take the lead. These men appreciated women who would take the first step in lovemaking by stimulating them. "What turns me on," says one man, who describes his partner as very active, "is knowing that she wants it as much as I do." As with many others who felt that their sex lives grew more fulfilling as the years passed, this man didn't play the macho man role of exclusive initiator. Each was a partner in the fullest sense of the word—both giving as well as getting—and lovemaking was more intimate and more satisfying. A number of men we interviewed were fortunate to have active, communicative partners and were able to work as a team to solve some of the problems that arose as a result of the aging process.

Many found that changing intercourse positions was one way to solve the problem of less than rock-hard erections. The way Clarence, sixty-seven, and his wife solved this difficulty was for her to straddle him. Being on top, she could lower herself onto his semi-erect penis. That way, Clarence was freed from the need to stay rigid and continue thrusting as he would have had to do in the missionary position.

Forrest, sixty-eight, found that, if he lay on his side and faced his partner, his penis could be "almost soft" during intercourse but both could still have a fulfilling experience:

It's just by accident that I discovered this other position. It's the one they advise for female patients who are pregnant and can't have the man lying on top of her. Instead, he lies to one side and puts his leg between hers. Then you can insert your penis, even if it is almost soft. It's a wonderful position because you're able to feel the woman's breasts and the woman enjoys it too.

When Gene, age sixty-six, found that his penis wasn't as hard as it used to be, his wife understood the dilemma and helped the process along:

With great skill she would put her hands between her legs when I was on the top and, by pulling the vulva apart a bit, made her vagina more receptive. At the same time, she had her finger around my penis so it didn't collapse. This way the penis, though not fully erect, still stayed in and did its job. If your partner understands and can do what she did with my bend in the middle, you don't need to make excuses for it.

Several of the men we interviewed preferred the male-superior position because it facilitated ejaculation. One man told us:

I can pump faster and harder in the missionary position. I know damn well that, when I was younger, it didn't make that much difference. But as I'm getting older, I'm a little less quick, so I sustain much longer, with a great deal of enjoyment. But when I get near ejaculation, I really need to thrust in and out, very, very rapidly. And I can do that best from the male-superior position.

No matter what position older men used, ejaculation was not always a sure thing. Sporadic ejaculation was cited by many of the older men we interviewed as one of the most disconcerting sexual changes they experienced. Brent, age sixty-four, for instance, says that the first time he didn't have an orgasm was frightening:

It brought up all sorts of crap about, "God, I *am* getting old." I worried that it was all going to stop and there'd be no more. And so for a while I began to say, "Am I?" "Will I?" or "How can I?" Ultimately, it just took relaxing and loving. And now if I have an orgasm, fine. If I don't, it's not fine, but it's not a great tragedy, either.

Richard, age fifty-three, discovered that, far from being a tragedy, not coming was actually beneficial:

When I don't come as frequently, I'm more interested in sex. I'm still a little bit turned on the next day. It's a Tantric-like approach where you focus on certain sensations to make them last, and you don't have to come. When that happens, I'm more available for sex the next time. Whereas if I came today, it's less likely that I'd be interested in sex as soon.

Another man felt there would be a time in his life when he probably wouldn't be able to come and so he consciously practiced holding back his ejaculation in preparation:

It's been great for me to discover that it's not some kind of urgent thing to have an ejaculation. I thought it would be bad for me physically, I'd be in pain, or so out of control I would have to go all the way. So I experimented. It took a little practice and there is a sense of depriving myself, but it's great. And the next day I'm even more aroused.

SEX GETS BETTER AND BETTER

And now for the good news! According to those we interviewed, men who are healthy, for whom money is not an ever-present anxiety, and whose relationships are steady and positive can look forward to increased satisfaction in their sexual pleasure as the years go by.

The satisfaction they reported was not a miracle. No one had discovered a fountain of youth. Instead, the success seemed to come from accepting their age and all the possibilities it afforded, rather than attempting, through a magic potion or the equally futile reliance on nostalgic memories, to recapture their youth.

Leo's concern about his changing sexuality was assuaged by his acceptance and subsequent appreciation of himself as an older man:

The more anxious I got about the sexual changes I was experiencing, the longer it took to get an erection. Finally I told myself, "I really am changing. All the willing it or thinking about it isn't going to slow it down. It's perfectly natural, so don't kick yourself about it. You can still have a whole bunch of fun." So I read books that described what goes on with males and I talked with other men. Finally I began to talk openly with the woman I was with, and I discovered I was far more interested in my physical changes than anyone else was. So I have learned to be patient with myself, not to be quite so demanding or quite so focused on whether my dick is hard enough, and this has helped me become more aware and more accepting of myself.

These men were attuned to the harmony their years offered and they appreciated and enjoyed its music thoroughly. A man who had lived sixty-five years could draw on many years of experience when he reached out to love his partner. The intimacy clearly could be subtler, deeper, and more satisfying than the urgency of more youthful sexual encounters. The men who achieved this level of interplay with their lovers had learned to explore the fragility as well as the power of sex. They considered sex to be better with time because they had discarded some of the baggage of their youth. Many, freed from the stresses of the workaday world, were more relaxed and had more time for sex. They were also freed from having to "score" and the worry of getting the woman pregnant. Companionship and intimacy, as opposed to sexual performance, formed the cornerstone of their sexual pleasure.

"It's a fallacy that sex is not enjoyable for older people," says Forrest, age sixty-eight:

There are many things that give you a lot of sexual pleasure. You can just lie there and caress each other or, if you have intercourse, you don't have to worry about the woman getting pregnant. If you're out with people you've known for a long time, you don't worry about disease. You can have an erection for twenty or thirty minutes and enjoy the whole process of lovemaking. And when you do come, it has all the satisfaction of when you were younger.

Many men even found that sex improved over the years. This was the experience of sixty-six-year-old Gene: "I would say sex has gotten much more intense now over the past few years." He attributes this enhanced enjoyment to increased relaxation and the absence of worry over birth control:

All the kids are out and taken care of and there's no worry. As the tensions of life begin to diminish you can allow yourself more spontaneity. My wife has had a hysterectomy and she's completely relaxed. There's no more fear about the diaphragm not working, the foam not working, or the condom coming off. And I think that does a lot for your relaxation.

Bob, who has been married twenty-five years, says that the passage of time has had a positive effect on his sexual relationship. He and his wife have become more skilled at lovemaking and better partners. As he says:

> Sex is better now than it was in my twenties. I think that as we mature we learn how to handle ourselves and our partners. We learn what pleases them and eventually it gets back to pleasing us even if it's something different from what we like. And sex is just as exciting. After twenty-five years of marriage, I can even say it's better now. We have experimented and expanded our sexual repertoire to include exciting and stimulating things. Our communication has improved too, so we're both just happier with our sex life.

But all of the positive changes were not limited to the mental aspects of worry-free, relaxed intimacy. Some benefits were clearly derived from the physiological slowing-down process—the very process that was anticipated with dread. For what these men realized was that being slower to get erect and to ejaculate meant prolonged lovemaking and increased pleasure. Realizing this, many men, some for the first time in their lives, were able to relax and leisurely savor their lovemaking sessions, much as they would relish a fine meal. As Dan, sixty-eight, a retired airline pilot said, "There's no urgency about it anymore. Nobody's in a hurry to get it on or get it over with, and I can certainly prolong the experience much longer than I could twenty-three or twenty-four years ago."

Alvin, who is seventy-two, wishes that he could have attained the same degree of pleasure as a young man that he now has during intercourse:

> As a younger man, ejaculation came rather normally. Ejaculation now is more delayed, stretched out. It's something that I have to admit I wish I could have done then. It's much more pleasurable now because it all takes longer. Before, erection was almost immediate. Now there has to be an interest on the part of my partner to caress my penis. And I'm caressing parts of her body, so erection now is much more pleasurable. It takes longer, but it's more beautiful.

A delightful bonus, which many older men say they hadn't expected with aging, was the discovery that, as their sexual responses slowed down, they were more in tune with their wives' and lovers' sexual rhythms. As younger men, they were often running ahead of their female partners by being quicker to erect and ejaculate. Women often needed and wanted more foreplay to get primed for intercourse. And men who cared for their women learned to restrain themselves. They learned to thwart their natural processes. But as those physical processes changed and slowed, this was no longer necessary. As older men, their sexual response cycles more closely resembled those of their female lovers. Accordingly, older men were now more interested in engaging in foreplay and exploring the sensuality of sex.

Frank, a minister, finds that at sixty-three years of age he's reached an appreciation of the sensual aspect of sex:

> The only way I can explain it is that I didn't know there was such a thing as being sensuous. I find I'm much more sensuous now, and much less active sexually. In other words, I'm much less aggressive when it comes to sex.

Those like Frank, who had come to appreciate sensuality in their later years, often experienced a heightened interest in fulfilling their partners' needs. For sixty-eight-year-old Don, satisfying his partner was a turn-on in itself:

> Sex has gotten much better as I've gotten older. I don't have an orgasm in a hurry, and sometimes I don't have one at all. It doesn't make any difference to me whether I do or not. I know eventually it's going to take care of itself. But now, I'm much more turned on by experiencing the woman's orgasm. I like the feeling of oneness this gives me. And the lady happens to be lucky too, because I can be there as long as she wants me to.

Even though older men were more in tune with their partners' needs and better able to satisfy them, they were still interested in peak sexual experiences for themselves. And while much of the literature says that one consequence of the aging process is that ejaculations and orgasms are often not as intense, this runs contrary to what some men told us. For many of them, the quality and intensity of the orgasm is still there. Gene, age sixty-six, felt that "the orgasm itself is definitely better, even better than when I was in my twenties or thirties." From what we learned of these men, this response made sense to us. They were more relaxed, and often more open to experiencing the subtleties of sex, the sensual delights. They were experienced lovers, they were more turned on by the satisfaction that they were able to give to their partners—and there were more feelings involved. As fifty-year-old Nicholas expressed it: "My sexual feelings have become more intense because there is more involvement of my feelings. My feelings have become stronger and clearer as I've gotten older, and with that has come a lot more sexual feeling."

For sixty-seven-year-old Barry, orgasm itself is more intense and sex in general is more of a sensual thrill than it used to be because he has lost some of the inhibitions of his youth:

My experience of orgasm now is definitely better, much better. It's a groovier experience, it feels better, it's a greater high, it's more of a sensual thrill than it used to be and I think it's probably all in the mind. I'm not as uptight about sex as I was. I had some pretty severe inhibitions placed on me when I was a boy and quite a bit of guilt to overcome, but I managed it pretty well. The passage of time and people I knew, books I read, psychotherapy, and experiences I had all added to my gradual realization that it's nonsense to feel guilty about something as natural as sex. And while I can't say that there isn't still a little gnawing feeling of guilt around the edges, it's not the way it used to be. Consequently, my moments of orgasm are more intense now than they were when I was younger. There is more pure physical pleasure and I think more personal pleasure too, because I feel much closer to my partner than I used to. There is less fear, less hostility, and more empathy.

A number of men felt that their orgasmic pattern had changed in a positive way. Some, like Mel, age fifty-nine, mentioned "waves of pleasure and multiple orgasms":

Although orgasm is less frequent, my orgasms are much, much more powerful. I think it has to do with a heightened awareness I've developed. It's a multiple kind of thing which I didn't experience in my youth at all. It's like these waves that keep coming and coming and it's really a tremendous experience. The refractory period is much longer, it's like a day or so, or sometimes a week or so, but when the orgasm occurs, it's so much more powerful and longer-lasting than it was before that there's just no comparison.

Some men in their seventies whose ejaculate often seeped out as opposed to bursting forth as it had in their youth spoke of their new sense of continuous orgasm. Alvin, at seventy-two, finds that his orgasmic response, which he calls "coming down the other side of the mountain," holds more pleasure for both him and his partner than it did in earlier years:

> There are times when I don't ejaculate completely. It's a slow ejaculation, a seepage as it were. When my partner and I are really at it, she informs me that I'm leaking and I'm aware of it, but the leaking goes on and on and on. Not in spurts, but a seepage that I really enjoy. It's difficult to describe it, but it's wonderful because there isn't this sudden thing and it's over. The seepage allows me to show a continued interest in my partner. My climax is stretched out so we can both come down the other side of the mountain together. That's our expression for it. And it's done gradually. I can stimulate her with my fingers, with my tongue, with my legs, with whatever part of my body is close because I'm not so preoccupied with my orgasm that it interferes with attending to her. And I enjoy it because she is coming down gradually also. Afterward I don't turn over and go to sleep, I have no interest in sleep. So my partner and I have as much afterplay as foreplay.

The evidence seems to be in. If men can overcome the cultural messages that their sex lives are finished once their erections and ejaculations slow down, there can be more physical pleasure, more involvement of feelings, and more sexual intimacy. Armed with accurate information, the ability to rethink old attitudes, continued physical and sexual activity, and the cooperation of a loving partner, the golden years can be as good or even better sexually than the youthful years.

Men who understood this expressed a desire to enjoy their remaining years to their fullest. As sixty-eight-year-old Forrest put it:

> I'm looking forward to getting all the sex I can before I die—

and getting in all kinds of other things too. My aim is to enjoy life to the fullest in everything I do.

Perhaps all those deprecating sexual jokes about older men ought to be replaced with more realistic images, such as those that gave forty-eight-year-old Justin more positive attitudes about aging:

I have friends who operate nursing homes. I heard one nursing home manager say, "I can't keep that old guy out of the room with that woman." And I looked at this woman dragging this guy away and saw the bulge in the man's robe, and I knew they were going to do it. And every once in a while I break down and buy this magazine called *Horny* and I read letters from these old guys who are still masturbating two or three times a day, and guys who are saying, "I live in a senior home and I'm still raring to go." When I see these kinds of things, my whole outlook changes. And I think there's hope for me yet!

There's more than hope for Justin and other older men. From what we learned in our interviews, it seems that Sadie made a serious mistake. Though we doubt that older men can fly, they certainly can make love!

NOTE: One problem the older men didn't have that was experienced by the women interviewed for *Shared Intimacies* was difficulty finding partners. Because there are so many more females than males over sixty, men were more likely to declare, "Are you kidding? Difficulty finding partners? They're all over me!"

CONCLUSION

As far as William knew, he had it all. At age thirty-five, his career was finally taking off and it looked as if his financial worries were behind him. Susan, his wife of ten years, had a part-time job that supplemented the family income, but she knew she could quit to have a baby if she wanted to since William's salary could more than cover their monthly expenses. After his last raise, William expected the coming years to be financially secure. There would be more time to relax and be together. They could now afford a live-in housekeeper and could even take that trip to Paris they weren't able to afford on their honeymoon. But those dreams were abruptly shattered. Susan announced one evening that she wanted a divorce. Her reason? She didn't feel she was getting the emotional intimacy she needed. The material comforts he provided were nice, but they weren't enough.

William was devastated. As far as he was concerned he had carried out his male script impeccably. He was a responsible and successful breadwinner, respected by his peers, and he had never strayed from his marital bed. Didn't they have the requisite American Dream—an impressive suburban home with two cars and an American Express Gold Card? What could Susan be talking about? No intimacy! What did that mean, anyway?

Almost overnight, William was forced to confront the very real question of what had caused the loss of the only thing that was really important to him. In his attempt to make his wife happy, the best way he knew how, he had lost her. His basic assumptions about being a man which he had always lived up to were being challenged and finally discarded by his wife. And nowhere in his masculine script was "intimacy" even mentioned.

So William, like many men, had to embark on an inner journey. By taking a critical look at his life and at himself as a man, he hoped to understand why he had been unable to develop an intimate relationship.

Others went through a similar process of reevaluating their masculine scripts, but at a more gradual pace. Those who had made a conscious effort to change their attitudes and expectations of themselves as men said they did so because of an amorphous sense of emptiness that consistently nagged at them. For some, the spark had gone from their marriages, or their sex lives had become routine, or they had a sense of being a stranger to their children. Whatever the cause, these men concluded that intimacy and a feeling of connection with those they loved was absent from their lives.

Still other men—primarily younger bachelors or older men who were reentering the social circuit after separating from a longstanding partner—were changing in reaction to a new kind of woman. These women were more assertive and self-assured; they were accustomed to paying their own way, propositioning a man, or getting "on top" during intercourse. They were a new breed of women who wanted to be with a new breed of men. Emotionally, these new men were supposed to be versatile and able to express a wider range of feelings. And in the sexual realm they were expected to be playful, tender, occasionally passive, and certainly not threatened by women who might at times take control of the lovemaking.

Whatever prompted a man to reevaluate his sexual role script, the conclusion was generally the same. The old "shoulds" about being a man were antithetical to achieving intimacy, particularly in the sexual realm. Machismo, with its emphasis on scoring, performing, and controlling feelings ran counter to the expression of loving, caring, and tender feelings.

Two years after his divorce from Susan, William says he is just beginning to emerge from his state of shock. However, this experience has forced him to examine his attitudes in a way he might never have without Susan's ultimatum. And he has taken it upon himself to change things. He realizes that if Susan can rewrite her script and refuse to play out certain roles and carry out certain tasks solely because she is a woman, then he can do the same and, in the process, get more overall fulfillment as a man.

A number of men we interviewed had similar insights. They were openly experimenting, in some cases, even adopting behaviors, activities, and roles that previously had been assigned to women. Many men, for example, are enjoying cooking gourmet meals, decorating their homes, and learning new art forms. Sexually, more men are experimenting with a wider range of behaviors and experiencing a broader spectrum of emotions. The evidence we've accumulated from the men we interviewed points to an upcoming societal change in sexual behaviors and attitudes, but by no means suggests that we are in the throes of a full-scale revolution of sex roles. Men have taken longer than women to examine and evaluate their role scripts because, at least in part, women were able to look to one another for support. Men, meanwhile, are often struggling through these changes alone. Usually a shift in sexual attitude or behavior is a private experience for a man, done in the confines of his bedroom, with only his partner as witness. Due to a deeply ingrained ethic of male competition, men who are experimenting with removing their macho-man mask are naturally reluctant to share their concerns and, in so doing, expose their vulnerabilities to other men's judgment.

The men we interviewed were bolder than most and risked allowing us in on their innermost thoughts. By agreeing to a detailed interview, they, in a sense, took us on a tour of their evolving ideas about masculinity. Perhaps they felt comfortable doing this because we were women and *not* men, or possibly because we were professionals and could assure them of confidentiality. Whatever the case, this opportunity to take a closer look at the fine print in their new role scripts gave us a unique perspective on men in the midst of change.

The following are some of the changes the men we interviewed perceived that they had undergone. Some are slight shifts in attitude, others entail enormous behavioral change. We believe the sum, however, points to impressive gains made by men who want to express themselves as fully as they can. The old expectations are not as valid anymore, and men are now saying that you don't have to:

- feel that an erection is necessary in order to enjoy sex

- feel you have to maintain an erection for hours to be a good lover

- feel you have to ejaculate every time you make love

- feel obliged to have sex just because it's available

- feel you should already know everything there is to know about sex or feel embarrassed about wanting to learn more

- feel emasculated if your partner suggests there are ways you could improve your lovemaking

- feel that you are less of a man if your partner wants sex more often than you

- feel that your partner has to have one or more orgasms or you're not a good lover

- feel that if you take longer to attain an erection as you get older your sex life is over

The former taboos are being dropped and men are now saying that it's okay to:

- be sexually passive at times

- wait awhile after meeting someone before having sex

- ask for physical affection instead of sex—if all you want is a hug or some nurturing

- feel anxious sometimes

- talk about your feelings and let your partner know how you like to be stimulated

- choose to be with an assertive woman who can take initiative in bed

- keep the romance alive in the relationship and plan for sex

- be monogamous if it feels right for you

- masturbate because you enjoy your body and it feels good

- be intimately involved in your wife's pregnancy whether it means being sexually active or not

- require more direct physical stimulation in your later years to attain an erection

These lists should be considered carefully. As encouraged as some men and women might be in hearing that men are breaking out of long-standing, rigid behavioral patterns, it is important to proceed cautiously and not to lose sight of the end goal, which is greater fulfillment and intimacy. The danger is in discarding the former "shoulds" of machismo for a set of new "shoulds." If men see these evolving behaviors and attitudes as dictates instead of options, and begin once again to judge themselves according to how closely they match up to this new list, they may find themselves locked into a new but equally restrictive straitjacket. And at worst, the standards may be completely unattainable as both men—and women—begin expecting men to act macho and liberated at the same time. No such Superman exists here on earth. While men can pick and choose from among the range of possibilities, they cannot expect to be all things at all times.

Women who are expecting such diversity from one man are placing unrealistic expectations on him and are likely to be disappointed. As the following joke illustrates, this pressure is becoming more and more evident in some relationships:

After making love, the man and woman ease back against the pillows, each smiling and relaxed, lost in their own thoughts as they bask in the afterglow of their shared experience. Self-satisfied, the man puffs on his cigarette. The woman begins to speak, "You know what I really like in a man?" She flexes her muscles and says, "I love strength . . ." and then she cradles her arm, adding, "and I appreciate tenderness. And I really go for a guy who's supportive but doesn't mince words, a man who's completely honest with me, and, of course, highly intelligent, but modest about it." As she becomes more enraptured with her words, he looks on skeptically. "I like a guy who can go with equal ease to see a Shakespeare play and a punk rock concert—a man who's cool and together on the outside, but really in touch with his emotions on the inside. Yes, someone who's very assertive but who also gives me enough space of my own." Impatient and exasperated, the man snaps back, "If you find a man like that, *I'll* sleep with him!"

No wonder he was angry. No man can—or perhaps would even want to—display such a range of contradictory emotions and attitudes. In the same way, a woman cannot attain the Superwoman ideal—a successful career woman/homemaker/mother/wife/lover and yet have the energy and time left over to be nurturing and caring. Rather than have these larger-than-life models loom as yet another societal pressure, these changes can represent a new freedom to pick and choose from among the options in attitude, behavior, or emotions that express how you feel and what you want. If a man wants to be tender, he can be. If he wants to sweep a woman into bed, he can; and if, the next night, he wants to relax and be pleasured, he can feel free to ask her to make love to him. The point is that he need not be locked into a strict role. He can feel comfortable asking for what he wants, knowing he can expose his true desires and express his deepest feelings without giving up any shred of his masculinity.

It's this freedom to express their innermost selves that the men we interviewed felt was most important in allowing them to develop intimate relationships that were truly satisfying. As you examine your own life, do you find that your script for being a man matches your emotional makeup and allows you to express your true feelings? Does your script help or hinder the expression of intimacy in your relationship? If it fails to reflect your inner feelings or stands as a barrier to intimacy, you can make changes in your script without putting your masculinity on the line. In truth, it takes courage to change—especially when male conditioning stresses strength and stoicism at the expense of vulnerability. Men who are able to express their warmth, vulnerability, and tenderness have gone through an extraordinary amount of personal growth to overcome this societal conditioning. It requires great courage and strength of character to alter these deeply ingrained societal scripts. It takes a real super-man to do it, and there are more and more of these men around.

NOTES

CHAPTER ONE

1. Jerry Siegel and Joe Shuster, *Superman: From the Thirties to the Seventies* (New York: Crown Publishers, 1971), p. 9.
2. Harold Robbins, *The Betsy* (New York: Pocket Books, 1978), pp. 101–3.
3. Bernie Zilbergeld, *Male Sexuality* (Boston: Little, Brown & Company, 1978), p. 21.
4. Susan Goldberg and Michael Lewis, "Play Behavior in the Year-Old Infant: Early Sex Differences," *Child Development*, Vol. 40, No. 1, March 1969, p. 29.
5. Clark R. Clipson, Ph.D., *Variability in Sex Role Identity Development During the Adult Years: a Sample of Heterosexual Men* (Unpublished doctoral dissertation, California School of Professional Psychology, San Diego, 1980).

CHAPTER TWO

1. Bill Cosby, "The Regular Way," *Playboy*, December 1968, pp. 288–89.

CHAPTER FOUR

1. Daniel Rudman, *Hold Me Until Morning* (Berkeley, Calif.: Fred Cody Books, 1975), pp. 13–15.
2. J. Semans, "Premature Ejaculation," *Southern Medical Journal*, Vol. 49, 1956, pp. 353–58.
3. Read *Male Sexuality* by Bernie Zilbergeld for a detailed description of the stop/start method.

CHAPTER FIVE

1. Dan Greenburg, *Scoring: A Sexual Memoir* (Garden City, N.Y.: Doubleday & Company, 1972), pp. 9–10.

CHAPTER SEVEN

1. Ralph Rosenblum, *When the Shooting Stops . . . the Cutting Begins* (New York: Viking Press, 1979), p. 287.

CHAPTER EIGHT

1. Barry W. McCarthy, *What You (Still) Don't Know About Male Sexuality* (New York: Thomas Y. Crowell Co., 1977), p. 17.
2. Ibid., p. 166.
3. Lonnie Barbach, *For Each Other: Sharing Sexual Intimacy* (Garden City, N.Y.: Doubleday & Company, 1982), pp. 213–26.

CHAPTER NINE

1. Kathleen Woodiwiss, *The Flame and the Flower* (New York: Avon Books, 1972), p. 311.
2. Nathan Cabot Hale, *The Birth of a Family* (Garden City, N.Y.: Anchor Press/Doubleday, 1979), p. 8.
3. Helmuth Vorherr and Robert Messer, "Breast Cancer: Potentially Predisposing and Protecting Factors," *American Journal of Obstetrics and Gynecology*, Vol. 130, No. 3, February 1978, p. 347.

CHAPTER TEN

1. Lonnie Barbach and Linda Levine, *Shared Intimacies: Women's Sexual Experiences* (New York: Bantam Books, 1981), p. 321.
2. National Center for Health Statistics, "National Estimates of Marriage Dissolution and Survivorship," *Vital Health Statistics*, Series 3, No. 19, November 1980.
3. Educational Reviews, Inc., "The Effects of Divorce on Children," Practical Reviews in Psychiatry (a cassette tape), Vol. 6, No. 8, 1981.
4. U.S. Dept. of Commerce, Census Bureau, "Household and Family Characteristics," *Current Population Report*, Series P-20, No. 271, March 1981.

CHAPTER ELEVEN

1. Bernard D. Starr and Marcella Dukur Weiner, *The Starr-Weiner Report on Sex and Sexuality in the Mature Years* (New York: Stein & Day Publishers, 1981), p. 253.
2. Ibid., p. 8.
3. Ibid.
4. Digby Diehl, "Looking at Forty," *Esquire*, March 1981, pp. 25–31.

BIBLIOGRAPHY

Alberti, Robert E. and Emmons, M. L. *Your Perfect Right* (San Luis Obispo, Calif.: Impact, 1974)

Bach, George R. and Wyden, Peter. *The Intimate Enemy* (New York: Avon Books, 1968)

Barbach, Lonnie. *For Each Other* (Garden City, N.Y.: Anchor Press/Doubleday, 1982)

———. *For Yourself: The Fulfillment of Female Sexuality* (Garden City, N.Y.: Doubleday & Company, 1975)

——— and Levine, Linda. *Shared Intimacies* (Garden City, N.Y.: Anchor Press/Doubleday, 1980)

Bing, Elizabeth and Colman, Libby. *Making Love During Pregnancy* (New York: Bantam Books, 1977)

Bradley, Robert A. *Husband-Coached Childbirth* (New York: Harper & Row, 1965)

Brenton, Myron. *The American Male* (New York: Coward-McCann, 1966)

Butler, Robert N. and Lewis, Myrna I. *Sex After Sixty* (New York: Harper & Row, 1976)

Calderone, Mary S. and Johnson, Eric W. *The Family Book About Sexuality* (New York: Harper & Row, 1981)

Carrera, Michael. *Sex: The Facts, The Acts, and Your Feelings* (New York: Crown Publishers, 1981)

Castelman, Michael. *Sexual Solutions: A Family Guide* (New York: Simon & Schuster, 1980)

Comfort, Alex. *Good Age* (New York: Crown Publishers, 1976)

———. *The Joy of Sex* (New York: Crown Publishers, 1972)

Ellis, Albert. *Sex and the Liberated Man* (New York: Lyle Stuart, 1976)

Farrell, Warren. *The Liberated Man* (New York: Random House, 1974)

Fasteau, Marc Feigen. *The Male Machine* (New York: McGraw-Hill, 1974)

Goldberg, Herb. *The Hazards of Being Male* (Plainview, N.Y.: Nash Publishing Corp., 1976)

Gordon, Sol. *Let's Make Sex a Household Word: A Guide for Parents and Children* (New York: John Day, 1981)

Hale, Nathan Cabot. *The Birth of a Family* (Garden City, N.Y.: Anchor Press/Doubleday, 1979)

Hite, Shere. *The Hite Report on Male Sexuality* (New York: Alfred A. Knopf, 1981)

Hunt, Morton. *Sexual Behavior in the 1970s* (Chicago: Playboy Press, 1974)

Kinsey, Alfred C. et al. *Sexual Behavior in the Human Male* (Philadelphia: W. B. Saunders Company, 1948)

Lamaze, Fernand. *Painless Childbirth: The Lamaze Method* (Chicago: Henry Regnery Co., 1970)

Lichtendorf, Susan and Gillis, Phyllis. *The New Pregnancy* (New York: Random House, 1979)

Masters, William H. and Johnson, Virginia E. *Human Sexual Response* (Boston: Little, Brown & Company, 1966)

McCarthy, Barry. *Sexual Awareness* (San Francisco: Boyd & Fraser Publishing Co., 1975)

———. *What You (Still) Don't Know About Male Sexuality* (New York: Thomas Y. Crowell Co., 1977)

Morin, Jack. *Men Loving Themselves* (Burlingame, Ca.: Down There Press, 1980)

Offit, Avodah K. *Night Thoughts: Reflections of a Sex Therapist* (New York: Congdon & Lattès, Inc., 1981)

Otto, Herbert and Otto, Roberta. *Total Sex* (New York: Signet, The New American Library, 1972)

Pleck, Joseph and Sawyer, Jack. *Men and Masculinity* (Englewood Cliffs, N.J.: Prentice-Hall, 1974)

Pomeroy, Wardell B. *Your Child and Sex* (New York: Delacorte Press, 1974)

Schiengold, Lee and Wagner, Nathaniel N. *Sound Sex and the Aging Heart* (New York: Human Sciences Press, 1974)

Starr, Bernard D. and Weiner, Marcella. *The Starr-Weiner Report on Sex and Sexuality in the Mature Years* (New York, McGraw-Hill, 1981)

Woodiwiss, Kathleen. *The Flame and the Flower* (New York: Avon Books, 1972)

Zilbergeld, Bernie. *Male Sexuality* (Boston: Little, Brown & Company, 1978)

INDEX